Recognition of Kafala in the Italian Law System from a Comparative Perspective

Recognition of Kafala in the Italian Law System from a Comparative Perspective

By

Adele Pastena

Cambridge Scholars Publishing

Recognition of Kafala in the Italian Law System from a Comparative Perspective

By Adele Pastena

This book first published 2020

Cambridge Scholars Publishing

Lady Stephenson Library, Newcastle upon Tyne, NE6 2PA, UK

British Library Cataloguing in Publication Data
A catalogue record for this book is available from the British Library

ISBN (10): 1-5275-5508-9
ISBN (13): 978-1-5275-5508-2

TABLE OF CONTENTS

INTRODUCTION

In the legal panorama of modern societies there are several areas where the dynamics of identity intersect. Jurists, then, are often called upon to deal with legal models and tools deriving from different cultural contexts which sometimes need to be recognised within our own political structures. In this sense, a particularly interesting case is that of kafala, which is typical of the Islamic world, though with few, very rare exceptions. This is a form of protection for the child but without formal adoption or the recognition of a status equal to that of a legitimate child, and falls at some distance from the legal coding of secularized legal systems.

The study of this particular institution cannot, however, be simplistically reduced to a relationship between private rules of sovereign and independent state systems and/or the norms of private international law alone. Given that kafala gives rise to a number of concrete problems in Western society, arising principally to the fear of circumventing legislation on family reunification and the strict criteria established in terms of international adoptions, kafala cannot be parameterized solely with respect to the principles of respect for international public order.

An analysis of kafala in comparison with our own legal and cultural systems reveals a sort of legal short-circuit when laws of a religious nature (which imply the respect and observance of a divine law) come up against the rules of secular law and its associated rights recognized to all, regardless of any private, religious conviction. In addition, the rules governing kafala are known to be part of a particular category of norms which refer to 'personal status' and thus go beyond national boundaries, affecting all Muslims (who adhere to the majority of interpretative legal schools) and requiring public recognition in the host countries. This way then, a sound methodological approach entails considering the culture of the recipients of legal rules as a technical variable rather than a neutral parameter. This implies that the cultural norms used by the protagonists of any legal relationship must be increasingly taken into account, and at the same time law must be evaluated as a cultural product by adopting an appropriate perspective of legal analysis.

The use of religiously determined normative systems may create obvious systemic differences, with a number of consequences affecting the life of the individual and might sometimes lead to a limitation of rights as recognized in our legal systems. Being unable to analyze the multi-centric Islamic universe in its universality, we have thus focused our attention on a particular territorial area, the Maghreb, which is close to Italy's borders, and is particularly interesting in the case of Tunisia since the latter attempted to use the Italian legal system within the specific religious context of Islam.

Italy's non-ratification of the 1996 Hague Convention where it relates to kafala does highlight the legal difficulties of implementing this regulatory model in our own legal context, which is based on secularism and is profoundly respectful of the right to enjoy religious freedom and adhere to any religious faith (which can be freely accepted and changed). It is also important to underline the impossibility of using legal frameworks which were formerly present in our own legal system (consider kafala's affinity with the institution of 'affiliation' created under Fascist law in Italy), but which have been superseded by social and, above all, legal developments regarding non-biological parenting and the rights of legitimate children. It is not easy to contemplate suppressing or limiting those hard-won rights in the name of respect for religious dictates.

It is necessary, therefore, to carefully evaluate how a democratic legal system, largely secularized, if not non-religious, can accept the respect of religious rule which translates into law and deeply affects the absolute rights of the subjects involved. The risk is that the adoption of a dogmatic approach based on cultural relativism may impede a correct balance between respect for cultural identities and measures to safeguard individuals. Adopting this hermeneutical perspective would mean placing all different cultures on equal footing, but it would also mean placing individuals in a position of inequality, favouring collective protection. In the current phase of conceptual elaboration on issues of human rights it would no longer be possible, for example, to accept any discrimination towards natural / legitimate and adoptive children on the basis of religious precepts alone, and the fundamental right to religious freedom should be considered as an inalienable right in respect of the person and his / her rights.

A rethinking of these issues from the perspective of religious freedom of individuals and the necessary neutrality of legal rules might therefore be particularly significant for the protection of fundamental human rights, which must be perceived as right and necessary by the individuals concerned in order to be effective.

In this sense, therefore, a correct hermeneutical viewpoint cannot be simplistically addressed to the identification of possible 'universal' legal principles falling upon the institutions of law, nor should it be oriented towards studying the various systems with a mere comparative approach. What is needed, instead, is a focus on the connections between the various areas of cultural experience in order to analyze the regulatory instruments within a broader theoretical framework, and ultimately strike a difficult balance between the different fields of experience and the recognition of complex cultures. This is the main thrust of this book presented in four important chapters.

The Author
May 2020

CHAPTER ONE

THE PROTECTION OF CHILDREN IN THE ISLAMIC ORDER OF MAGHREB: RELIGIOUS IDENTITY AND CIVIL LEGISLATION

1. Non-biological Parental Construction in Religiously Oriented Contexts

Kafala is a form of family construction typical of the Islamic world that involves the particularly sensitive sector of parenting and 'non-biological' kinship. It is coupled with an important juridical operation which manages to develop a synthesis between religiously oriented and other largely secularized regulatory systems of law by applying the fundamental principle of axiological neutrality.[1]

---

[1] Human rights organizations increasingly report a distortion of this institution, used improperly as a tool for exploiting child labour, although in this study the focus is on kafala as an alternative tool to foster-adoption. In contractual terms, this term designates an important control system for immigrant workers established by the oil companies of the Arabian Gulf countries and has become a *conditio sine qua non* for residing and working in these states. All workers must have the legal guarantee of the kafil/employer, who acts as an intermediary with the company. In this way through kafala the State delegates a part of the control and regulation of foreign workers to civil society: I.L.O., *Tricked and trapped, Human trafficking in the Middle East,* 2013, in http://www.ilo.org/wcmsp5/groups/public/---arabstates/---ro-beirut/documents/publication/wcms_211214.pdf; G. BEAUGÉ, *La kafala: un système de gestion transitoire de la main-d'oeuvre et du capital dans les pays du Gulfe,* in *Revue Européenne des Migrations Internationales*, vol. 2, n. 1, 1986, pp. 109-122; A.N. LONGVA, *Keeping Migrant Workers in Check: The Kafala System in the Gulf*, in *Middle East Report,* n. 211, 1999, p. 22 *et seq*.; C. JEANGEY, *Il sistema della kafala e la tutela dei lavoratori migranti nella penisola arabica,* in *Studi in onore di Claudio Zanghì,* L.PANELLA, E. SPATAFORA (eds.), Turin, Giappichelli, 2012, p. 397 *et seq*.. On the usual meaning of kafala cf. *Islam and European legal systems*, S. FERRARI, A. BRADNEY (ed.), Aldershot, Ashgate and Dartmouth, 2000; M.L. LO GIACCO, *Religione e cultura nell'adozione internazionale*, in *Diritto e*

In recent years, Italy and other European countries have been increasingly forced to deal with the transfer of values due to growing migration, and the spatial-temporal shift linked to this has given impetus to a dynamic of redefining membership in contexts where religion, or a particular confession, is no longer the only key to reading cultural norms. In the search for a healthy balance in a liberal and democratic society, a multicultural/intercultural perspective is needed, which cannot be guaranteed by stigmatization of otherness, but through inclusive forms of diverse cultural models that respect our fundamental and mandatory rights.[2] The current and unavoidable demands of multiculturalism affect the consolidated order of the construction and codification of filiation relationships, giving rise to the problem of parenting separated from the concept of family, as traditionally structured.

The institution of kafala, the only legal instrument that guarantees abandoned Muslim children a childhood of sorts, comes into conflict with Western legislation. As is the case with Italian legislation, this raises problems as to its recognition as adoption, highlighting a dangerous legislative vacuum to the detriment of the minors themselves, whose very protection is at the heart of any liberal legal system. It is therefore particularly interesting to reflect on these institutions alongside their legal configuration and underlying rationale, in an attempt to implement the necessary regulatory connections that are indispensable in open societies.

Given the heterogeneity of the polycentric Islamic universe, it is more useful to limit the study to the Mediterranean area, closer to the Italian reality, and in particular to that of the Maghreb, on account of multiple factors. Firstly, for historical reasons, subjection to a common colonial dominion has long determined the imposition of a uniform Western legal model. Secondly, because of migratory flows, geographical proximity has also given rise to a considerable number of couples of mixed nationality. And, finally, the peculiarity of Tunisian legislation which recognises

---

Religione, 1, 2015, pp. 341-359; M.C. LE BOURSICOT, *La kafala ou recueil légal des mineurs en droit musulman: une adoption sans filiation*, in *Droit et Culture*, 2010, pp. 283-302; G. CAROBENE, *Kafala islamica e protezione dei minori in Italia dopo la ratifica della Convenzione dell'Aja,* in *Le proiezioni civili delle religioni tra libertà e bilateralità: modelli di disciplina giuridica,* A. FUCCILLO (ed.), Napoli, ESI, 2017, pp. 197-224.

[2] For a general overview of Islamic law cf. F. MILLOT, F.P. BLANC, *Introduction à l'étude du droit musulman,* Paris, Dalloz, 2001; on recent issues with particular attention on Egypt and Syria, B. BOTIVEAU, *Loi islamique et droit dans le société arabes,* Paris, Karthala, 2013.

adoption legally as it is based on a more modern conception of law and above all its interpretation.

Filiation is characterized by a principle of a social nature with which an identity is acquired and the transmission of kinship is codified; it is not only a private but above all a social act. Some anthropologists, moreover, prefer to use the term descent rather than filiation.[3] Functionally, adoption is a new model of representation of descent that consecrates a model of filiation built upon the desire to have a child. Each regulatory system is characterized by a specific model of parenting, a particular view of the family, precise childcare methods and the greater or lesser importance given to the child's best interests.

The tools for creating non-biological bonds in the family unit are strongly influenced by cultural background and allow us to identify different objectives in different social contexts, namely, demographic rebalance, ways of strengthening social ties, emotional or economic functions and compensation, and migratory phenomena. Sometimes, adoption is perceived as a legal institution aimed at the promotion and protection of abandoned children, therefore, as a tool of social policy.[4] In addition to these needs, kafala itself responds to a precise religious precept which prohibits adoption, and in this sense its regulatory translation should be evaluated in the light of the principles of religious freedom and secularism.

Recent studies on these issues in the fields of sociology and anthropology have pointed to the plurality of concepts of childhood and its socio-cultural foundations in the world that characterize and condition taking charge of a minor when the state of abandonment has been legally ascertained. It is generally known that in the African context the child does not belong to its biological parents alone but to the larger nucleus of the extended family, and sometimes, in rural contexts, to the whole village.[5]

---

[3] Cf. C. LÉVI-STRAUSS, *Les Structures élémentaires de la parenté,* Paris -La Haye, Mouton, 1949, and more recently M. VERDON, *Contre la culture. Fondements d'une anthropologie sociale opérationnelle,* Paris, Éd. des Archives contemporaines, 1991.

[4] Cf. G. PIZZOLANTE, *Le adozioni nel diritto internazionale privato,* Bari, Cacucci, 2008, in particol. p. 23; K. O'HALLORAN, *The politics of adoption. International prspectives on law, policy and practice²,* Dordrecht, Springer, 2009; G. CATTANEO, *Adozione,* in *Digesto discipline privatistiche,* Utet, Turin, vol. l, 1987, p. 98 *et seq.*; F. BOULANGER, *Enjeux et défis de l'adoption. Étude comparative et internationale,* Paris, Economica, 2001; P. MURAT, *L'évolution du droit de l'adoption en Europe,* in *Le statut juridique de l'en/ant dans l'espace européen,* Brussels, Bruylant, 2005, p. 121 *et seq.*

[5] Cf. V. DELAUNAY, *Abandon et prise en charge des enfants en Afrique: une problématique centrale pour la protection de l'enfant,* in *Mondes en*

It has also been observed that in Islamic societies (where the social context is closely linked to a specific religious view) filiation is not bound to a mere biological component – natural descent is not actually recognized – and the concept of son/*ibn* is conceived as a legal principle,[6] based on procreative ties whose legitimacy results only from marriage.[7] Thus, a family system has been built on alliance and consanguinity in which adoption, which distorts the legitimate filiation system, constitutes a form of transgression, first religious and subsequently social, since it calls into question the bonds of commitment and descent.

Adoption, then, is therefore prohibited coherently with the many precepts of a religious matrix that prevent the breaking of the natural bond underlying filiation.[8] What Islam expressly forbids, however, is not

---

développement, 146, 2, 2009, pp. 33-46 and at https://www.cairn.info/revue-mondes-en-developpement- 2009-2-page-33.htm which stresses that "*la question de la prise en charge de l'enfant et de son abandon, prend dès lors piace dans un contexte social et culturel caractérisé à la fois par cles systèmes de représentations et de normes dans lesquels les comportements de rejet, y compris extremes (infanticide), prennent leur signification et par des pratiques de circulation et de confiage des enfants, ou fosterage selon la terminologie adoptée par les anthropologues*" (p.34). it may be observed that "*le don d'enfants en Afrique n'a pas pour condition d'exiger l'instauration d'une distance entre donateurs et adoptants, et encore moins d'un secret*": N. JOURNET, *De l'abandon au don: l'adoption dans le monde,* in *Sciences Humaines,* Hors série *45,* L'enfant, 2004, pp. 64- 67 (qui p. 65). In general cf. D. BONNET, C. DE SUREMAIN, *Quelle place pour l'anthropologie de l'enfance dans le développement?* in *Sciences au Sud, 2008,* 44, p. 16 *et seq.*; *Enfants d'aujourd 'hui. Diversité des contextes, pluralité des parcours,* vol. l, AIDELF/INED, 2006; F. EZEMBÈ, *Don et abandon des enfants en Afrique,* in *Le bébé face à l'abandon, le bébé face à l'adoption,* M. SZEJER (ed.), Paris, Albin Michel, 2003, pp. 225-246; A. MARIE, *Les structures familiales à l'épreuve de l'individualisation,* in *Ménages et familles en Afrique. Approche des dynamiques contemporaines,* M. PILON, T. LOCOH, E. VIGNIKIN, P. VIMARD (eds.), Paris, Ceped, 1997, pp. 279-300.

[6] Under a law of 1998, further amended in 2003, the Tunisian code recognised natural filiation with the attribution of a patronymic name to abandoned children of unknown paternity. This allowed children to be given a complete social identity.

[7] On filiation within the legitimate marriage, cf. Surah LXX, *The Ways of Ascent* verses 9 and 29 - 31. On marriage cf. A. CILARDO, *Marriage: Islamic Law,* in *The Oxford International Encyclopedia of Legal History,* ed. Stanley N. Katz, vol. IV, 2009, pp. 163-169; D. PEARL – W. MENSKI, *Muslim Family Law,* London, Sweet & Maxwell, 1998.

[8] Only Indonesia, Turkey and Tunisia among the Muslim countries, recognize the *adoption/Tabbani*. Turkey has a strong historical and institutional background in the protection of minors, which has its roots in the early twentieth century, with the

adoption itself, but its essential effects arising from the dominant model of adoption as currently accepted in countries of a Western cultural matrix, that is, expression of the constitution of an exclusive legal relationship of filiation between the adopted child and the adopting parent.

The Quran expressly prohibits equating biological children with adopted children, signifying that the family is an institution of divine origin so that it is not possible to determine the bonds of filiation independently. However, among the duties of a good Muslim there is undoubtedly also the duty to take care of the needy and in particular orphans; in this way, kafala is therefore the legal instrument through which protection to minors in need may be offered, without breaking any divine law.[9] Many Sunnah *hadiths* declare that the adoption of an individual of

---

creation of the 'Child Protection Organization' and the protection of minors and the care of children acquiring considerable cultural importance in society especially since 2005, when a broad 'Child Protection Law' (CPL) was adopted as part of the series of legislative reforms for EU membership. This law provides for a global system for the protection of minors, with a specialized judiciary (with public prosecutors for minors, special courts and social workers) capable of adopting the necessary protection/support measures. In 2013, Turkey launched a political and media campaign to recover the children of Turkish emigrants in Europe, adopted by foreigners to place them in families where they can preserve their cultural identity. Even Somalia, before the exhausting civil conflict, was an Islamic country that allowed adoption.

[9] References to the Quran are in the third verse of Surah XXXIII, *The Combined Forces,* which deals with elective kinship, and in particular in verses 4, 5 and 37. Verse 4: "Allah has not made for a man two hearts in his interior. And He has not made your wives whom you declare unlawful your mothers. And he has not made your adopted sons your [true] sons. That is [merely] your saying by your mouths, but Allah says the truth, and He guides to the [right] way." Verse 5: "Call them by [the names of] their fathers; it is more just in the sight of Allah. But if you do not know their fathers - then they are [still] your brothers in religion and those entrusted to you. And there is no blame upon you for that in which you have erred but [only for] what your hearts intended. And ever is Allah Forgiving and Merciful." Verse 37: "And [remember, O Muhammad], when you said to the one on whom Allah bestowed favour and you bestowed favour, 'Keep your wife and fear Allah,' while you concealed within yourself that which Allah is to disclose. And you feared the people, while Allah has more right that you fear Him. So when Zayd had no longer any need for her, We married her to you in order that there not be upon the believers any discomfort concerning the wives of their adopted sons when they no longer have need of them. And ever is the command of Allah accomplished." at https://quran.com/ Cf. A. CILARDO, *Il minore nel diritto islamico. Il nuovo istituto della kafala*, in *La tutela dei minori di cultura islamica*

known parents would constitute an act of apostasy,[10] although some jurists prefer instead an interpretation aimed at regulating rather than prohibiting this practice.[11]

Kafala is legally definable as a 'delegation of parental authority' or 'legal protection'; it confers the *wilaya* which, in a broad sense, includes authority, power and representation. It indicates a guarantee, but also acceptance and care;[12] it is actually implemented through the appointment – judicial or by notarial deed – of a guardian, the *kafil*, with a view to providing assistance to a minor, the *makful*. As a way of superimposing parental functions and interpersonal relationships, this concept determines a legal and social relationship. Lawmakers chose the word kafala, which derived from the commercial sphere and was understood as a guarantee, a surety. The semantic field of the same was thus used to describe the behaviour of adults towards the child. The underlying rationale seems therefore to emphasize the essentially contractual nature of this type of obligation.

In the Quran itself, this term appears only twice in the sense of entrusting care, appointing someone as guardian.[13] From a legal point of view, it represents the commitment to take charge of a minor, but in no

---

nell'area mediterranea. Aspetti sociali, giuridici e medici, A. CILARDO (ed.), Naples, ESI, 2011, pp. 219-264.

[10] Cf. L. PRUVOST, *Intégration familiale de l'enfant sans généalogie en Algérie et en Tunisie: kafala ou adoption,* in *Studi arabo-islamici del* PISAI, 8, Rome, Pontificio istituto di studi Arabi e d'Islamistica (PISAI), p. 163 *et seq*.

[11] F. C. ZIDANI, *L'enfant né hors mariage en Algérie,* EAP, Alger, 1992, in particular p. 82.

[12] J. BARGACH, *Orphans of Islam. Family. Abandonment and secret Adoption in* Morocco, Boston, Rowman & Littlefield Publishers inc., 2002 stresses that "the etymology of the word kafala has two distinct meanings in classical Arabic: to guarantee (*damăn*) and to take care (from the root verb of ka-fa-la). In its former meaning of guaranteeing, the word kafala has been mainly employed in the realm of commerce and business transactions...the semantic field of kafala being diffused between these two realms - contract and a guarantee- is then employed to describe, in part, the behaviour of the adopting adults towards a minor" (p. 29).

[13] Surah XX, *Tâ- Hâ,* verse 39 "[Saying], 'Cast him into the chest and cast it into the river, and the river will throw it onto the bank; there will take him an enemy to Me and an enemy to him.' And I bestowed upon you love from Me that you would be brought up under My eye." And Surah III, *Family of Imrân,* verse 37 "So her Lord accepted her with good acceptance and caused her to grow in a good manner and put her in the care of Zechariah. Every time Zechariah entered upon her in the prayer chamber, he found with her provision. He said, 'O Mary, from where is this [coming] to you?' She said, 'It is from Allah. Indeed, Allah provides for whom He wills without account.'" at https://quran.com.

case is the *kafil-makful* bond recognised as filiation. The latter, in fact, does not take the name of the former nor does s/he have any inheritance rights (since the rules of succession, determined by the Quran and reproduced in positive legislation, are based exclusively on consanguinity and alliance). The child is not registered in the family status record and finds him/herself in a particular administrative position because s/he could be 'returned' by the *kafil* and again placed under the responsibility of the State. Kafala thus remains a temporary and revocable instrument. It also ends upon reaching the age of majority, except in the case of an unmarried girl or a disabled person; upon the death of the two parents or in the event of their being unable to take care of themselves. It may be annulled by the judge (in the event of a breach of obligations and always bearing in mind the interest of the minor) and, finally, it may be brought to an end if the Court finds that this measure is no longer founded.

Two forms of kafala are normally contemplated: judicial (emanating from the Juvenile Court) which applies to children of unknown parents, and notarial (a sort of contract drawn up before a notary), which is used for non-abandoned minors, of known parents and with their consent. Formed to protect endangered children, it subsequently extended to children who were not in a position of total abandonment, formalizing any transfer that took place within the circle of kinship as well. At an intra-family level, this system has also developed in migratory contexts and currently involves older children, sometimes entrusted by biological parents to emigrated relatives to allow their children a better level of education in Western countries or give better access to the job market. After some years or on reaching adulthood, the children might then decide to return to their family and country of origin.[14]

The Western adoption model, on the other hand, determines a definitive and irreversible change of identity and is based on the principle of exclusivity and an emphasis on the wishes of those involved. It tends to cancel the ties of origin of the adopted child as a precondition to the construction of exclusive filiation by substitution, from the legal point of view assimilated in all respects to the natural parent-child bond.[15]

---

[14] Cf. C. OPPONG, *Les systèmes familiaux et la crise économique*, in *La famille africaine. Politiques démographiques et développement*, A. ADEPODJU (ed.), Paris, Karthala, 1999, pp. 221-254; *Abandoned children*, C. PANTER-BRICK, M. SMITH (ed.), Cambridge, Cambridge University Press, 2000; M.VOORHOEVE, *Family Law in Islam, Divorce, Marriage and Women in the Muslim World*, London - New-York, I.B. Tauris, 2012.

[15] J. LONG, *Ordinamenti giuridici occidentali, kafalah e divieto di adozione: un'occasione per riflettere sull'adozione legittimante*, in *Nuova giur. civ. comm.*, II,

The legal need to allow the entry of sub-kafala minors or the use of this tool by Western citizens for the construction of a parental bond with a child of an Islamic country in legal cultures such as our own, largely secularized, culture thus brings about a mismatch with the legal system that Italy's recent ratification of the 1996 Hague Convention aims to resolve.[16]

Law no. 101 of 2015 finally incorporated this fundamental international document in Italy, but faced with the evident difficulties of adapting kafala's rules to the Italian legal system, Italian legislation scrapped the rules referring to the Islamic kafala that will have to be the subject of separate regulation to avoid the risk of legal discrimination towards 'invisible' children. Although the removed section regards essentially the procedures to be followed for the placement of the foreign minor who is not in a position of abandonment, it is clear that this important legal institution needs to be regulated. It is increasingly used not only in migratory contexts, but also to facilitate the path of international adoptions towards new geographical areas, as already implemented in other European countries. The urgency to intervene in these matters has been underlined by the many organizations and institutions dedicated to children that complain of the impossibility of monitoring the effective

---

2003, p. 175 *et seq*. and *La kafalah come banco di prova per un diritto "interculturale"*, in *Minori e giustizia*, n. 2, 2012, p. 254 *et seq*.; T. TOMEO, *La kafala*, in *Comparazione e diritto civile*, 2013, www.comparazionedirittocivile.it/prova/files/ncr_tomeo_kafala .pdf; R. CLERICI, *La compatibilità del diritto di famiglia mussulmano con l'ordine pubblico internazionale*, in *Fam. Dir* ., 2009, p. 208 *et seq*.; M. ORLANDI, *La Kafala islamica e la sua riconoscibilità quale adozione*, in *Dir. fam. Pers*. 2005, p. 635 *et seq*.; P. STEFANÌ, *Kafalah islamica e uguaglianza religiosa: laicità e società multiculturale*, in *Diritto e Religione. L'evoluzione di un settore della scienza giuridica attraverso il confronto fra quattro libri,* G. MACRÌ, M. PARISI, V. TOZZI (eds.), Salerno, Plectica, 2012, pp. 433- 447; P. DIAGO, *La Kafala islamica en España*, in *Cuad. der. tran.*, vol. 2, n. 1 2010 p. 140.

[16] This law came into force on Jan. 1. 2016, but was ratified with L. 8 Jun. 2015, n. 101. Having delayed this ratification considerably (the Council of the European Union, with Decision 2008 / 431 / CE, had imposed the deadline of 2010 on the member countries), Italy ratified urgently and, considering that on kafala there are divergences of views and complications related to the different legal systems, Parliament chose to approve for ratification a text of the law that would exclude the legislation of kafala, postponed to a later date. Cf. Il Rapporto CRC, *I diritti dell'infanzia e dell'adolescenza in Italia.* 9° Rapporto di aggiornamento sul monitoraggio della Convenzione sui diritti dell'infanzia e dell'adolescenza in Italia, anno 2015-2016 http:://www.gruppocrc.net/IMG/pdf/ixrapportocrc2016.pdf, esp. p. 95 *et seq*.

presence of sub-kafala minors in our social fabric without any regulatory protection.

For a definition of kafala, the *Lisan Al Arab* - the quintessential Arabic dictionary - refers to a verse of the Quran, roughly translatable as: "And her Lord accepted her with full acceptance and vouchsafed to her a goodly growth; and made Zachariah her guardian. Whenever Zachariah went into the sanctuary where she was, he found that she had food."[17] Interestingly, many interpretations have been given of this verse. According to current editions of the Quran, Zachariah is the second direct object and designates the person subjected to the action of God, but who is responsible for enforcing the action with regard to Mary. This implies that God gave Mary to Zachariah to be his guarantor; he was therefore selected to guarantee his protection/*hadana*. O the contrary, another reading considers Zachariah the subject so that the sentence would mean '*Zachariah* is the guarantor of Mary': this would allow the person to consider him / herself free and voluntarily accept to guarantee for someone. The *Lisan Al Arab* seems to reinforce this interpretation of kafala on the basis of a *hadith* of the Prophet narrated by Sahl Ben Sa'd: In Heaven, I and the one who took charge of an orphan will be like this and showed his two fingers together, forefinger and middle finger, which in the familiar language of Arabs meant that they would be together, united. In another *hadith* it emerges that the best example of care is that of the Prophet: "You are the best of those who have been supported / taken care of since childhood, nurtured, educated to the point of becoming great".[18] In this text, therefore, meanings and definitions revolve around three main semantic axes: protection, guarantee and fulfilment of promises.

In the traditional exegetical reading, it is also customary to quote the episode of Zayd ibn Haritha, formally known as Zayd ibn Muhammad: "Allah has not made for a man two hearts in his interior. And He has not made your wives whom you declare unlawful your mothers. And he has not made your adopted sons your [true] sons. That is [merely] your saying by your mouths, but Allah says the truth, and He guides to the [right] way. Call them by [the names of] their fathers; it is more just in the sight of Allah. But if you do not know their fathers - then they are [still] your

[17] Il *Lisan Al Arab* di I. MANZŪR è. Reference is to Surah III, verse 37, cit.
[18] N. AÏT ZAÏ, *La kafala en droit algérien,* in *Les institutions traditionnelles dans le monde arabe*, H. BLEUCHOT (ed.), Paris, Karthala, 1996, pp. 95-105.

brothers in religion and those entrusted to you."[19] These statements have been interpreted as an explicit declaration against adoption.

In order to explain these verses, however, it is necessary to tie them in more properly to the circumstances of the time[20] and to take into account underlying events.[21] To this end, it is necessary to read these words carefully and to emphasize that in the commentary to the Quran it is clear that they draw attention to the unnatural state of certain situations: a woman cannot be the mother and wife of a man at the same time; a man cannot have two hearts, and a man cannot be a father if he is not so naturally. The parent-child relationship can only derive from a biological link and not from a series of linguistic ties. The symbols of these bonds - marriage and adoption - must then be reworked to adapt to the visions of a particular culture in which cohesion was essentially built on the parameters of loyalty, or based on common religious faith.

The Quran's revelation does not therefore seem to deny the possibility of accepting a child who cannot claim paternal recognition or agnatic filiation, but affirms the pre-eminence of blood kinship and kinship rights

---

[19] Cf. Surah XXXIII, vv. 4-5, cit. on their interpretation Cf. M. REZIG, *Les aspirations conflictueles du droit à l'adoption: étude comparative*, in *Arab Law Quarterly*, vol. 19, nn. 1-4, 2004, pp. 147-168, esp. p. 153.

[20] M. ARKOUN, *Lectures du Coran*, Paris, Editions Maisonneuv e et Larose, 1982: "*lier les versets a la circonstance, c'est accrediter, comme on l'a fait, l'idée positiviste d'un e Revelation opportuniste, d'un prophete appelant Dieu au secours dans les moments utiles; c'est figer dans la contingence la portée d'un texte dont l'intention premiere et le résultat effectif est d'activer l'histoire. C'est le temps de reviser cette attitude mortelle de la theologie essentialiste developpée au Moyen Age*" (p. 26). The ban must therefore be framed in the social framework of the time and connected with Muhammad's revolutionary message of social renewal, of brotherhood in Islam regardless of personal and social conditions. This message helped to determine the crisis in the tribal system on which pre-Islamic society was founded, where adoption was frequently used to allow childless individuals to pass on their names and property.

[21] "This incident being that on one of the Prophet's visits, Zaynab bint Jahsh (his patemal cousin and wife of his then adopted son Zayd) hurriedly opened the door in her eagerness not to let the Prophet wait while she was still inappropriately dressed. Upon seeing her, the Prophet hastily left, declining her invitation to enter and wait for Zayd. When Zaynab reported the incident of the Prophet's hasty leaving to her husband, the latter went to his adopted father saying that he was ready to divorce Zaynab if the Prophet wanted to marry her. The Prophet declined Zayd's offer. Revelation then came in which a divine sanction was given to his marriage with Zaynab": J. BARGACH, *Adoption and wardship (kafala) in Morocco*, in *Rect van de Islam*, 18, 2001 pp. 77-98, esp. p. 87.

over elective ties.[22] What is more, prohibiting adoption can be interpreted as a way of defending the bonds of descent and protecting a specific family model.[23] The kafala system is the result of a compromise since it does not question the legal mechanism of inheritance, patronymic or property, but allows a social need to be met in terms of the reality of children without families and couples who cannot bear offspring, without prejudice to laws and morals. This prohibition, justified by the Quran and the life of the Prophet himself (who married the wife of his adopted son),

---

[22] As explicitly stated in verse six of Surah XXXIII, cit.: "The Prophet is more worthy of the believers than themselves, and his wives are [in the position of] their mothers. And those of [blood] relationship are more entitled [to inheritance] in the decree of Allah than the [other] believers and the emigrants, except that you may do to your close associates a kindness [through bequest]. That was in the Book inscribed."

[23] This prohibition is present in most Muslim countries with some exceptions. There are: "*Countries with strict application of a 'non international kafala'*: Iran, Mauritania, Egypt. They reject kafala at the international level, based on a strict interpretation of the Sharia and rejecting all equivalence between kafala and adoption. Thus, abandoned children only have limited possibilities to leave their country in order to benefit from a placement abroad, except by relatives. At national level, child placements in non-biological families exist, but remain very limited or outside the legal framework (for example, traditional family placements). *Countries with a 'case-by-case' solution:* Morocco, Algeria, Jordan and Pakistan. They estimate that the situation of children deprived of family and the lack of national applicants for kafala is such that it may be necessary to allow international kafala, as long as the applicants respect some of the procedural conditions for a kafala (for example, the conversion to Islam). Morocco allows for international placements of abandoned children, in favour of nationals living abroad, but also by foreigners. In Pakistan, according to law, non-Muslim children may be adopted by non-Muslim applicants, whether nationals or foreigners. However, it is very difficult to find evidence of this practice and to know how the procedures are dealt with. Algeria and Jordan have systems which privilege national candidates, but both countries allow for the placement of children abroad, either with nationals or with foreigners, under the condition that they have the same religion as the child, meaning that they are Muslim. However, international placements remain rare and documented to a limited extent. It is to be noted that in Jordan, the word kafala refers to the monthly financial support granted to children living with a single parent (for the greater part the mother). *Countries having legislation on adoption or on the 'conversion' of kafala:* Tunisia and Indonesia. Even though they are very much attached to Islamic values, these countries allow for adoption, with full legal consequences in relation to filiation. However, by law (in Indonesia) or by practice (in Tunisia), adoption is limited to national applicants, living in the country or abroad, but of the same religion as the child.": http://www.crin.org/en/docs/Kafalah.BCN.doc.

should be read as a founding element of societies characterized by a well-structured kinship system and a specific normative model of the family.

In Arabic, the notion of kinship is reflected in the term *qarâba*/affinity, blood ties, and has three aspects: *nasab* (descent), *musâhara* (alliance) and *ridâ'a* (milk kinship). In general, *nasab* refers to the origin and defines the family in terms of descent.[24] The North African system is unilineal and patrilineal, it fits into a context of cultural anthropology and is established on the basis of kinship groups, from father to son, in which the entire social structure is based on the genealogy of the male line and is not simply dependant on blood ties, but on the status and power of the group.[25]

The male *nasab* is, in actual fact, linked to a tribal logic and has a specific political meaning: it allows men to think of themselves as 'peers' and this equality guarantees social stability. The rule in Muslim law requires that each individual take the patronymic name from the legitimate father and this constitutes the guarantee of the origins of the family.[26]

It is thus necessary to consider also the particular value that the name holds in Arab societies: it is made up of various elements, each indicating a trace of the family history.[27] Here, the crux of the matter is *nasab*, meaning lineage.[28] This places the individual in the male line of the family, with the list of the names of the male ascendants and may be

---

[24] C. HAMES, *La filiation généalogique (nasab) dans la societé d'Ibn Khaldoun*, in *Rév.de l'homme*, 1987, vol. 27, 102, p. 99 *et seq*.

[25] *Quaraba* in Arabic refers to kinship but etymologically speaking means closeness/proximity and is not related to procreation. Cf. C. FORTIER, *Le droit musulman en pratique: genre, filiation et bioétique*, in *Droit et Cultures*, 59, 2010, p. 1 *et seq*.; C. LACOSTE- DUJARDIN Au Maghreb, *l'enfance innomable. in Autrement (Abandon et Adoption)*, 1986 96, pp. 85-90; S. LALLEMAND, *La circulation des enfants en société traditionnelle. Pret, don, échange*, Paris, L'Harmattan, 1993; M. PILON, K. VIGNIKIN, *Ménages et famil les en Afrique subsaharienne*, Paris, Ed. des archives contemporaines/AUF, Savoirs francophones, 2006.

[26] Surah XXXIII v. 5, cit. though these principles are also emphasised in the *Sunnah*.

[27] The first is called *ism*: it is a name attributed at birth, then comes the *nasab*, genealogical name placing the individual in the male line of the family, the list of names of male ascendants; the third element, the *laqab*, is a sort of honorific nickname that underlines the individual's qualities and can become a patronymic name; this is followed by the *kunya* as a sign of friendship and respect and the *nisba* or 'name of relationship' which places the individual in the fabric of social relationships.

[28] Filiation is also called 'history of the name': Cf. N. SAADI, *Le nom, le sang ou la filiation exhortée par le droit*, in *Rev. alger. sciences ju ridiques économiques et politiques*, 29, n. 1-2, 1991, p. 55-64.

known or not.[29] To protect the honour of minors, in many Islamic countries the term 'parents unknown' (a shameful and deeply damaging term socially speaking) is no longer included in the birth certificate, but is replaced by the names of a father and a mother of Arab tradition, fictitiously assigned by the registrar.

It is understandable therefore how the fiction of adoption appears in opposition to this idea of the family, founded as it is on the truth of 'blood' ties. According to this kinship system, an essential principle of which is that the chain should not be broken, traditional Islamic society measures the importance of fertility and the highly social nature of the desire to have children, defined as a duty so that the necessary descendants can be guaranteed. It is thus easy to see how celibacy and sterility may be considered a threat to the social balance or an offense to the community itself. While fertility is one of the main concerns of those anxious to perpetuate their lineage, infertility is seen as a drama, a harbinger of rejection and shame. The barren woman has failed in her role, becoming worthless and the couple find themselves on the margins of society.[30]

In this sense the prohibitive rules of adoption have always been subtly sidestepped in Muslim countries, with diversified stratagems devised by families' intent on respecting this traditional social model. Although adoption has always been formally prohibited, there were in actual fact forms of 'cultural' adoption that are still widespread in rural contexts.[31]

The most widespread was *customary adoption*, which involved the gift of a child from one family to another. In general, a couple without children or with few males would ask a member of their own extended family for the gift of a child or a woman with multiple pregnancies would generously give one of her children to a close relative who was sterile. In North Africa, as was customary in Western countries at one time, a family member, more 'fortunate' in terms of the number of children or gender

---

[29] P. BORDIEU, *Sociologie de l'Algérie*, Paris, PUF, 2001 observed that Islam wished to create "*une communauté universelle fondée sur d'autres liens que ceux de la parenté ... a laissé subsister des communautés sociales telles que le clan et la tribu, en sorte que les liens du sang ont continué longtemps à l'emporter sur ceux qui découlent de l'appartenance à la communauté musulmane*" (p. 99). Article 2 of the Algerian code, for example, spells out that the family is the basic cell of society and is made up of people united by marriage or kinship ties, *nasab* or filiation, *musâhara* or alliance and *ridâ'a* or milk kinship); Article 142 of the Moroccan code specifies that filiation derives from procreation by the child's parents.

[30] C. LACOSTE-DUJARDIN, *Des mères contre les femmes, maternité et patriarcat au Maghreb*, Paris, La Découverte, 1985.

[31] J. BARGACH, *Orphans of Islam*, cit., esp. pp. 27-28.

distribution, would typically give up a part of his children. Nevertheless, it was simply the transfer of a minor to another family, that is, an informal transfer without legal consequences typical of a peasant culture in which the identity of the child remained unchanged and was the result of multiple parenting relationships; the child thus belonged to the extended parental group. While this practice still continues in isolated areas, modern and urbanized infertile couples currently rely on other methods such as adoption or kafala and medically assisted procreation.

A second form was the *secret adoption*, based on a secret agreement between two parties, in which a young woman, normally a single mother or an adulterous woman would give up her child - the 'fruits of her sin' - to a sterile couple. With the fraudulent complicity of some professional figures and the use of secrecy and various reuses (for example, simulating a pregnancy), the couple would then register the child as their own. In this way they would obtain the triple advantage of compensating for the three forms of dishonour or shame: that of the single mother, the sterile woman and the 'bastard' child.[32] It was and is an absolutely illegal measure which, by altering biological ties, also violated a precise religious dictate. This form was called *tabanni* in classical Arabic, a verbal noun derived from *ibn* / son, meaning the process by which a minor is transformed into a child.

With regard to international measures to protect children, the reference to a *Declaration sur les droits et la protection de l'enfant dans le monde islamique* of 1994 is important.[33]

2. Personal Status and Family Structure in the Islamic Legal Culture

As already mentioned, the legal development of kafala may be more broadly assessed within the context of individual and social relationships within the Muslim world. Any juridical analysis of kafala necessarily implies a reference to certain legal categories typical of the Islamic context where, first and foremost, the concept of Personal Status comes into play

---

[32] N. AÏT- ZAÏ, *L'enfant illégitime dans la société musulmane*, in *Rev. alger. sciences juridiques économiques et politiques*, 1990, pp. 229-239 and ID., *L'abandon d'enfant et la loi*, in *Rev. alger. sciences juridiques économiques et politiques*, 1991, p. 17 *et seq.*

[33] Article 4 of the *Déclaration*, adopted in Casablanca 15 Dec. 1994 by *O.C.I.*, *Organisation de la Conférence Islamique*. In the subsequent Convention, no mention was made of the issues surrounding filiation or adoption: Cf. *Convention des droits de l'enfant en Islam*, 2005, adopted in Sana'a (Yémen).

at least in the Maghreb. The indissolubility of the link between the spiritual and the temporal powers together with the undisputed authority of the Quran are the cornerstones of the Codes of Islamic countries where Personal Status is deeply involved. This phrase was not in use in classical Islamic law nor is there any documentation in European law of the modern day; its object is constituted by marriage, the dissolution of the conjugal bond, filiation, capacity and inheritance. Basically, these are the areas that concern the individual's development from birth to death, and are all treated by respecting religious dictates.

While the civil codification of the colonised Islamic world was carried out under the decisive influence of European legal systems, family law and Personal Status have their roots in the sacred law of Islam, in the *Sharia*, reformulated in codes and laws by various Arab states during the last century.[34] It is also important not to confuse Islam as a religion with classical Muslim law presented as a part of that. Part of the Islamic doctrine has sought to emphasize that Muslim law could be defined as secular, though this might give a particular meaning to the concept of secularism, at some remove from our own cultural parameters.[35] Others, instead, prefer to emphasize that Muslim law is a historical product, just as Roman law is for Latin countries; in other words, it is a set of legal rules

---

[34] The expression Personal Status arises from the recent evolution of Arab legal systems and did not belong to traditional legal vocabulary but was coined by the Egyptian jurist Muhammad Quadri Bàù. This expression does not refer to the subject matter of the rules, since in addition to issues of status and capacity of persons, marriage, personal and property relations between spouses, family relationships and related maintenance obligations, protection and care, filiation, etc, are included. It represents a characteristic position of Islamic legal systems and includes matters in which Sharia law has never ceased to be applied, and therefore represented the most conservative part of Islamic legal rules. Cf. I. GOLDRIHER, *Le dogme et la loi dans l'Islam,* Paris, Librarie orientaliste Paul Geythner, 2005; M. BENJEMIA, *Libertè de religion et statut personnel,* in *Rivista di Filosofia del Diritto e Cultura Giuridica*, 2009, 9, pp.91-106; D. SOURDEL, *Droit musulman et codification*, in *Revue française de théorie, de philosophie et de cultures juridiques*, n. 26, 199 , pp.33-50; J.F. RYCX , G. BLANCHI, *Références à l'Islam dans le droit public positif en pays arabes*, in *Pouvoirs*, 1980, n.12 ; S. PAPI, *L'influence juridique islamique au Maghreb*, Paris, L'Harmattan, 2009.

[35] It was developed by Muslim jurists in the first three centuries of Hegira and did not have distant or indirect relations with Islam, as a religion: Cf. C. CHEHATA, *Nature, structure et division du droit musulman*, in *Rev. alger. sciences juridiques économiques et politiques*, 1973, p. 555 *et seq*.; M. CLARET DE FLEURIEU, *L'Etat musulman, entre l'idéal islamique et les contraintes du monde temporel*, Paris, L.G.D.J, 2010; D. SOURDEL, *Droit musulman et codification, in Revue française de théorie, de philosophie et de cultures juridiques*, 26, 1998, pp.33-50.

that might serve as a base and explanation for the current regulatory developments, but which are essentially anachronistic.[36]

Another important cultural factor to take into consideration is the historical-political direction taken by Arab countries once freed from colonization. In contrast to the French revolutionaries of 1789, who strove to free secular power from its enslavement to religion, in the North African context Islam actually represented a conduit and catalyst during liberation from foreign invasion as a new national identity was being constructed.

The expression Personal Status / *al-ahwāl al-šaĥşiyya* itself stems from the recent evolution of Arab legal systems and did not belong to the traditional legal vocabulary.[37] The personal character of the code does not only refer to the object of the rules and, in particular, it should not be understood in the sense given by private international law, but refers to the applicability, on a personal basis of this set of rules.[38] The concept of Personal Status derives from that of 'personality of law' that classical Islamic law took from pre-existing juridical traditions, presenting it as one of the foundations of its own doctrine.

The legal framework of Personal Status is a characteristic partition of these legal systems, which can be defined historically as the area of

---

[36] Cf. N. BERNARD-MAUGIRON, J.N. FERRIÉ, *Les architectures constitutionnelles: introduction*, in *Égypte/Monde arabe*, Troisième série, 2, 2005, in http://ema.revues.org/1049; Y. BEN ACHOUR, *Politique, religion et droit dans le monde arabe*, Tunis, Casablanca, Cerès- Eddif 1992; J. R. HENRY, *Droit et société au Maghreb: quelques nouveaux enjeux de la recherche juridique*, in *Politiques législatives: Égypte, Tunisie, Algérie, Maroc, Centre d'études et de documentation économiques, juridiques et sociales* e in http://books.openedition.org/cedej/398; H. SANSON, *Laïcité islmique en Algerie*, Paris, CRESM, 1983. Worth noting also that most countries declare Islam as the state religion but do not define themselves as Islamic states.

[37] Cf. A. CILARDO, *Personal Status Law: Personal Status Law in Islamic Countries*, in *The Oxford International Encyclopedia of Legal History*, S.N. KATZ (ed.), New York, Oxford University press, vol. IV, 2009, pp. 295-299; D. TECHOUAR, *Lacunes de la législation des lois de status personnel au Maghreb, la question de la filiation*, in *Rev. alger. sciences juridiques économiques et politique*, 39, l 2002, p. 147 *et seq*.; L. ASLAOUI, *Le statut juridique de l'enfant au Magreb*, in *Rev. alger. sciences juridiques économiques et politiques*, 1990, 28, 2, pp. 241-257, in http://biblio.univalger.dz/jspui/handle/1635/508.

[38] In addition to the status and capacity of the person there is also marriage, personal and property relationships between spouses, family relationships and related maintenance obligations, protection and care, donations, successions, last will and testament and in general acts after the subject's death and endowments to charitable causes (*waqf*).

maximum resistance opposed by Muslim law to modernization and above all westernization.[39] It is the area in which reference to Muslim law is stronger, relating as it does to the more intimate sphere of the individual and his or her social relations. At present, however, what we are observing is a phase of re-conceptualization of the Muslim family that aims to put an end to relationships of subjugation and subordination, in line with a more modern vision, more akin to our own. Only the adoption of a global perspective that is not simply juridical but also social and political, may bring about any significant changes.

The institution of marriage, like the family and filiation, is placed fully within those areas subject to *ius personae* or personal law, not only as essential institutions for the development of society, but also as a fundamental tool in the context of relations with other religious confessions. The principle of the 'personality of law' constitutes, as mentioned, the origin of the system of Personal Status since it affirms the submission of each individual to the laws emanated by the ethnic, religious, linguistic community to which the subject belongs rather than the state in which the subject resides or holds citizenship. The community to which the individual belongs is thus not necessarily religious; the essential nucleus of this principle, in fact, is not the definition of the characteristics of this group, but rather the provision of legislation that is not valid indiscriminately for all those who reside within the territorial boundaries of a state structure.[40] It is based on the personal rather than the territorial aspect of the law and has a dual autonomy: judicial and legislative. The first is realized through the existence of religious tribunals for all confessions present in the territory; the second in respect of the internal religious norms of the individual communities. It thus creates an exclusive right devoid of any external communication or interference, permanently linked to the reading of the religious text, which can be modified only through careful interpretation/*ijtihâd*. This pluralism of Personal Status, even within a common religious framework as in some multi-community Islamic States (e.g. Lebanon), leads to the coexistence of

---

[39] The attitude adopted by individual state legislation in codifying these norms is extremely diversified: while Egyptian legislation did not call into question the continuity of the formal validity of Sharia law and only amended individual rules, Tunisian reformism, supported by a strong desire to re-found and renew society led to such radical results that it is judged by some to be foreign to Muslim juridical tradition.

[40] Cf *Statut Personnel* in F. MESSNER, *Dictionnaire de droit des religions*, Paris, ed. CNRS, p. 666.

a multiplicity of legal forms within the same state structure, which are not always free from conflict.[41]

The Islamic conception of the *ius personae* is in any case based on religious belonging: the law applicable to a subject is determined solely by his or her faith. According to some *Surahs* or chapters of the Quran, it is Muhammad himself who invites the 'nation' of Christians and Jews to follow the prescriptions indicated by the Bible and the Torah and to indicate the divine origin of these norms, established by God for each 'nation'.[42] Sharia law is, in fact, applied to all Muslims by a Muslim judge, leaving non-Muslims to be governed by their own rules, administered by their respective denominational courts, and inspired by the legal principle of the privilege of religion. This, then, determines that the law applicable

---

[41] S. FERRARI, *Religioni, Diritto e Conflitti sociali*, in *An. Der. Ecl. Est.*, 2007 states that "where there are conflicts between religions, the element that is most important today is the growth of their identity. In many parts of the world it was and still is frequent for people who, despite having a different religion, share the same culture and live together. This is the case, for example, of Christians and Muslims who live in Egypt, Syria and other Middle Eastern countries: though different in terms of religion, they are part of the same Arab cultural world. This situation did not raise particularly serious problems until the identity components of religion took over, accentuating the importance of belonging to a community, the symbols that express it and the boundaries that define it: at this point it became difficult to reconcile the difference of faith and cultural identity, since religion is perceived and experienced as a producer of cultural diversity. Religious alterity generates cultural extraneousness and makes the coexistence of different communities in the same territory more problematic, generating tensions that induce phenomena of ghettoization and marginalization or lead to open conflicts" (p. 46).

[42] Quran, Surah V, *Al Mâ'ida*, verses 51-54: "51 O you who have believed, do not take the Jews and the Christians as allies. They are [in fact] allies of one another. And whoever is an ally to them among you - then indeed, he is [one] of them. Indeed, Allah guides not the wrongdoing people; 52 So you see those in whose hearts is disease hastening into [association with] them, saying, 'We are afraid a misfortune may strike us.' But perhaps Allah will bring conquest or a decision from Him, and they will become, over what they have been concealing within themselves, regretful; 53 And those who believe will say, 'Are these the ones who swore by Allah their strongest oaths that indeed they were with you?' Their deeds have become worthless, and they have become losers; 54 O you who have believed, whoever of you should revert from his religion - Allah will bring forth [in place of them] a people He will love and who will love Him [who are] humble toward the believers, powerful against the disbelievers; they strive in the cause of Allah and do not fear the blame of a critic. That is the favour of Allah; He bestows it upon whom He wills. And Allah is all-Encompassing and Knowing."

must always be religious law. But after independence, this term indicated the law applicable across the territory, necessary to build a strong national identity.

With the birth and spread of Islam and its body of legislation in the conquered lands along with the juridical principle of *cuius religio, cuius lex* was formed: everyone had their religion, hence their law.[43] Thus, a close connection between the juridical norm and the religious command took root and, on the basis of the Quran's dictate, since the stipulation of the first pacts between the followers of Muhammad and the Christian and Jewish communities, the exclusive jurisdiction of the judge was recognized and appointed by each religious authority authorized by its own law to hear all cases concerning relations between the faithful of their own community, both in the religious and civil sphere. By contrast, in the cases of a dispute between parties of different religions, if one of the two belonged to the *Umma*/Islamic community, the judge would necessarily be Muslim. This system of relationships between legal systems remained unchanged over the centuries.

Within the Islamic states, or at least the geographical area of the Maghreb, it is necessary to distinguish between a family comprising two non-Muslim foreigners and a family made up of a Muslim and a non-Muslim. In the first case, the system is extremely liberal and will allow the application of the couple's own laws, but in the second the notion of the privilege of religion will prevail since in Muslim law there is no distinction based on nationality, but only from belonging to the *Umma* / community of believers.[44] The unitary identity expressed in this concept is a basic social characteristic of Islam in which the individual defines his/her inclusion in the group, his/her identity and his/her humanity. It appears as an all-embracing process that places emphasis on the subject's position in relation to the *Umma* rather than on the application of internal rules, and this determines precise consequences in terms of belonging and organization.[45]

---

[43] Cf. A. FATTAL, *Statut légal des non-musulmans en pays d'Islam,* Beirut, ed. Imprimerie catholique, 1958, esp. p. 71.

[44] Cf. *Intercultural Relations and Religious Authorities: Muslims in the European Union*, W.A.R. SHADID, P.S. VAN KONINGVELD (eds.), Leuven, Peeters, 2002.

[45] Membership is structured starting from a public declaration of faith which consists of two affirmations, an individual declaration made to at least two Muslims from whom they obtain a social position and personal obligations. The declarations are "there is no divinity other than God" and "Muhammad is the messenger of God". The concept of *Umma*, the religious and social community, has a complex meaning, endowed with a strong emotional charge. It refers to pre-

It is particularly important to highlight how classical Islamic law, in outlining the material scope of the inapplicability of Islamic law to non-Muslim residents, did not actually arrive at an exhaustive list of matters falling under Personal Status, up to the first definition which dates back to 1875. While Islamic law was assigned a predominant position in some countries, the material scope of Personal Status was reduced and, importantly, religion fell under state authority. This allowed civil institutions to control and contain religion and promote the reforms necessary for modernization, as well as raising the possibility of legal adoption in some Muslim countries.

The code of Personal Status present in Arab states could, therefore, be applied in Europe when foreigners coming from these geographical areas require the application of their own legal rules, as indeed already occurs. What is necessary, then, is a study of the normative processes of conflicts of jurisdiction that might lead to the introduction of institutions which carry forward the value of diversity. This, though, could risk exacerbating the conflict between legal systems, especially in the delicate area of family law.[46]

Islamic Bedouin categories of community and solidarity and, at the same time, to the spirit of the body/*'asabijja*, one of the fundamental categories for understanding the socio-political organization of the Arab world that concerns solidarity. Another element that characterizes it is that it includes the concept of community. Cf. H. DAJAÏT, *La grande discorde. Religion et politique dans l'Islam des origines*, Paris, Folio, 2008; S. MERVIN, *L' Islam. Fondamenti e dottrine*, Milan, B. Mondadori- Paravia, 2001. The concept is based on a social contract "The *Umma* being founded on a universal belief system is non-territorial insofar as it is aimed to restoring the ideological unity of mankind (*Umma wāhida*). Being non-territorial, the *Umma* naturally cannot be equated with the territorial concepts of modern state and nationality": A. MANZOORUDDIN, *Umma: the idea of a universal community,* in *Islamic Studies*, vol. 14, n. l, 1975, pp. 27-54, qui p. 50. For an historical approach cf. O. BUCCI, *Le radici storiche della Shari'a islamica*, in *Iura Orientalia*, 6, 2010, pp. 232-259 and at http://www.iuraorientalia.net/IO/IO_06_2010/IV_01_Bucci.pdf.

[46] Cf. J. SCHACHT, *An introduction to Islamic law*, Oxford, Clarendon Press, 1964 (Italian translation by P. GUAZZETTI, E. LANFRANCHI, *Introduzione al diritto musulmano*, Turin, Fondazione G. Agnelli ed. 1995); F. CASTRO, *La codificazione del diritto privato negli stati arabi contemporanei*, in *Rivista di diritto civile*, XXXI 1985, l, pp. 387-447; F. CASTRO, *Il modello islamico*, Turin, Giappichelli, 2007; M. BORRMANS, *Statut personnel et famille au Maghreb de 1940 à nos jours,* Paris - La Haye, Mouton, 1977; M. BORRMANS, *Cours de Droit Familial musulman*, Rome, Pontificio Istituto di Studi arabi e d'Islamistica, 1977; M. BORRMANS, *Documents sur la famille au Maghreb de 1940 à nos jours (avec les textes législatifs marocain, algérien, tunisien, et égyptien en matière de Statut*

In migratory contexts, Islamic public order remains religiously characterised and the fundamental values to be defended are anchored in Sharia law. The sphere of private international law is limited by the preference accorded to the principle of the nationality / religion of the subject as a preponderant, if not exclusive, criterion. While European countries currently tend to anchor their rules to the criterion of domicile or residence, based on the presumption that foreign subjects will be more inclined towards integration and assimilation, in North Africa the principle of nationality prevails from a legislative/judicial point of view.[47]

Any analysis of the laws regarding the personal sphere as related to the family environment or the sensitive issue of the rights of minors within that environment, does bring to light a series of 'short-circuits' that may occur when Islamic and Western regulations meet, as they do for instance in regard to legal recognition of kafala. In this sense, the study of this instrument and its legal translation into Western legal systems could highlight the resilience of a political structure we like to think of as liberal and democratic.

The notion of public order must therefore be the normative parameter of reference, an indispensable tool for assessing the moment when foreign law does not affect the fundamental principles of our system and can therefore be applied.[48] It is clearly a particularly complex area especially because of the difficulty of defining such a notion, which is essentially of jurisprudential creation and subject to the mutability of space-time coordinates. However, it represents the only possible regulatory anchorage to refer to which is able to highlight a specific ideological conception of the national system.

Personnel), in *Oriente Moderno*, LIX, 1- 5, 1979; R. ALUFFI BECK-PECCOZ, *La modernizzazione del diritto di famiglia nei paesi arabi*, Milan, Giuffré, 1990; *Le leggi del diritto di famiglia negli stati arabi del Nord-Africa*, R. ALUFFI BECK - PECCOZ (ed.), Turin, Fondazione Giovanni Agnelli, 1997; *Tradizioni culturali, sistemi giuridici e diritti umani nell'area del Mediterraneo*, V. COLOMBO - G. GOZZI (eds.), Bologna, Il Mulino, 2004; G. VERCELLIN, *Istituzioni del mondo musulmano*, Turin, Einaudi, 2002; A. AL-NA'IM, *Islamic Family Law in a changing World*, London, Zed Books ed., 2002.

[47] Cf. *Ordre public et droit musulman de la famille en Europe et en Afrique du Nord*, N. BERNARD -MAUGIRON, B. DUPRET (ed.), Brussels, Bruylant, 2012, esp. p. 17; more generally Y. EN ACHOUR, *Politique, religion et droit dans le monde arabe*, Tunis, Cérès, 1992.

[48] *La famiglia si trasforma. Status familiari costituiti all'estero e loro riconoscimento in Italia tra ordine pubblico e interesse del minore*, G.O. CESARO, P. LOVATI, G. MASTRANGELO (eds.), Milan, F. Angeli, 2014.

In this framework, it is also important to emphasize that the reacquisition of independence from the French in the Maghreb resulted in a plurality of codes within Personal Status, which gave rise to a form of legal decolonization in which state policy proposed different regulatory solutions. Thus, in Morocco the choice was made for respect to be paid to Muslim authenticity through re-establishment of traditional law, albeit modernized to a certain extent. In Algeria, a coexistence of traditional and modern law was created in varying proportions, though this led to a series of social and cultural conflicts and political instability. Tunisia, on the other hand, chose to go its own way with a modern twist, structured as an evolution of traditional law. So, it is precisely this plurality of legislative approaches to the current sector which is of interest to us, and makes a specific focus on this geographical area particularly interesting.[49]

3. Kafala in the Kingdom of Morocco. Evolution of Islamic Family Law

Having regained its independence from French colonial rule in the twentieth century, Morocco decided to ban adoption as a tool to create a legal relationship of filiation, with explicit reference to Sharia law.

Here, it is interesting to note the evolutionary framework of Moroccan legislative policy oriented towards providing more protection. It should be emphasized that the Code of Personal Status continuously evolved, albeit within a strictly religious framework, due to the political transformations that affected Morocco since its reacquisition of independence and this led to the promulgation of a unique code applicable to all Moroccan Muslims.[50] The condition of 'foundlings' was regulated by the 1993 laws which clarified that the civil status of the child must be regularized and the kafala procedure accelerated after a short a stay as possible in a specialized institute. The child and the foster family have the right to social welfare through both public and private support. In a modern perspective, the basic

---

[49] Cf. Y. BEN ACHOUR, *Politique, religion et droit dans le monde arabe*, Tunis, ed. Cérès Production, 1992; N. ROULAND, *Les colonisations juridiques de l'Arctique à l'Afrique noire*, in *Journal of legal pluralism*, 29, 1990, p. 39 *et seq.*; K. MEZIOU, *Le droit de La famille au Maghreb*, in *Etudes maghrébines*, 9, 1999, p. 4 *et seq.*; A. MOULAY RCHID, *Un horizon de la modernité qui pass e par l'ijtihâd*, in *Etudes maghrébines*, 9, 1999, p. 23 *et seq.*

[50] M. TOZY, *Monarchie et Islam po litique au Maroc*, Paris, Presse de la Fondation nationale des sciences politiques, 1999; *Trente ans de vie constitutionnelle au Maroc*, D. BASRI, M. ROUSET, G. VEDEL (eds.), Paris, L.G.D.J., 1993.

rights of women within the family and in the workplace were made subject to specific protection.

However, the first codifications date back to 1957 up to the most recent reform of 2004. Such a reform did not affect its strong religious origins but took shape in a renewed context of change whose central node was represented, at a political and regulatory level, by the need to adapt family legislation, structured according to traditional Muslim law, to social changes. The Code of Personal Status was thus called the *Mudawana al-usra*, i.e. the family code.[51]

The protection of the child in the family environment is an obligation for both parents, or the minor's guardian in the event of their separation.[52] They have the obligation to take care of the health and education of the child. Any forms of brutality or neglect are also punishable under criminal law, and the most serious form of negligence is represented, of course, by abandonment. Children's rights received particular attention in compliance with the international conventions adopted on this matter, of which Morocco is practically the only signatory among Islamic countries. The only condition of legitimate filiation however derives from a legitimate marriage, according to more traditional interpretations of the Quran.

---

[51] The Preamble states that it presents a "*formulation dans un style juridique contemporain, en conformité avec les prescriptions tolérantes de l'Islam ... en prévoyant des solutions équilibrées, équitables et pratiques qui reflètent l'effort jurisprudentiel éclairé et ouvert et consacrant les droits de l'homme et de la citoyenneté pour tous les marocains, tant hommes que femmes, dans le respect des références divines*". In assessing the reform, it is also necessary to consider the particular role of the king in the political structure of Morocco who embodies the symbolic figure of the Muslim tradition, that of *Amir al Mu'minin*, who holds a dual power: religious (therefore he must direct the community of believers) and political (he must apply the commandments of Allah): Cf. F. TOBICH, *Les Statuts Personnels dans les Pays Arabes. De l'éclatement à l'harmonisation*, Aix-en-Provence, Presses Univ. d'Aix-Marseille, 2008, esp. pp. 55-88; S. MERNISSI, *Quelques aspects de la codification du statut personnel marocain*, in *Le statut personnel des musulmans, droit comparé et droit international privé*, J.Y. CARLIER, M. VERWILGHEN (ed.), Brussels, Bruylant, 1992.

[52] Law 70-03 of 3 Feb. 2004 in O. MOUNIA, *La Mudawana. Le nouveau droit de la famille au Maroc*, Rabat, ed. Marsam, 2005. The Moroccan Code of Personal Status, codified in 1958 under the reign of King Mohammed V, was amended in 1993 by King Hassan II and revised in February 2004 by the Parliament of Morocco, promulgated by King Mohammed VI, and is still in force. Interestingly, at the discretion of the judge, men who abandon women after leaving them pregnant are punishable: Article 54 and Articles 155-156.

The rules contained in the Family Code of 2004 find their justification in the reference to religion and to the desire to preserve a national, ethnic and religious identity. The problems faced at the time of the reform of the regulatory system and the protection of minors came up against several politically complex issues which interconnected with cultural identity, the rights of the individual towards the community, and the protection of its weakest members represented by women, and above all, minors.[53]

The Moroccan Family Code thus constituted significant evolutionary progress with political recognition of the concept of minor that was up until then practically invisible at the regulatory level. The *Moudawana* distinguishes between kinship/*bunuwwa* (relationship with the father and the mother) and paternal filiation/*nasab* (the male line only), considered one of the rights of the child resulting from the conjugal bond. According to a modernist view, one of the objectives of marriage is the foundation of an Arab family and only if the father is unknown can filiation be matrilineal.

Article 149 of the Code, based on traditional Muslim/*fiqh* law, states that adoption has no legal value and does not produce any of the effects of filiation.[54] However, a testamentary legacy is possible which allows an unrelated individual to benefit from a part of the inherited rights. In Morocco, despite its prohibition, adoption did exist explicitly as a habit of donating a child at an intra-family level and in secret.

The legal provision of kafala derives, therefore, on the one hand from the refusal on the part of the political authorities to accept the institution of adoption, and, on the other, from a growing awareness of the need to develop a policy of management and care for abandoned children. This phenomenon intensified in the eighties as a result of profound socio-economic change (decolonization, rural migration, urbanization, re-distribution of family groups), and of compliance with the 1996 Hague Convention to which only Morocco joined, among other Islamic countries. Kafala, therefore, is the instrument through which illegitimate and abandoned children are allowed a second chance. What is more, ignoring a relationship of filiation between parents and children avoids the transgression

---

[53] Cf. A. AHMED, *Le thème de la filiation en droit et Charie*, Koweit, ed. Dar el Kalam, 1983. For an overview of the evolution of Islamic feminism with important repercussions on family law in Morocco Cf. S. BORRILLO, *Femminismi e Islam in Marocco*, Naples, ESI, 2017.

[54] Pursuant to article 142 of the same code, filiation occurs only with the procreation of the child by the child's parents. Article 83 of the Code of Personal Status and Inheritance/*Moudawana* was absorbed without change into the current Family Code of 2004.

of mixing blood and the community is reassured because the child taken in does not threaten the rights of blood relatives.

Only in 1983 did the Moroccan government express the desire to control the abandonment of children through institutionalized forms of legal custody seen as a purely charitable act, but consecrated legally only ten years later with a single, solitary law on abandoned children.

From Morocco's independence in 1956, until 1993, only administrative circulars provided for this important legislative instrument, which was subsequently regulated more fully by a law enacted in 2002.[55] This law contained important changes in a more modern sense. It recognized the possibility even for a single woman to claim custody, and, above all, allowed the fictitious names of the father and mother to appear on the birth certificate, avoiding social discrimination for orphans of unknown parents.

The modern type of kafala, now completely legal, is reserved exclusively for abandoned children, but does not exclude a similar notarial system which applies to the non-abandoned minors of known parents. In addition to kafala, Moroccan law provides another method of integration of the minor into a host family, the so-called 'gratification' adoption/*jazâ* or testamentary adoption/*wasiyya* or *tanzil*, a measure that allows parents to transfer a part of their estate to a beneficiary, without creating bonds of filiation.

Though it had given judicial authorities limited control over the procedure, the 1993 law left ample room for administrative bodies to turn to kafala to regulate the position of abandoned minors, minors whose parents were unworthy or whose parents, for reasons beyond their control, were unable to manage or educate their children.[56] By this legislation, on ascertaining the state of abandonment as a precondition to access to kafala and with a simple motion from the King's Prosecutor, the court could then decide on custody, without proceeding with an inquiry. It could, however, be granted only to Muslims who had been married for at least three years and after an administrative board had ascertained their suitability. In

[55] The institution of kafala was initially regulated by Law no. 1-93-165 of 10 September 1993, and subsequently by '*Dahir*' (Moroccan variant of the term '*zahir*', which in classical Arabic means decree) no. 1-02-172 of June 13, 2002 with law 15-01. The 2002 law is divided into Chapter I, which concerns general provisions; Chapter II on the conditions of kafala of an abandoned child; kafala procedure; Chapter III on monitoring and control of kafala; Chapter IV on the effects of the ordinance relating to the concession of kafala; Chapter V which has as its object the causes of the end of kafala; Chapter VI and Chapter VII which concern the final provisions.

[56] The law of 9 June 1984 was replaced with the *dahir* of 10 Sept. 1993.

practice, however, this decision was essentially referred to the local authority/*wali* and materialized in a simple act of commitment by the *kafil*. The Court was involved only in the event of conflict. However, these measures were not able to offer adequate protection to minors and judicial protection was excessively simplified.

Currently, the legislative text of reference is Law no. 15-01,[57] which indicates the abandoned child in its first article as: the eighteen-year-old child born of unknown parents; an orphan or with parents unable to satisfy their needs or who do not have legal means of subsistence; the child with dissolute parents who do not fulfil their role. The state of abandonment can result from a matter of fact or a decision by the judge. The law punishes the abandonment of children unless they arc placed with someone in care. It is the duty of the Prosecutor to verify the state of abandonment and open an investigation at the Family Court.

If the minor is of unknown parents s/he will be given a name and surname as well as an indication (fictitious) of names of parents. Even if the religious affiliation of the minor is not clear, the registrar will automatically assign names from the Arab-Muslim tradition, thus reintegrating the child into the *Umma,* the community of believers from which the child was excluded by being ‘illegitimate’. The condition of abandonment effectively means that the child is assigned a new identity, definitively cutting any ties with the ‘blood’ family. The registrar will give the child the name of a father and mother, as well as a name and surname that must be, also phonetically, Arabic-Muslim.[58]

The Court will then proceed to investigate the state of abandonment with a tutelary judge – a judge supervising cases concerning guardianship – also qualified to judge kafala applications. In the case of unknown parents, a declaration will be issued and made public to allow natural relatives possible recognition.[59]

Following a declaration of the state of abandonment, the Prosecutor will decide whether to entrust the child in kafala to an institution or a family. This may take place by judicial means, by order of the judge after

[57] Law 15-01 regarding kafala, *dahir* 13 June 2002, B.O. n. 5036, 15 Sep. 2002.

[58] The King’s Prosecutor will choose a name and surname for the child as well as the surnames of parents or father, if the mother is known. In the margin of the birth certificate, the registrar will note that these names have been chosen in accordance with the law (Article 16 law 37-99). This will help to avoid discrimination and integrate the child perfectly into the community. All abandoned children in Morocco automatically acquire Moroccan nationality.

[59] It is important to remember that Article 490 of the penal code punishes sexual relations outside marriage, which is the main reason why children are abandoned.

careful investigation. In granting kafala the Court must also take into account the religious affiliation of the parents, who must fulfil certain conditions: they must be of age, morally and socially suitable to take on this responsibility; they must not be in dispute with the child whose protection they are requesting, nor have been convicted of crimes and must not suffer from infectious disease. Where more than one couple is involved, priority is given to families without children or to couples who offer greater assurances.

Kafala may therefore be granted to a Muslim couple who can guarantee conditions of morality, health and safety for the child.[60] The length of time the couple have been married or whether or not they have children is no longer taken into account. Kafala can also be granted to a single woman as long as she meets the conditions required by law: she is a Muslim and is morally and materially suitable. The application is presented by the interested parties and any minor over the age of twelve must give his/her consent.

The tutelary judge entrusts the investigation to a committee after which an order attributing kafala is issued and is open to appeal. When it becomes enforceable, this decision is transcribed in the margin of the birth certificate but has no effect on civil status and does change the patronymic name. However, the judge continues to play a role even after the attribution of kafala through mandatory monitoring. In addition, should the couple decide to move abroad or if there are donations, legacies or a *tanzil*, authorisation must be granted by the judge.

Kafala ends when the child comes of age, with the exception of unmarried girls, handicapped individuals or those who are in no position to take care of themselves.[61] Kafala may also come to an end on the death of the parents or the single mother, if the foster parents are accused of incapacity or violation of the obligations set by the judge or if the court, on the parents' request, ascertains that this measure is no longer necessary. In the event of a separation, the judge will have to decide in the interests of the minor, and after obtaining the child's consent, whether to entrust the child to one of the parents or appoint a guardian.

---

[60] In Morocco, unlike Algeria, where this practice does not exist, tens of thousands of children, girls in particular, are domestic workers. Kafala can therefore be employed for different ends as many are used to having a 'maid' at home and may sometimes become an instrument for national and international trafficking and abuse of minors.

[61] Article 198 of the family code specifies that as far as women are concerned, kafala ends when the woman marries or when she is able to support herself financially.

Article 29 provides that once the reasons for abandonment have ceased to exist, both or either of the two biological parents, may apply to the judge to recover their child. If the child is over twelve years of age,[62] the Court will listen to the child and if s/he has no wish to return, the court will decide in the best interest of the child.[63] The King's Prosecutor may then place the child at a health facility or in a child protection centre.[64]

Moroccan laws allow the *kafil* to leave the country to settle abroad, but do not consider the hypothesis of the international kafala. Being a Muslim is obviously fundamental to claiming kafala and religious identity – conceived as an innate character, a legacy transmitted through birth from parents to child – is essential. Even abandoned minors are no exception to this rule and this indisputable transfer requires the coincidence of religious identities for kafala to be legally granted. The abandoned child must therefore be welcomed by people of the same religion. There are different categories of foreign candidates for the Moroccan kafala, that is, couples in which both members come from Islamic countries, mixed or foreign couples. In the first case, they are considered Muslims in an inherited ethno-cultural sense, while in the second case the non-Muslim spouse is not deprived of his/her kafala aspirations. However, it is essential, as well as for foreign couples, that there be a formal conversion. In general, it can be said that it is the parents who assign and transmit a religious identity to their children, whether biological or not.

We therefore understand that, with any kafala application, it is absolutely necessary for couples to prove in advance that they belong to the *Umma* / Muslim community. Particular problems could derive from a possible non-recognition of kafala in the destination country. This issue was the subject of a circular issued by the Ministry of Justice in 2003, concerning the authorization to transfer a kafala child abroad, in order to

---

[62] The law does not specify the age at which a child may be heard but applying by analogy Article 214 of the family code it could well be 12 years of age.

[63] The person or organisation to which the child is entrusted under kafala must perform the obligations relating to the care and protection of the child and ensure that s/he grows up in a healthy environment, taking care of his/her basic needs up to adulthood (for girls up to marriage), in accordance with the rules of the family code (Articles 22 to 24). It is up to the local judge to carry out checks. Cf. H. ZEKRÌ, *La kafala en el Derecho marroquì*, in *Kafala y adopciones en las relaciones hispano-marroquies*, Madrid, FIIAPP, 2009, p. 12 *et seq*.

[64] Cf. UNICEF, *Enfance abandonnée au Maroc. Ampleur, état des lieux juridique et social, prise en charge, véecus*, in www.unicef.org/morocco/french/2010-Etude_Enfance_abandon_UNICEF-LMPE.pdf. Unicef reports that very often, in the absence of suitable facilities, these children are practically hospitalized. Even though they are in separate wings they are still kept in health facilities.

solve the problem of residence outside Morocco. To bypass situations that could derive from the non-recognition of kafala in the new state of residence of the *makful* and to avoid judicial procedures in the event of non-compliance or correspondence with the legislation of the host country, the Ministry deemed it preferable to provide for the preventive release of authorization to leave Morocco to ensure the existence of a legal agreement authorizing the kafala system or a certificate issued by the local authorities, confirming the legitimacy of the legal position that the kafala minor will acquire.

In recent years, particularly, Moroccan authorities have shown a greater and more rigorous respect for the conditions and aims pursued by the kafala institution, and made greater efforts to ensure that the underlying principles are well identified in respect of the origins of the child, his or her education in the Muslim faith, and maintenance of his/her Moroccan nationality. It is clear that when minors move to Europe, such control becomes impossible or at least extremely difficult when delegated to the consular authorities or embassies. This circular was also followed by a legislative proposal (as yet still awaiting approval) for a reform of the judicial kafala in Morocco and its requirements in order to slow down requests from Western citizens. The current objective therefore seems to be to provide Moroccan minors with better guarantees, avoiding the legal uncertainties of the transnational kafala.[65]

4. The Kafala Institution in Algeria. Identity Continuity of a Cultural and Religious Nature

Adoption as structured in the Western tradition has no equivalent in Moroccan and Algerian law, but this does not exclude the existence of other forms of legal/social (elective), institutionalised (kafala) or non-institutionalised kinship. To understand these institutions, a single religious perspective that tends to reduce the complex reality of North Africa to the single practice of Islam simply will not do. What is needed is to analyze the "structural affinity between the lifestyle favoured by the Muslim religion and the lifestyle specific to Algerian [and Moroccan] society", and how "the Quran's message could have penetrated so deeply

---

[65] Following this Moroccan government circular, the Spanish authorities decided, from 16 October 2012, not to accept requests for kafala from Moroccan minors and to suspend the processing of applications for kafala. Such a decision has obvious implications, especially for Spanish citizens who were awaiting the custody of a Moroccan minor or awaiting the certificate of eligibility.

into these societies".[66] On a sociological level, Islam represents "the language in which the unspoken rules of conduct are stated",[67] going some way to explain and legitimise the choices, practices, rules and prohibitions society has made. But it is a society in which the religious argument turns out to be insufficient to justify the ban set on adoption in Moroccan and Algerian law.

The three well-known verses of Surah XXXIII relating to elective kinship have been interpreted as prohibiting the adoption process commonly in use among the ancient Arabs as a means to overcome the quantitative and qualitative defects of lineage, or to open the field to more marriage options.[68] Under the Muhammad Ali ruling dynasty, therefore, family institutions were revised not so much as an actual break with the past but to adapt to new social relations. The objective of this reform was to underline the primacy of the rights of blood relatives and to oppose adoption, which jeopardized the organisation and legitimacy of kinship groups.

It is also important to underline that before the declaration of independence in Algeria, four personal statuses were recognised legally, which allowed different populations to follow their own traditional regulations, especially regarding family law. Algerian Muslims were thus granted the possibility of opting between their own law and French law in the matter of personal status. This made it possible for them to use French law to disregard prohibitions laid down by the Quran, especially in the sphere of adoption and inheritance and to turn an otherwise fictitious bond into a legal and legitimate kinship. In actual fact, in addition to prohibiting adoption, Muslim law only allows the recognition of paternity following

---

[66] P. BOURDIEU, *Sociologie de l'Algérie*, Paris, PUF, 2001, esp. p. 99; Cf. anche M.C. IVALDI, *La religione nell'ordinamento algerino tra previsioni costituzionali e normativa ordinaria in materia di esercizio dei culti diversi dal mussulmano*, at www.statoechiese.it, Nov. 2012.

[67] P. BOURDIEU, *Sociologie ...*, cit., p. 100.

[68] E. CONTE, *Alliances et parenté élective en Arabie ancienne. Éléments d'une problématique*, in *L'Homme*, 102, XXVII (2), 1987, pp. 119-138; E. CONTE, *Entrer dans le sang, perceptions arabes des origines*, in *Al-ansâb. La quéte des origines. Anthropologie historique de la société tribale arabe*, P. BONTE, E. CONTE, C. HAMES, A. WEHOUD OULD CHEIKH (eds.), Paris, Éditions de la maison des sciences de l'homme, 1991, pp. 55-100; E. CONTE, *Choisir ses parents dans la société arabe. La situation à l'avènement de l'Islam*, in *Épouser au plus proche. Inceste, prohibitions et stratégies matrimoniales autour de la Méditerranée*, P. BONTE (ed.), Paris, Éditions de l'école des hautes études en sciences sociales, 1994, pp. 165-186.

marriage, which substantially amounts to legitimacy gained by subsequent bond rather than by proper adoption.

In the phase following the reacquisition of independence from French colonial rule, the country restored its previous legislation, but with the new rules emerged the need for a revision of the Family Code, which took place only in 1984.[69] This Code is based on classical traditions and establishes that filiation derives only from a valid marriage that allows for the father-son bond, but also establishes that the institution of kafala is legally formalized.[70] An extramarital relationship based on consequent filiation constitutes an infringement that can also be criminally punishable, and the natural child has no legal or social recognition.[71] Due to the pressure of the community, an illegitimate pregnancy is also considered unacceptable and it is to save the girl's 'honour' that children are frequently abandoned in Algeria as well as in the whole geographical area of the Maghreb (as happened in the past also in our continent).

In the case of an illegitimate child there is no possibility of legal recognition as the child will never be able to take the father's surname. The registrar will be able to give the child two names but no paternal surname, at best the surname of the mother. The 1976 Public Health Code

---

[69] Law no. 62157 of 31 Dec. 1962, *Journal officiel de la RADP*, 11 Jan. 1963. This rule referred back to French legislation and in particular to the decree of March 6 1907, which allowed adoption in Algeria of the French law of 27 June 1904 (amended by Law 182 of 15 April 1943 relating to childcare). By organizing assistance to minors in France, that provision entrusted its execution to a public service. The application of these provisions in the colony allowed Algerian families to legally adopt abandoned children. Until introduction of a 1966 circular that imposed the application of Muslim law, full adoption was allowed and until 1984 childcare contracts included the statement 'with a view to adoption'. Cf. M.C. SALAH- BEY, *Le droit de la famille et le dualisme juridique*, in *Rev. alger. sciences juridiques économiques et politiques*, 1997, 3, p. 923 *et seq*.

[70] Law no. 84-II of 9 June 1984, Code de la Famille, *J.C.* n. 24. Articles 116 – 125 refer to kafala.

[71] Unlike other legislation enforced in the Maghreb, the Algerian family code does not qualify the child born out of wedlock as 'natural'. It simply makes no mention. The Code of Algerian nationality, on the other hand, makes no distinction so that all children born in Algeria are presumed to be of Algerian nationality. Cf. M.C. SALAH-BEY, *La filiation naturelle dans le projet du Code de la famille*, in *Rev. alger sciences juridiques économiques et politiques*, 3, 1974, who stressed that "*la position du droit musulman classique est encore plus rigoureuse que celle du droit canonique. Il ne reconnait qu'une seule catégorie d'enfants, les enfants légitimes et ignore toute forme d'illégitimité, qu'il s'agisse de la filiation adultérine ou encore de la filiation incestueuse entre lesquelles, il n'opère pas de distinction*" (p. 85); finally cf. G. BENMELAHA, *Le droit algérien de la famille*, Alger, OPU, 1993.

envisaged the establishment of shelters for pregnant unmarried women in order to stem the incidence of abandonment, as well as the provision of monthly subsidies and care for the needs of mother and child. But this was repealed eleven years later without any of these measures ever being applied.[72] This Code had also provided, albeit in a very meagre way, the legal possibility of kafala as the only legal form of a 'fictitious' parental bond.[73]

In the debate that surrounded family law reform, there were clashes among modernists versus traditionalists concerning above all the matter of family law and filiation – that is, those supporting the authenticity of the interpretation of the Quran/*asala* against supporters who leaned towards openness/*tafattuh*.[74] Adoption, as a legal solution to protect abandoned minors was not adopted by legislation, even though the certificates of minors awaiting a solution contained the expression "in view of adoption".

Between 1984 and 1992, rare rulings of kafala in favour of abandoned children took place in the utmost secrecy to avoid social discrimination against thc couple (sterile) and the child (fruit of sin). The child was given only two names, and this constituted a serious problem in Muslim society

---

[72] N. Aït Zaï, *L'enfant illégitime dans la société musulmane*, in *Peuples Méditerranées*, 1989, p.48 *et seq*. and Id., *L 'abandon d'enfant et la loi*, in *Rev. alger. sciences juridiques économiques et politiques*, 1991, XXIX, 3, pp. 473-493; F. Chihab Zidane, *L' enfant né hors mariage en Algérie*, Alger, ed. Entreprise algérienne de presse, 1992; A. Bencheneb, *Le droit de la famille entre la tradition et la modernité*, in *Rev. alger. sciences juridiques économiques et politique*, 1982, l, p. 25 *et seq*.

[73] Ordinance no. 76-79 of 23 Oct. 1976, Code de la Santé Publique. A single article regards the protection of minors: the basic idea is that one task of executive power is to encourage kafala by seeking a family within which a child without a family will be able to live a well-balanced emotional and social climate (Article 256). The whole of Section 1 regards children without a family whose interests they seek to protect by creating a public childcare service. Cf. Article. 256, 2, which spells out that the commitment to welcome and educate a child without a family is sanctioned with the act of kafala. According to article 252, the tutor (prefect) or the family council give their consent to this act of kafala. Children who are not the subject of kafala should be entrusted, as far as possible, to a family as a free offer, or, failing that, through a paid placement (Article 257). Legislation paves the way for the legal drafting process. G. Lahlou-Khiar, *La kafala en drot algérien: une transgression d'intéret supérieur de l'enfant*, in *Varia, Rev. Franco-maghrébine de droit*, 2013, 20, pp. 23-220; M. Mawan, *Les causes de l'interdition de l'adoption et la kafala camme substituton en droit musulman et en droit de la famille algérienne*, in *Revue myiiar*, 9, 2004, p. 479 *et seq*.

[74] Cf. A. Bencheneb, *La formation du lien de kafala et les silences législatifs*, in *Rev. alg. sciences juridiques économiques et politiques*; 1991, n. 1- 2, p. 47 *et seq*.

where, as mentioned, filial status defines individuals socially. In 1992, legislation finally decided to correct this inconvenience and source of prejudice, allowing the use of the patronymic name *kafil-makful*. It is, in actual fact, permitted to give the child a name without creating a legal bond of filiation.[75]

The legal commitment of those applying for kafala can be defined as the desire to take care of the welfare, education and protection of a child in the same way as a father would his child, an apparently unilateral act as it expresses a single desire: that of an adult.[76] The next article in the Family Code clarifies, however, that in the presence of biological parents their consent is required.[77] This form of custody (originally provided for by the Public Health Code) thus became a legal instrument with a notarial deed or following a judgment by the Court.

Here, the first condition is that the *kafil* must be a Muslim, regardless of his nationality; must be 'reasonable' and honest and be able to financially support and protect the child.[78] This kind of condition involves fulfilling the family and scholastic obligations of legitimate children, but does not determine matrimonial impediments between adopter and adopted.

While Algerian law provides that in the event of the death of the father, guardian of the minor, this guardianship is transferred to the mother, Article 125 of the Family Code establishes, instead, that in the event of the death of the *kafil*, guardianship is transferred to the heirs, if they accept, otherwise the judge will entrust the minor to the proper institution for support. No mention is made of the wife of the *kafil*, who is subject to the will of the heirs. If the child is at the age of discernment, s/he can decide

---

[75] There is an unresolved disfunction on the concordance of the *kafil-makful* name between the 1992 decree, which allows the child to obtain the name of the foster family and a circular dated 1994 of the Minister of the Interior (often disregarded), which prohibits inserting the *makful* in the family status record.

[76] Article 116, family code.

[77] Cf. Article 117. The code is silent about the consent of the child of unknown parents.

[78] Cf. Article 118. The original filiation is retained if the child has known relatives (Article 120). Otherwise, Article 64 of the civil code applies, which assigns two names to the child, one of which will serve as patronymic. This provision of Article 64 has been extended to the abandoned child. But assigning two names to the child helps to marginalize him even more in a society that rejects illegitimate children. In this sense, the 1992 decree, complementary to the decree of 3 June 1971, no. 71157 on the change of name. Cf. Y. BETTAHAR, *La construction sociale de la parentalité: l'exemple de l'Algérie*, in *L'Anné du Maghreb*, II, 2005- 2006, pp. 155-167.

whether or not to return to his/her biological parents, if they ask for the child to be returned to their protection, otherwise the judge will have to make an appropriate judgement. The *kafil*, moreover, can bequeath or make a gift, of up to one third of his estate, in favour of the child, but in case of pre-death of the minor / *makful* the *kafil* does not acquire inheritance rights. Though it may destabilize the child psychologically, kafala can be revoked at any time: Algerian law, in fact, remained faithful to religious thought that proclaims that there is no legal relationship between the adopter and the adopted.

It is also necessary to consider the legal and practical difficulties of applying the rules on kafala in private international law. Unlike Morocco, the Algerian rule on kafala bases its needs on the issue of name and nationality. Assuming that the code strictly applies to Algerian citizens, at an international level, only Algerian immigrants will be able to aspire to it. As in Morocco, Islam is the state religion, and in Algeria everyone is substantially Muslim. But in granting kafala the Algerian authorities are much stricter than their Moroccan counterparts, although the objective is the same: to match the religious identity of the child with the adoptive parents. For this purpose, Algeria does not accept a formal conversion.[79] Thus the abandoned child is mainly Algerian and Muslim; the name, a powerful sign of identification, must always be Arab-Muslim. In Algeria too, kafala is perceived as the transmission and continuity of an identity of a cultural and religious nature.

It must always be considered that by regulating the phenomenon of emigration where kafala is concerned, North African countries aim to ensure cultural continuity, and above all make sure that children will continue to be raised according to the principles of Islam, even outside national borders. But caution is necessary even in the case of simple custody of a Muslim minor, meaning that if the foster parents are not Muslims, the provision could come up against the sensitivity of the Islamic community, whose main concern is that the child grows up in an appropriate environment from a religious and moral point of view.

5. The Normative Provision of Adoption in Tunisia between Religious Command and 'Western' Legislation

It is interesting to note that Tunisia presents a unique form of the Personal Status code. Under the political impulse of Bourguiba, the first

---

[79] Cf. *Anthropologie du politique*, M. Abélès, H.P. Jeudy, (ed.), Paris, A. Colin, 1997.

president of the Republic, lawmakers made an important innovation not only to choose the path of codification, but also to reorganise family relationships in a more modern sense.[80] It succeeded in developing a modern code that founded its innovation within religion, by taking a completely opposite approach from, for example, Ataturk for the construction of the modern Turkish State, eliminating any reference to the religious and affirming the principle of secularism within the Constitution as well.[81]

The Tunisian Constitution continues to declare Islam the state religion but omits the common formulation to the Constitutions of Islamic countries whereby Sharia is the main source of law.[82] While its promulgation was favourably received in the West, reaction in Muslim countries was

---

[80] M. CHARFI, *Le droit tunisien de La famille entre l'Islam et la modernité*, RTD, 1973, observed that "*les conservateurs ne sont pas encore rétablis de la maladie de la colonisation; ils se croient obligés de lutter pour garder leur authenticité contre le danger de l'assimilation coloniale devenu pourtant aujourd'hui, purement imaginaire, et ils n 'ont pas encore compris que l'ère de la domination étrangère est à jamais révolue. Pour résoudre les problèmes du présent, ils ne cessent de regarder en arrière vers un passé vieux de quatorze siècles. Pour les conservateurs, les modernistes, victimes de leur propre formation occidentale, sous-produit de la périod e coloniale, sont prisonniers d'une certaine culture et d 'une idéologie étrangères. lls sont condamnés à rester des déracinés et ils constituent un danger dès qu'ils veulent plaquer leurs idées impor- tées sur nos réalités arabo-musulmanes*" (p. 13).

[81] M. KERRROU, *Laicité, sécularisation et islam dans la Tunisie de Bourguiba*, in *Revue Franco-Maghrébine de Droit*, 15, 2007 observes that "*le projet politique bourguibien offre des similitudes avec l'expérience kémaliste dans la mesure où, dans les deux cas, le culte de la personnalité s'accompagne d'une mise en tutelle de la société par l'État moderniste. L'islam était perçu par les deux "grands hommes" comme étant un obstacle au progrès et à la modernité. Il devait donc être exclu ou domestiqué. Mais, alors que Mustapha Kémal entreprend une lacisation radicale sur le pian juridique. et symbolique (abolition du califat, suppression de l'enseignement islamique, interdiction des confréries, prohibition des vètements religieux en dehors des lieux de culte, adoption de l'alphabet latin, laicité de l'État, etc.), Habib Bourguiba compose avec la société et l'islam tout en tenant à les séculariser progressivement. Le bouguibisme n'est ainsi pas une idéologie cohérente mais une démarche pragmatique et souple basée sur la "politique des étapes". Dans sa démarche sécularíste, Bourguiba tend à écarter ses concurrents religieux et traditionalistes en sapant leur assise économique et idéologique et en leur offrant la possibilité d'ètre récupérés, par l'octroi de fonctions officielles*" (p. 43). As regards Turkey cf. R. BOTTONI, *Il principio di laicità in Turchia. Profili storico-giuridici*, Milan, Vita e Pensiero, 2012

[82] F. TOBICH, *Les Statuts Personnels ...,* cit, esp. pp. 89-126.

lukewarm and within the most traditionalist part of society and among Tunisian intellectuals, decidedly hostile. Political discourse therefore heavily emphasized the relationship of the code with *ijtihad* / religious interpretation, based on a modern and innovative reading of religious texts, which still remained the primary source.[83]

In the area that interests us, the prohibition of adoption respected in most Muslim countries is applied with few exceptions, as in the case of Indonesia, Turkey, Somalia (before the dreadful internal conflict) and Lebanon which, like Tunisia in 1958, legalized this practice. Though the normative religious reference of the polycentric Islamic world is one alone, debate on the application of Sharia law is an important component of contemporary dynamics: the legal system does constitute one of the most important concrete expressions in which society establishes a set of shared values on the basis of which it builds its own idea of the state. In this sense, all Islamic societies transitioning towards modernity have felt the need to look to new values, which derive from both their own internal evolution and from other social realities and diverse cultural models. It is in this sense that the fundamental innovations of Tunisian law in the recognition of adoptions may now be understood.

In the post-war period, the state took over the legislative function in the modern sense and introduced Sharia law into the codified laws. Put differently, the law became written and schematic, taking on the shape of general and abstract law with the Divine Revelation channelled into structured provisions. The end of colonization, at least in North Africa, meant that many institutions similar to those which arose out of contact with European countries, were maintained and also led to a rethinking of the role of women and the family based on the cultural patterns of the West.

Given the relevance of classical Islamic law, the legal recognition of adoption was understood as an absolute novelty since it created a real relationship between adopter and adopted,[84] with reciprocal rights and duties of parents and legitimate children.[85] As in Morocco and Algeria,

---

[83] Y. BEN ACHOUR, *Une révolution par le droit? Bourguiba et le Code du statut personnel*, Cérès, CERP, 1992; M. BENJEMIA, S. BEN ACHOUR, M. BELLAMINE, *Le droit tunisien de la famille entre modernité et tradition*, in *Ordre public et droit musuman de la famille en Europe et en Afrique du Nord*, N. BERNARD- MAUGIRON, B. DUPRET (eds.), Brussels, Bruylant, 2012, pp. 161-196.

[84] Cf. S. BEN ACHOUR, L. CHEDLY, *Actualités du droit international privé de la famille en Tunisie età l'étranger*, Tunis Latrach, 2015

[85] Cf. B. HAJ HAMOUDA, *A la recherche d'une autre famille: la famille nourricière. Cas du droit tunisien*, in *L'enfant et les famills nourricières en drot comparé*, J.

Tunisian law also proposed and defended a concept of family, in which growth and development were possible only if there were blood ties, sanctioned by a legitimate union. However, the legalization of adoption in Tunisia did demonstrate a desire to give priority within the Constitution to other values and to the demands of the most modern social realities.[86]

In the first place, it should be considered that the Tunisian Code of Personal Status of 1956 arose in a very particular moment, historically and politically speaking. Immediately after independence, Bourguiba – leader of the struggle for independence, founder of modern Tunisia and the first President of the country for thirty years – profoundly reformed the state, the law and the institutions, preparing the way for modernisation, by revolutionizing in particular the condition of women.[87]

The decision to legalize adoption was therefore the result of this modernist policy and an attempt to adapt the law to the needs of a re-reading of the sacred texts and to the modern demands of society. Given the existence of orphans and abandoned children, the State decided to intervene to organize the necessary support, guaranteeing an alternative family (adoption) or shelter (through unofficial protection or kafala). Thus, at this time, Tunisian family law occupies a special place in the Arab-Muslim world, constituting in some respects a unique example. It equipped itself with a Code which was as audacious in its reform as it was innovative. Legislation did not limit itself to codifying personal status, but went further still, acting on the content of the law itself and modernizing it to help society evolve. Through these reforms, legislation foresaw an evolution of mindsets, still latent in large sections of the population, especially in rural areas.

The introduction of a law in this area implied the political desire to redefine the family and male-female social roles whose relations were subject to state regulation. The written law thus represented the instrument by which to affirm, spread and impose new models of social behaviour.

There are two main legislative references regarding filiation: Articles 68 to 76 of the CSP - *Code de Statut Personnel* - and the law of 1998 concerning the attribution of the patronymic to abandoned children or of

---

POUSSON-PETIT (ed.), Toulouse, Presses de l'Université des Sciences Sociales de Toulouse, 1997, p. 280 *et seq*.

[86] M. ARENA, *La maternità in Tunisia, in Spazio privato, spazio pubblico e società civile in Medio Oriente e in Africa del Nord*, D. MELFA, A. MELCANGI, F. CRESTI (eds.), Milan, Giuffré, 2008, p. 206 *et seq*.

[87] Proclaimed in 1956. The day of its proclamation is still celebrated as a national holiday. The following year the Republic was proclaimed and the Constitution in 1958.

unknown parents. The rules make no distinction between natural or legitimate filiation, preferring to use the generic term of *nasab* or *ubua'a*/paternity, although an important part of the doctrine nevertheless admits the existence of two distinct types of biological filiation.[88] Legitimate filiation is linked to birth within a valid marital bond. In Tunisian law it is specified that the natural child is excluded from the succession line of the father, but after the promulgation of the 1998 law it appeared that legislation was anxious to include a paternal natural filiation as well.[89]

In Tunisia, there is a strong regulatory conflict between ethics and law since adoption is, as mentioned, permitted legally though prohibited by religion. The 1958 law, which took as its model the analogous French law, regulated the three forms of custody for abandoned children, that is, public protection, unofficial protection and adoption.[90] The first form of custody

---

[88] S. BEN HALIMA, *La filiation naturelle en droit tunisien*, in *Mélanges en l'honneur de Mohamed Charfi*, Tunis, Centre de publication universitaire, 2001, p. 459 *et seq*.; A. MEZGHANI, *Le droit tunisien reconnait ses enfants naturels*, in *Mélanges of ferts au prof Sassi Ben Halima*, Tunis, Centre de publication universitaire, 2005, p. 651 *et seq*.

[89] Jurisprudence is not in agreement as to the interpretation of the norm, so sometimes decisions were limited to attributing the patronymic name to the child born out of wedlock without establishing the child's filiation: M. BENJEMIA, S. BEN ACHOUR, M. BELLAMINE, *Le droit tunisien de la famille...,* cit. esp. p.181. It must be considered that the very modern nationality code provided that there is no reference to religion for the definition of the concept of nationality; it eliminated tribal, religious and maraboutic eponyms and reduced the patronymic to the father's surname. Currently in force is Law no. 98-75 of 28 Oct. 1998, regarding the attribution of a patronymic to abandoned children or whose parentage is unknown at
http://www.delegue-enfance.nat.tn/images/legislation/loi_75_1998_fr.pdf.

[90] Cf. Law no. 58-27 of 4 March 1958 regarding public guardianship, informal guardianship and adoption, J.O.R.T. 7 March 1958, p. 236. For comments cf. R. BOUKHARI, *L'adoption internationale vue à travers le prisme de la loi tunisienne du 4 mars 1958*, in *Revue Jurid. Thémis*, 2011, 45, pp. 115-148 at
https://ssl.editionsthemis.com/uploaded/revue/article/21124_rjt451-115a150.pdf.
The author also descibes an interesting and previously unknown decision of the Court of Tunis of 26 June 2000, which underlines at note 96, p. 136, that "*l'alinéa 2 de l'article 10 de la loi n. 58- 27 du 4 mars 1958 relative à la tutelle publique, à la tutelle officieuse et à l'adoption dispose que le Tunisien peut adopter un étranger. Il découle donc de cette règle que le droit tunisien interdit à l'étranger d'adopter un Tunisien*" (Trib. de 1ère inst. de Tunis, jugement n. 34256, 26 juin 2000 (inédit); A. MEZGHANI, *L'adoption internationale en droit tunisien*, in *La*

is the responsibility of the head of a public institution – often an orphanage – which takes in the child. Civil liability lies with the State, the municipality or the institute. Abandoned children are the responsibility of *Inpe* (*Institut National de Protection de L'Enfance*) founded in 1971, with the dual task of providing a reception centre for children and a laboratory for ideas for the development and protection of children.[91]

Unofficial protection coincides with kafala of which it retains some characteristics: transfer of the child and separation of adopting-adopted genealogies. The agreement derives from a contract that must be approved by the judge. In his parental role the *kafil* has the same rights and duties as the 'blood' parents. The code governed kafala through Articles 77-80, but a more detailed discipline of the institution of kafala was introduced subsequently by Law no. 27/1958.

Adoption, on the other hand, is characterized, as in the West, by the transmission to the adopted of the name of the adopter and by the attribution of reciprocal succession rights. It is established by a court judgment in the presence of the adopters, the biological parents or, in their absence, the head of the institute. The registrar transcribes the adoption provision in the margins of the birth certificate and from that moment the adopted child acquires the rights and duties of the legitimate child. If the biological parents are known the marriage impediments foreseen by the code remain. Direct adoption is possible at the time of birth, if the father and mother consent and appear before the judge after the birth.

The main effects of filiation are care/*hadana*, which can be considered as domestic protection of the child, and tutorship / *wilaya*, external or social protection. There are three types of protection: legal, attributed by law; judicial, following a decision of the judge and testamentary, all of which last until the child reaches the age of majority, regardless of gender. The reforms of family law, which took place between 1966 and 1993, modified the classical rules on the subjects of these forms of protection, with the advantage of greater openness towards mothers, though still not on a level of equality. Alongside traditional rights, maintenance obligations are placed.

However, adoption before the judge throws up two kinds of problems, one religious and the other relating to the identity of the child. The Quran's ban on the transfer of the name and the creation of a new bond of filiation constitutes in many cases a deterrent to the use of this institution.

---

passion du droit. Mélanges en l'honneur de Mohamed Larbi Hachem, Tunis, Orbis, 2006, p. 372 *et seq*.

[91] Cf. A. ZUNDEL BEN KHEMIS, *Enfance privé e de famille (1956-2000),* Tunis, Unicef, 2000.

Furthermore, adding the name of the adoptive parents creates considerable problems because the name in Islamic culture is the vector of identity. In this perspective, the cancellation of the original name and its replacement are equivalent to the cancellation of the basic structure of the individual. This aspect is more incisive for direct adoptions where the name of the biological parents is known. In addition, if the adoption is revoked, unlike the typical Western adoption, the child will reacquire his/her biological name, demonstrating the indissoluble link with the *nasab* of origin.

The adoption deed is ratified by an enforceable judgment of the judge and can be revoked if the minor's interest requires it. Nothing is said about the difference in religion between adopter and adopted, but a Muslim minor can presumably be adopted only by a believer of the same religion, based on the general principles governing Tunisian family law. Legislation provides that in order to adopt a child, it is necessary to be in possession of certain requisites including having contracted marriage for at least three years without separation, a consensual request by both spouses, moral and material suitability, a limit of age difference between eighteen and forty-five years, and a declaration of state of adoptability by the Court concerned.

Once these requirements have been met, an application for adoption is presented by the couple to the Juvenile Court nearest to their place of residence, requesting that the Court declare them suitable. After ensuring that the conditions required by law are met and having obtained the consent of all parties, the judge pronounces the adoption judgment. However, assistance to the adopted child can be withdrawn by the Court of First Instance when adoptive parents fail in their obligations. This failure can only be proven when the social worker continues to visit the adopted child at his/her new home to ensure that the conditions for his/her development and growth are in place.

A series of obligations obviously derive from this commitment: the father must support the children; if he does not have the means, the mother must provide; support continues up to the age of majority or until the completion of studies up to 25 years old; a daughter without income, however, remains dependent on the father until marriage. Child care is entrusted to both parents, who cooperate in their children's education and provide for their needs; in the event of separation, custody is attributed to the surviving parent or to the person that the judge considers meets the best interests of the child. The guardian – whether it be the father, mother or tutor/*walī*, have full powers to manage the affairs of the child in terms of development and education; if it is the mother who exercises custody, she is given the powers of the *walī* as regards travel and study and representation in matters of property.[92]

The Tunisian Code of Personal Status, with subsequent modifications, contains various provisions. Some protect minors as well as the mother while others exclusively safeguard the rights of the latter. In light of the latest reforms made to the code, in particular with amendments no. 32/2007 and no. 20/2008, many provisions sanctioning gender differences were repealed or amended. Worthy of note is the provision that governs a typically Islamic institution, *hadana*, the right to take care of the child and, at the same time, the right of the latter to be protected, both from a material and psychological point of view, the provisions relating to the safeguarding of filiation, the foundling and the rules concerning inheritance.[93] All these rules are indicative of the high degree of protection that the Tunisian legal system wished to recognize for the minor, paying attention to the regulation and to the safeguarding of the minor's basic rights. Central to this is the Child Protection Code within Law no. 92 of 1995, promulgated in 2004, which is, by far, the first specific national codification aimed at protecting the interests of minors issued by an Arab-Islamic state. As such, it appears particularly innovative, adding as much to the developments on intra-Islamic international and regional regulations, as to the national legislation of the Tunisian Code of Personal Status, and in some points even exceeding these provisions.

These rules must be linked to the provisions of the Code of private international law for all cases of involvement of subjects of different nationalities. Tunisian legislation too looked to the general option of Islamic countries to benefit national law, but in some cases allowed the connection to the home and eliminated the automatic favour against the

---

[92] Dossier Mondo Islamico, 4, http://www.fga.it/uploads/media/Dossier_Mondo_Islamico_4.pdf. For a list of documentation cf. https://darna.tn/wp-content/uploads/adoptio.pdf. The legal reference is Law n. 1958-0027 of 4 March 1958 concerning public guardianship, informal guardianship and adoption at http://WWW.jurisitetunisie.com/tunisie/codes/csp/L1958-0027.htm.

[93] On *hadana*/custody cf. A. CILARDO, F. MENNILLO, *Due sistemi a confronto. La famiglia nell'Islam e nel diritto canonico*, Padua, Cedam, 2009, pp. 39 and *et seq.* In addition, for an examination of the institution according to dogmatics, H. SAFAI, *La garde des enfants en droit musulman chiite et dans la législation iranienne*, in *Revue internationale de droit comparé*, 1972, XXIV, 3, pp. 551-562 and at http://www.persee.fr/doc/ridc_0035-3337_1972_num_24_3_15017; D.C. FELLER, *La garde (hadana) en droit musulmmane et dans les droits égyptien, syrien, et tunisien*, Geneva, Droz, 1996; V. M. CAMAU, *Tunisie au présent. Une modernité au-dessus de tout soupçon?* Paris, CNRS, 1987.

husband, introducing alternative conflict rules. A jurisprudential examination allows us to highlight two different conceptions of the principle of public order: a more traditional one on the subject of adoption and a more modern one with reference to natural filiation.[94]

It should be noted that according to the Tunisian Code of Private International Law, "the conditions of adoption are subject to the law of the adopter and that of the adoptee, each as far as s/he is concerned" (Article 53). The text highlights a conflict rule that postulates a distributive application of two different rules: the personal law of the adoptee and that of the adopter. The effects of adoption are governed by the law of the former and this seems to be in conformity with a tendency expressed by a resolution of international law of 1973.[95] The most appropriate legislative solution here regards the necessity of using the method of consultation to allow that a juridical institution "can be recognized within the framework of the foreign legal system or systems where it is intended to be located and to take place".[96]

The legalization of adoption in 1958 was justified by the historical-political need to protect abandoned children or children of unknown parents in a country that had just regained independence. Taking advantage of this momentum and its rediscovered autonomy and with a desire to give a modernist image, political leaders supported a change in society through the law. The codification of Personal Status, in this sense, was one of the stages of this reforming fervour.

But the observation *de iure condendo* highlights a different scenario. First of all, adoption was legalized under a special law, which has not been incorporated to date in the Code of Personal Status. On the other hand, Article 10 of the law is formulated in such a way that it is not in favour of international adoption, at least when a child of Tunisian nationality is being adopted. Finally, the identification of the applicable law is anchored to a classic reference (Article 53 of the Code of Personal Status), which does not allow us to speak of a *favor adoptionis*. It is also noted that the

---

[94] The Tunis Court of First Instance in 2000 refused the *exequatur* of an Austrian ruling of adoption of a Tunisian child, stressing that Tunisian law does not recognize adoption by a foreigner unless s/he has converted to Islam. This decision therefore seemed contrary to public order: Cf. M. BENJEMIA, S. BEN ACHOUR, M. BELLAMINE, *Droit international public tunisien ...* cit., esp. p. 219-220.

[95] Institut de droit international, *Les effets de l'adoption en droit international privé*, 1973, art.1, at www.idi-iil.org/idiF/resolutionsF/1973_rome_03_fr.pdf.

[96] P. PICONE, *La méthode de la référence à l'ordre juridique compétent en droit international privé*, in *Recueil des Cours Academie de droit international de La Haye*, vol. 197, Leiden, Nijhoff, 1986, p. 229 *et seq*., and p. 244.

rare cases of jurisprudential intervention have shown a clear hostility in cases of adoption of a Tunisian child by a foreign couple of different religious affiliation.[97]

[97] Cf. R. BOUKHARI, *L'adoption internationale vue à travers le prisme de la Loi tunisienne du 4 mars 1958,* in *Revue Juridique Thémis*, 45, 205, 2011, pp. 115-160, esp. p. 148 *et seq*.

CHAPTER TWO

RIGHTS OF CHILDREN AND RELIGIOUS IDENTITY IN MULTICULTURAL INTERNATIONAL LAW

1. Human Rights and the Rights of the Child. Protection of Identity in Multicultural Contexts

The concept of freedom – one of the most important, if not the most important concept of political language, philosophy and ethics – is closely linked to the relationships between individuals or social groups and the *powers*, particularly the power of the state. Tackling the subject of *rights to freedom* and *basic human rights* from a 'universal' viewpoint is no easy task. The *universalisation* of human rights and the wider – especially legal – debate on how to guarantee their effective protection does raise an important question: how do we define exactly the freedoms that we wish to guarantee? This issue is particularly evident in the field of what has traditionally been defined as *spiritual liberty*, concerning freedom of thought, conscience and religion. Because it is to do with the inner self, *spiritual liberty* here is hard to define with a reasonable degree of precision.[98]

Basic human rights are, in a sense, a recent juridical *discovery* and the relationship with the transcendent and the conscience exercises a very particular function among those rights as part of the freedom to practise religion – that is, the freedom to choose what is most intimate in the human soul. For the jurist, a study of these rights and freedoms means venturing into areas that are beyond his/her normal scope to embrace the

---

[98] Cf. S. FERLITO, *Diritto soggettivo e libertà religiosa. Riflessioni per uno studio storico e concettuale*, Naples, Jovene, 2002; M. RICCA, *Art. 19, in La Costituzione italiana. Principi fondamentali, diritti e doveri dei cittadini. Commento agli artt. 1-15*, R. BIFULCO, C. CELOTTO, M. OLIVETTI (eds.), Turin, Giappichelli, 2006, p. 421 *et seq.*; G. CAROBENE, *Sulla protezione internazionale della libertà religiosa*, in *Il Diritto Ecclesiastico*, 1998, 2, pp. 363-383.

field of philosophy and ethics. Once the debate extends to the universal level, one inevitably *slips* into the *impasse* created by the political universe, guided as it is by different and sometimes antithetical rules with respect to those of rationality and juridical development. Clearly, providing a unitary solution, or a common paradigm, is hard to achieve. The international community's attitude to international provisions concerning human rights – among which freedom of religion is certainly included – did not begin to change until the 19th century. Indeed, the first forms of international treaties to protect individuals date back to this period, though they were aimed at achieving specific purposes or protecting particular situations. After the Second World War, a greater consideration towards the *individual* emerged in the international sphere. The individual began to be considered an autonomous entity and thus could become a direct recipient of international provisions. At the same time, many states began to abandon their position of centrality and authority.

The centre of gravity of international law thus shifted. From that moment onwards, the central pivot was no longer the *state*, but the *individual* seen as a new subject. The international community began to take a more concrete interest in the rights enjoyed by individuals, seen not just as *citizens* or simply members of a particular state, but as autonomous subjects. The recognition and protection of their freedoms were no longer left to arbitrary state regulation but took into account, at least in general terms, universal and supranational criteria.

At the same time, the need to protect and promote the right to diversity and to cultural identity began to be outlined in the collective sphere. The impossibility of separating cultural identity from cultural diversity was clearly underlined in the Mexico City Declaration on Cultural Policies (1982). This highlighted the unique and irreplaceable character of each culture which, through intercultural dialogue, could bring about the enrichment of the communion of universal values and constitute cultural pluralism. 'Cultural diversity' in this sense came to be identified as the common heritage of humanity, whose protection represented an ethical imperative inseparable from the respect for human dignity, and stood out as a guarantee of pluralism, democracy and social cohesion.

However, the use of particular legal instruments such as the kafala, with its strong religious connotation, in open and multicultural contexts, requires a careful reflection on the management of cultural diversity that has become one of the major challenges of international law over recent years. In addition to universal rights, the right to particularity has emerged so that it is not attributable primarily to individuals but to groups and communities and their cultural identity. Cultural relativism and pluralism of values call into question the universality of human rights because they tend to contextualize them in relation to different societies and cultures. At times, cultural differences almost seem to exercise a limitation or even an exclusion of universally recognized human rights.

Within multi-cultural social contexts, the acceptance of basic democratic principles – including those relating to non-discrimination and pluralism – obliges public authorities to provide the necessary tools to safeguard and promote the identities of single individuals as well as those of minority communities.[99]

In this way, the area of cultural diversity, intimately connected with the principles of respect for identity and social multiculturalism, obtained progressive recognition in the broad *genus* of human rights and cultural rights in particular. However, the evaluation and enhancement of cultural differences between individuals in their specificity and the definition of their rights does require a flexible approach, which is "focused on their needs and excludes both the rigid universalism of universal tradition and the crystallization of cultural heritage".[100]

Religion is known to be an important factor in the process of building legal systems and institutions, at both a national and international level, and allows respect for *identity* to be re-examined and reformulated. The starting point must, therefore, be a proper understanding of these concepts so that they can be given not only a positive philosophical-conceptual structure – but also a juridical one.[101] From this perspective, particular

---

[99] Cf. G. CAROBENE, *Il principio di non-discriminazione e la tutela delle minoranze in diritto internazionale*, in *Lo studio del diritto ecclesiastico. Attualità e prospettive*, V. TOZZI (ed.), Salerno, Edisud, 1996, pp. 133- 148.

[100] L. BACCELLI, *I diritti dei popoli. Universalismo e differenze culturali*, Roma-Bari, Laterza, 2009, esp. p. 115. The author also stresses that "recognizing the groundlessness of universalism favours the extension of rights. The activist, conflictual and emancipatory connotation of the language of rights can thus become the most useful element for 'other' cultures that come into contact with it." (p. 122).

[101] Cf. W. KYMLICKA, *La cittadinanza multiculturale*, Bologna, Il Mulino, 1999; P. CAVANA, *Nuove dimensioni della cittadinanza e pluralismo religioso: premesse per uno studio*, in *La cittadinanza. Problemi e dinamiche in una società pluralistica*, G. DALLA TORRE, F. D'AGOSTINO (eds.), Turin, Giappichelli, 2000, pp. 59-150; G. DAMMACCO, *Diritti umani e fattore religioso nel sistema multiculturale euromediterraneo*, Bari, Cacucci, 2000; V. TOZZI, *Società multiculturale, autonomia confessionale e questione della sovranità*, in *Dir.Eccl.*, I, 2000, pp. 124-147. M. VENTURA, in *La laicità dell'Unione Europea. Diritti-Mercato-religione*, Turin, Giappichelli, 2001 also stresses that "the competitive model of the community approach to the religious phenomenon consists in denying juridical

importance is given to the reference to freedom of religion in the development of the general area of basic human rights, though framed within a view of neutrality of the public space.

From this perspective, then, the doctrine of human rights took on the subversive character of a Copernican Revolution in international relations, since it overturned and superseded the dogma of state sovereignty – the traditional conception of international law as a relationship between sovereign systems, firmly safeguarding domestic jurisdiction. The activation of jurisdictional or political instruments of control undermined the position of the state – an organism in the classic sense with absolute sovereignty over its citizens – since human rights could be claimed on the world scene regardless of the relationship with one's own nation.

With the centre of gravity of international law shifting from the state to the individual – with the first codifications of fundamental human rights – we are able to witness another Copernican Revolution. Modern, multicultural and pluralist societies in fact came up against the contrast between what might be the ideal development of human rights and the need to protect specific cultural, religious and political identities. In the current phase of transition from an internationalist, Westphalian system based on a relationship between sovereign states to one of relations / clashes between civilizations, what becomes clear is the underlying contrast between our own Western culture and the Muslim world, in which reference to the religious factor is particularly central.

Now that we have successfully witnessed the transition from the first generation of human rights, we are experiencing a phase of expansion in terms of the rights of minors viewed not only as autonomous subjects in their own right but as a new legal class as well, attesting to an increasing perception of the inadequacy of traditional legal tools.[102]

---

relevance to the specificity of the religious element itself, and enhancing the principle of equality and non-discrimination." (p. 149). Cf. also N. FIORITA, D. LOPRIENO, *La libertà di manifestazione del pensiero e la libertà religiosa nelle società multiculturali*, Florence, Firenze University Press, 2009.

[102] The EU's Charter of Fundamental Rights fits perfectly into this new legal context since it explicitly attempts to integrate our continent, and aims not only at building economic unity but also at codifying a new legal standard founded on common values, the only tool for social peace. Cf. M. T. BITSCH, *Histoire de la construction europèenne de 1945 à nos jours*, Brussels, Complexe, 2004; *The European Union and Human Rights*, edited by N. NEUWAHL, A. ROSAS, The Hague-Boston-London, Nijhoff, 1995; *The European Union and Human Rights*, edited by P. ALSTON, Oxford, Oxford University Press, 1999; J.H.H. WEILER, *I diritti umani nello spazio giuridico europeo*, in *L'Unione Europea. Istituzioni, ordinamento e politiche*, B. BEUTLER, R. BIEBER, J. PIPKORN, J STREIL, J. H. H.

In the regulatory sphere, only in the 20th century did the rights of minors slowly began to achieve recognition, with the identification of a statute for the protection of the growing child and the provision of instruments to ensure the support and welfare of the child in difficult circumstances. Roman law saw in the child the future of the lineage and the object of paternal power: the mother took care of the child's upbringing accompanied by the *pater familias,* whose job was to transfer to the child faith in the customs and virtues of his/her ancestors. This situation did not change during the Middle Ages, dominated as they were by a substantial indifference to the needs of children.

It was not until the end of the 19th century that the need was felt to grant special protection to the child, who was no longer considered as a mere object but as a subject with vested rights. It is really only since industrialisation, then, that the protection of minors has been addressed by international law, and this mainly regards the issue of the exploitation of children in the world of work, which was previously the exclusive prerogative of the internal law of each state. Thus, it was the International Labour Organization that internationalized the issue of children.

For the first time, the law – which had always dealt with adult interests – welcomed and listened to the needs of children and translated those needs into perfect subjective rights.While previous laws were structured to simply guarantee economic and property relations, they moved towards a commitment to help the person realise his/her potential, by removing the negative conditions that made personal development difficult. Child protection was based on the child's 'incapacity' and vulnerability and the impossibility of asserting his/her rights. As a 'child on the way to adulthood', particular protection is needed. First of all, this kind of protection must be translated into a strengthening of traditional human rights, which must help the child to grow and accompany him/her towards adulthood[103] and help him/her to build an identity, which might be a religious identity as well. Secondly, protection here affects the affirmation of specific and proper rights concerning the state of childhood - provisions on adoption, on the right to play and to grow in a free environment.[104]

WEILER (eds.), Bologna, Il Mulino, 1998, p. 346 *et seq.*; *Religioni e sistemi giuridici*, F. MARGIOTTA BROGLIO, C. MIRA- BELLI, F. ONIDA (eds.), Milan, Giuffré, 2000; F. ALICINO, *Costituzionalismo e diritto europeo delle religioni*, Padua, Cedam, 2011.

[103] F. DEFOSSEZ-DEKEUWER, *Les droits de l'enfant,* Paris, Presses Universitaires de France, 2001, esp. p. 4.

[104] M. BOSSUYT, *La Convention des Nations Unies sur les Droits de l'Enfant*, in *Revue Univ. Droits de l'homme*, 2, 4, 1990, p. 142 *et seq.*

Having the minor's interest at heart means fully implementing the child's right to education, by creating the conditions for an ample and thorough development of the child's personality and progressively develop the child's autonomy and responsibility. With the age of the subject still in focus, however, this not only implies protection for the individual, but also the whole family network (though it may be 'artificial') of which the minor is a part. In this sense, international adoption is fully qualified to benefit from the measures to protect the child in difficulty.

Public and private cooperation constitutes the area in which the promotion of children's rights should be encouraged, obviously in the countries of origin of the children, preventing family hardship and providing the means to effectively save minors without a suitable family from being abandoned, while respecting the cultural pluralism of national legal systems. In this hermeneutical perspective, the institution of international adoption is configured and justified, understood in terms of a strategy aimed at supporting minors in countries which offer fewer guarantees economically and socially speaking. However, it should not be seen as simply transferring children from poor geographical areas to richer areas of the planet.

The protection of children is currently at the centre of the international community's attention, though each country, respecting culture and tradition, adopts a different legal response in terms of how to take charge of the child, which tools to implement, and which methods for managing situations of abandonment to use.

In countries of Western tradition, the institution of adoption – which means considering the child as equivalent to a legitimate child of the adopting couple – represents a paradigmatic model codified both nationally and internationally. Having no juridical correspondence in secularized political structures, the kafala requires specific legislative action indispensable for the protection of the weakest section of the population, which is of greatest vulnerability on account of their state of abandonment.

Recent international conventions have affirmed the priority of child protection over and above other interests. Although this syntagm is hard to define, it is a prevalent interpretative canon that obliges those involved to pursue this and not other objectives. The first important aspect of the importance given to the minor's interest is that the principle of residuality has been established as the foundation of national and international adoption.[105]

---

[105] The principle of residuality was sanctioned not only by our national adoption legislation, but also by the Hague Convention on International Adoption of 29 May 1993.

Along with the principle of residuality in international adoption is the principle of subsidiarity whereby, after verifying the impossibility of reintegration into the biological family, one must attempt the path of adoption within the country of origin of the minor and only later, as a subsidiary hypothesis, i.e. residual, is it possible to authorize the transfer to a different state. This is based on the assumption that for the minor it is certainly less traumatic and responds more closely to the minor's needs to be welcomed by another family in his/her own country. It is important to reiterate that the value of solidarity lies at the basis of subsidiarity: what must be a priority is to guarantee the permanence of the child in his/her family, social, cultural (and sometimes religious) context, as a response to the state of abandonment.

The conceptual pivot of the debate should then be to achieve a proper balance of individual and collective rights, the latter attributable according to the membership of the group and its cultural identity. The starting point for the protection of human rights must be to ensure respect for human dignity, a fundamental value that implies the freedom granted to the individual to be able to conceive and pursue his/her own idea of what is 'good'. These rights find their place in a purely subjective dimension so that the role of the state is limited to prohibiting interference in the private life of citizens and abstaining from imposing a particular type of identity, thus guaranteeing, *inter alia*, freedom of thought, conscience and religion.

The positive effect of the interrelation between cultural relativism and the universality of human rights is essentially embodied in the protection of cultural diversity, which underlines the centrality of the concept of *recognition*. Diversity as a legal interest that may be protected by international law must therefore be understood as including every manifestation of human culture as long as basic principles, such as respect for the norms of *ius cogens*, human rights and the protection of individual dignity, are not violated. This innovative and more correct interpretation alone represents the best perspective from which to understand the current phase of international protection of human rights and the rights of the minor.

The transition to this new phase of human rights could thus develop through the construction of a model based on the coexistence of differences, while respecting their specific identity. This process does presuppose a progressive but definitive fracture of the religious sphere from the political sphere through a process of real secularism in a broadly tolerant and neutral society, capable of welcoming and assimilating diverse religious groups.[106]

This ideal should be built on the Greek concept of *laos,* which identifies a people united in their own idea of society, with a common commitment, founded on equality, "*l'unité du laos est donc simultanément un principe de liberté et un prince d'égalité*".[107] This principle is legally based on the affirmation of freedom of conscience, guaranteeing equality for all within the *res publica*. In its universal scope, secularism based on identification in the national community, is structured as a model of social integration. Rather than annulling differences it seeks out common values capable of translating the underlying multiculturalism of modern democratic societies into legal language. This approach must begin with a redefinition of the concept of religious freedom as well, in an active, positive way, which can be translated into concrete government action inspired by a specific political programme – aimed at educating citizens so as to guarantee a real freedom of choice – but also a social programme – allowing all to freely take their own cultural direction.

The neutrality of political power as far as religion goes is the only instrument capable of guaranteeing equal respect for all faiths and for all

---

[106] Cf. M. RICCA, *Oltre Babele. Codici per una democrazia interculturale*, Bari, Dedalo, 2008 and ID., *Pantheon. Agenda della laicità interculturale*, Palermo, Torri del Vento, 2013. The term *laicità*, with an analogous meaning also in Spain and France, is absolutely untranslatable in English where the corresponding '*laicism*' assumes an immediate negative meaning. The bibliography on the subject is, of course, boundless. I will limit myself to citing only a few brief doctrinal references: for an Italian overview *Ripensare la laicità. Il problema della laicità nell'esperienza giuridica contemporanea*, G. DALLA TORRE (ed.), Turin, Giappichelli, 1993; P. BELLINI, *Riflessioni sull'idea di laicità*, in *La questione della tolleranza e le confessioni religiose,* Naples, Jovene, 1991, pp. 29-50; F. MARGIOTTA BROGLIO, *La laicità dello Stato*, in *Le ragioni dei laici*, G. PRETEROSSI (ed.), Roma-Bari, Laterza, 2005, p. 79 *et seq*.; P. STEFANI', *La laicità nell'esperienza giuridica dello Stato*, Cacucci, Bari, 2007; P. CAVANA, *Interpretazioni della laicità. Esperienza francese ed esperienza italiana a confronto*, Roma, Ave, 1998; S. DOMIANELLO, *Sulla laicità nella Costituzione*, Milan, Giuffrè, 1999, esp. p. 58 *et seq*.; S. PRISCO, *Laicità. Un percorso di riflessione,* Turin, Giappichelli, 2009 and, by the same author, his definition of *Laicità*, in *Dizionario di Diritto pubblico*, vol. IV, edited by S. CASSESE, Milan, Giuffré, 2006, pp. 3335-3345.

[107] H. PENA RUIZ, *Qu'est-ce que la laïcité?*, Paris, Gallimard, 2003, p.21 who stresses how "*l'unité du laos est à comprendre par opposition à l'idée qu'un groupe particulier... pourrait se voir reconnaître davantage de droits, voire un role directeur par rapport à l'ensemble... L'unité référentielle du laos n'a alors d'autre fondament que l'égalitè de statut des convinctions de ses membres*" (p.22).

manifestations of religious feeling in the social fabric, also with reference to legal institutions and rules. In this sense, the values that form the bedrock of secularism, capable of opening up a society based on respect for all consciences and equal freedom of individuals, could provide the right political and legal tools to build up a single collective identity. This political approach would obviously mean redefining the rules on personal status - typically linked in the Muslim universe to religious faith - in non-homogeneous socio-political contexts.

Through neutrality, the state must guarantee its impartiality, so that all citizens, regardless of their private religious ties, can recognize themselves in a common social and state context. Respect for secularism as a mode of new *civil tolerance*, imposed on everyone, could guarantee a proper public debate. In this sense, it is a possibility and does not mean, of course, denying freedom to groups, but does place emphasis on the creation of a 'common' right, which is *super partes*. The role of the public authorities should thus be properly directed towards redesigning a space so as to prevent any religious groups from conditioning those areas that must remain public and collective.

The codification of this ideal cannot be simplistically reduced to the inclusion of the greatest possible number of values but must constitute an *open*, flexible system, free from any judgments as to the ethical compatibility of *different* religious values. This way of rethinking secular ethics in the modern state requires that individual religious identities are guaranteed by virtue of their full participation in social and political life. Correctly understood, the concept of pluralism should set forth a principle of dutiful ethics, based on respect for the identity of others, and must represent the founding value of what we understand as democratic societies. It implies acceptance rather than imposition of a culturally heterogeneous society in an effort to a real integration that is not simply a kind of forced assimilation.

Multiculturalism presupposes a pluralist society and demands equal respect for all cultures, based on the politics of recognition. It is not based on the simplistic equation freedom = equality – with its misleading expectation of guaranteeing equal juridical positions to situations, rights and demands which are profoundly different.[108] A multicultural project, not based on exchange, but on the affirmation of identity and on the recognition of the rights of all groups present in a given social fabric could lacerate the very foundations of our current democratic structures. The

---

[108] C. TAYLOR, *La politica del riconoscimento*, in J. HABERMAS- C. TAYLOR, *Multicultiralismo. Lotte per il riconoscimento,* Milan, Feltrinelli, 2001, pp. 9-62.

effectiveness of full legal equality depends on political powers creating the conditions intended for the use of the freedoms guaranteed at a legal level. What is needed, then, is a different, and more shareable development of such a project based on an attempt to construct a new world ethic that identifies with the foundation of human rights and in which tolerance is not simply accepting the other but means constructing a universally valid moral rule.

The goal that today's multicultural societies should set themselves is the construction of a global morality based on a sense of responsibility and justice that is able to break down the impasse imposed by politics, and includes minorities as well. It would be necessary to create a political structure able to mediate between the concept of diversity and that of equality and cooperation between different cultures. This is the challenge that is imposed – not only at the global level – and that raises more questions for the positivist jurist: the creation of a social and legal structure that is really and positively open to such a balance. In the area that interests us most – the peaceful coexistence of legal rules with a religious connotation – this structure should guarantee complete religious freedom. This new freedom of conscience in the fullest sense of the term includes the neutrality of public space – for which modern societies demand protection – and represents the centre of gravity around which the entire debate should be developed. Since the bond with the divine represents what most intimately characterizes the human soul and transcends all space and time, the codification of a right that is *just* as regards freedom of religion, would represent the parameter on which to base an evaluation of the development of a given culture and society. This, then, represents the only possible anchor in the reading of religiously structured rules, such as the kafala.

2. Recognizing the Child's Best Interest and Identity

The very first international text to refer to the rights of children was the Minimum Age Convention adopted by the International Labour Conference in 1919. However, it was only with the Declaration of the Rights of the Child of 1924, approved by the League of Nations, that children's rights were actually achieved, even though the declaration itself was basically concerned with welfare and thus essentially with the satisfaction of material needs, along the lines of a still very traditional approach.[109] In addition, the declaration did not call on individual states to

[109] A.C. MORO, *Manuale di diritto minorile,* Bologna, 2008, p. 9.

establish what their obligations were, but rather urged humanity in general to ensure protection for children. For the first time, the child was recognized as having some rights, albeit passive in nature, and was no longer viewed as being a simple recipient of the decisions taken by others. This was the result of a specific analysis on the issue of childhood taken in all its peculiarity, with a view to carefully examining and specifying what exactly child protection should be, over and above a general and abstract view of human rights. Special protection for the child meant achieving a healthy and complete physical, intellectual, moral and social development. Put differently, "the rights expressly attributed to the child represent only a small part of the attention he/she needs and must be interpreted in the broader sense".[110]

Following the approval of the UN General Assembly's Declaration on the Rights of the Child in 1959, some fresh new principles regarding the protection of the child were introduced. First and foremost was the right to a name and nationality in order to take on a well-defined status in society, as was essential to enable the child to grow and develop his/her personality in a healthy and serene environment, such as the family.

With the Declaration of the Rights of the Child a new concept of the child thus began to take shape, as reflected in the hierarchy of values protected by the declaration itself. The child was now recognised as having an inalienable and absolute subjective position, which surmounted any instrumental kind of mediation established by legal guardianship. Rather than describing what legal rules might be applicable, the Declaration was concerned with the guarantees that society should provide "to the end that he may have a happy childhood and enjoy for his own good and for the good of society the rights and freedoms herein set forth". By so doing, the Declaration established organically the fundamental rights that must be recognized and guaranteed to all children, "without any exception whatsoever [...] without distinction or discrimination [...] whether of himself or of his family".

According to common practice in international law, this solemn declaration was followed by the adoption of a legally binding document – the New York Convention on the Rights of the Child of 1989. Here, the term 'minor', evoking the cultural stereotype of the incomplete child with a status of personal and legal inferiority and subject to the authority of others, was replaced by the term 'child', meaning "every human being

---

[110] M. COSSUTTA, *Dai diritti dell'uomo ai diritti del fanciullo,* in *La protezione internazionale dei diritti del fanciullo,* Trieste, 1993, p. 277 *et seq*.

below the age of eighteen years".[111] It also declared that a "child temporarily or permanently deprived of his or her family environment, or in whose own best interests cannot be allowed to remain in that environment, shall be entitled to special protection and assistance provided by the State".[112]

This marked a shift in perspective from protection to social advancement, with particular attention being paid to the child as a person, which led to the birth of a notion, hitherto rather confusing, of 'childhood rights'. Full legal protection was thus granted to the child. For the first time in the history of international law, indeed, these rights were codified in the form of a document that would have binding force for ratifying states. Children were recognized as individuals, signifying that they were neither the possession of the parents nor the products of the state. Nations would have the moral and legal responsibility to recognize their rights as separate and independent citizens. This convention thus reconciled a wide range of diverse traditions, cultures, religions, stages of economic development, legal and political systems, so much so that it may be defined as the sum of all international agreements concerning the protection of children's rights.

The Preamble to the convention stated that "the family, viewed as the fundamental group of society and the natural environment for the growth and well-being of all its members and particularly children, should be afforded the necessary protection and assistance so that it can fully assume its responsibilities within the community", thus recognising a positive obligation for the state to act upon. The Preamble, then, introduced the idea of the child as a subject with rights rather than a mere object of protection. Alongside rights which had been universally acknowledged and approved (the right to a name, survival, health, and education) came a new generation of rights such as the right to the child's identity, respect for privacy, dignity and freedom of expression.

The convention was the first universal and multilateral treaty establishing internationally recognized children's rights, binding the states

---

[111] Article 1, International Convention on the Rights of the Child as adopted by the United Nations General Assembly of 20 November 1989 and ratified by Italy under Law no. 176 of 27 May 1991.

[112] Article 20, International Convention on the Rights of the Child. The convention expressly mentions the kafala in paragraph 3: "[s]uch care could include, *inter alia*, foster placement, kafala of Islamic law, adoption, or if necessary, placement in suitable institutions for the care of children. When considering solutions, due regard shall be paid to the desirability of continuity in a child's upbringing and to the child's ethnic, religious, cultural and linguistic background".

to actually respect them. As a matter of fact, it is worth considering that the words used in the texts provide evidence for a certain amount of realism adopted during its drafting process.[113] Almost all the articles begin with "State Parties undertake to …", or "State Parties shall …", rather than 'children have the right to', thus directly identifying state parties as having the main responsibility for the realization of those rights. The most innovative aspect of the convention, however, is the explicit reference to international cooperation, which is an important means of improving the living conditions of children in all states, particularly those in the developing world.

Article 3 stresses the notion of the child's best interest, which must always be the main reference parameter in all child-related decisions, taking into account his/her identity and nationality, as well as the needs of his/her person and any elements of particular vulnerability.[114] Now that it is a universally recognised principle, this notion appears in the English version of the convention with the plural 'best interests', designed as a guiding principle when balancing the various possible interests of the child. This usage, however, is not exempt from criticism because of the words being excessively generic and indeterminate in relation to the concept of 'children's rights', not least because of the terminology used in the article and the different meanings attributable to it.[115]

In the English text, it is stated that "the best interests of the child shall be a primary consideration". The use of the adjective 'primary' rather than 'paramount' has contributed to fuelling doubts among theorists as to what weight drafters of the convention wished to attribute to the notion of 'best

---

[113] F. RIGAUX, *La Convenzione delle Nazioni Unite sui diritti dell'Infanzia,* in *Violazioni dei diritti dei bambini – un metodo di approccio,* Rome, 1995.

[114] M. DOGLIOTTI, *Che cosa è l'interesse del minore,* in *Dir. fam. pers.,* 1992; P. ALSTON, B. GILMOUR-WISH, *The Best Interests Of The Child, Towards A Synthesis Of Children's Rights And Cultural Values,* Unicef, 1996; A. BEGHÈ LORETI, *La tutela internazionale dei diritti del fanciullo,* Padua, 1995; A. GLENN MOWER JR.., *The Convention on the rights of the child,* London, 1997; F. MOSCONI, *La protezione dei minori*, in *Convenzioni internazionali e legge di riforma del diritto internazionale privato,* edited by F. Salerno, Padua, 1997; C. BREEN, *The Standard of the Best Interests of the Child: A Western Tradition in International and Comparative Law,* 2002; C. FOCARELLI, *La convenzione di New York sui diritti del fanciullo e il concetto di 'best interest of the child'*, in *Rivista di diritto internazionale,* n. 4, 2010; R. RIVELLO, *L'interesse del minore fra diritto internazionale e multiculturalità*, in *Minorigiustizia*, n. 3, 2011.

[115] S. PARKER, *The Best Interests of the Child – Principles and Problems*, in *The Best Interests of the Child. Reconciling Culture and Human Rights*, P. ALSTON (ed.), Oxford, 1994, p. 26 *et seq*.

interests of the child'. Moreover, special emphasis has been placed on what 'paramount' may have semantically attributed to the interests of the child compared with 'primary'. The choice of the latter, however, is supported by the different meaning attached to the principle in non-absolute terms,[116] since the primary consideration does not preclude *a priori* the possibility that it should and may be balanced with further considerations, which would not be feasible if it were understood in more narrow terms. It should be acknowledged, though, that this is a principle of interpretation rather than a subjective right.[117]

Nevertheless, setting hermeneutics aside the child's best interests may be considered an important tool to balance the universal claim for the protection of the rights of the child with the cultural, social and religious traditions that are worth preserving in individual states.[118] It constitutes a general principle that underpins the recognition of specific rights to the child, together with the provision of substantive and procedural law safeguards ideally suited to achieving them. It also constitutes a general clause which, thanks to its wording, makes it possible to disregard substantive and procedural safeguards according to the peculiarities of the real situation.

As has been correctly emphasized, this principle plays different roles in the application of the rights enshrined in the provisions of the 1989 Convention. First and foremost, it serves as a supporting instrument justifying a particular approach to the realization of rights relating to children, as well as being a means of resolving conflicts between the rights that may arise in the general context of the convention. Through this principle, it is still possible to highlight the importance of 'best interests' – in view of their universal scope – when it comes to evaluating the 'laws and practices' of the state parties, including those areas not covered by the provisions of the convention. These principles, then, stand as a criterion for assessing the international responsibilities of each state in matters where the law puts the child first through several different interpretations

---

[116] M. FREEMAN, *Article 3. The best interests of the child,* in *A commentary on the United Nations Convention on the rights of the child,* A. ALEN, J. VANDE LANOTTE, E. VERHELLEN, F. ANG, E. BERGHMANS, M. VERHEYDE (eds.), Leiden-Boston, 2007, p. 60 *et seq*.

[117] N. MATHIEU, *Séparation des parents et garde d'enfant – Le point de vue sur la jurisprudence de la Cour européenne des droits de l'homme,* in *Rev. trim. dr. homme*, 93, 2013, p. 59 *et seq*.

[118] M. DISTEFANO, *Interesse superiore del minore e sottrazione internazionale di minori: in margine al caso Neulinger,* in *Studi in onore di Claudio Zanghi*, edited by L. Panella and E. Spatafora, Turin, 2011, p. 232 *et seq*.

of the law likely to be formed, and where the concrete interest of the individual child is established by considering factual elements typical of legal protection.

With a view to achieving this, the recognition of full legal subjectivity to the child translates into a series of rights primarily to ensure: a) provision, meaning fulfilment of those needs that reflect a particular state of psycho-physical vulnerability; b) protection resulting from the recognition of the child's independent ownership of guaranteed rights vis-à-vis state authorities and ethical-family relationships; and c) participation, meaning expression of the right to be heard in relation to public or private choices that may have an impact on the child's well-being.[119] In particular, the so-called right to a hearing has been envisaged, representing a definite change in perspective as compared to the traditional approach that relegated the child to a passive role.[120]

By representing the minimum standards of child protection to be guaranteed by individual state systems of law,[121] this convention has the validity of a legislative framework, which implies the need to interpret any other law in the light of its principles and rules.[122] In actual fact, all relevant international acts emanated after 1989 expressly refer to the principles of the 'child's best interests' not only by proposing their implementation in specific areas, but also by identifying them as the informative criterion in decoding the principles of residuality, subsidiarity and equality in international adoption practices. This, then, places them at the top of the hierarchy of principles – those rendered even more forcefully in Italy by Law no. 149/2001, which defined adoption as a child's right to a family.

---

[119] N. CANTWELL, *Monitoring the Convention through the idea of the "3P"*, in *Politics of Childhood and Children at Risk: Provision, Protection, Participation,* P.L HEILÖ, E. LAURONEN, M. BARDY (eds.), Vienna, European Centre, 1993; P. STANZIONE, *Garanti per l'infanzia e interesse del minore,* Salerno, Università degli Studi di Salerno, 2000; L. STRUMENDO, P. DE STEFANI, *Il Garante dell'infanzia e dell'adolescenza,* in *Tutela civile del minore e diritto sociale della famiglia,* edited by L. Lenti, vol. VI (II ed.), *Trattato di diritto di famiglia,* edited by P. ZATTI, Milan, 2012, p. 257 *et seq*.

[120] A. BISIO, I. ROAGNA, *L'adozione internazionale dei minori. Normativa interna e giurisprudenza,* Milan, 2009; GHIONNI C., *Adozione internazionale e diritto alla famiglia,* Naples, 2016.

[121] G. VAN BUEREN, *The international Law on the Rights of the Child,* The Hague-Boston-London, 1998.

[122] M. FRANCHI, *Protezione dei minori e diritto internazionale privato,* Milan, 1997.

At an international level, respect for this fundamental interest also means possibly accepting religiously-determined legal instruments that might threaten other fundamental human rights of individuals, children included. The kafala of Islamic law highlights a series of legislative shortcomings that call into question the phrase ‘best interests of the child’ as it presents itself as an internal legal instrument of various countries, as such to be safeguarded within the international respect of state sovereignty at the legislative level, but with significant repercussions on individual rights, absolute human rights, such as freedom of conscience and religion, more importantly. Reference to this as an instrument of child protection in international law has undoubtedly engendered fresh interest on the part of the international community when it comes to respect of cultural (and religious) diversity in the context of international adoption.

Religion, in fact, has an undeniable role in social aggregation and identification and helps to identify and preserve the identity of a community, whether it coincides with the population of a nation, or a minority social group that finds the basis of its ethical, historical, traditional and cultural values in religion. It draws attention to the most perceptible component of a certain cultural heritage, the ethical substratum of pre-juridical ethical values underlying social construction.

The reference to kafala in Islamic law thus represents a step forward in the recognition of human rights, of the rights of the child, and especially of the ‘cultural’ institutions of individual states, which cannot be ignored in a purely Eurocentric/Western perspective on human rights. It also implies accepting that the protection of an abandoned child is more important than guarantees provided to the child’s religious freedom. Nevertheless, it is a difficult path to follow with regard to the subjects involved, the child and the parents, simply because they fall within a certain religious viewpoint which is positively binding in itself. In this context, it may suffice to think of a child born in an Islamic country, where he/she is automatically considered as belonging to the Ummah/community of believers, with obvious limits as to his/her freedom to religious belief. Or, it may suffice to consider the difficulties of parents who might change their religious faith. Thus, the reference to kafala in Islamic law cannot be readily interpreted as a legal institution of another state with the uncritical use of the legal instruments of private international law, but must be properly framed in intercultural and transnational contexts.

3. Child's Best Interest and International Recognition of Religiously-oriented Instruments

Kafala is currently a legal concept recognized by international law. The 1989 International Convention on the Rights of the Child stipulates that all private children in their family group are entitled to protection that may take the form of kafala or adoption. Decidedly, the choice of the measure depends on the need for a certain continuity in the child's education and ethnic-religious origin.[123]

The goal is clearly to avoid creating a filial bond that may be contested. The adoption of a child under the kafala model actually produces a break between two official identities. Of course, this route is not without glaring contradiction between respect for and failure to comply with the child's national legislation. Sociological analysis, however, suggests that almost all children adopted under the kafala model are chosen by parents who share common origins with the child (at least one of the two), thus ensuring that cultural-religious identity is maintained.

The Hague Convention of 1965, now repealed, was fundamental in defining relations between states on the matter of adoption, by legally recognizing and unifying the system.[124] Two years later, another convention gave further impetus to the process of harmonization and outlined the fundamental principle in this area, providing the child with a family (not a family with a child) by complete change in perspective, so that the main focus was no longer on the couple and their right to a child but on the child and his/her right to a family.[125]

At the international level, two other important conventions dealt with this matter by placing great importance on the interests of the child, both at the legal and psychological levels, as the decisive elements of any political decision. These were the Hague Convention on Protection of Children and Co-operation in Respect of Intercountry Adoption (or Hague Adoption Convention) of 1993 and the Hague Convention of 1996, with further

---

[123] M.C. Le Boursicot, *La kafâla ou recueil lègal des mineurs en droit musulman: une adoption sans filiation,* in *Droit et Culture,* 2010, n. 59, p. 297 *et seq*.

[124] In the Convention of 15 November 1965 on the jurisdiction of the authorities, applicable law and recognition of the decisions on adoption were annulled following the coming into force of the Hague Convention of 29 May 1993 on 1st January 2003.

[125] B. Poletti di Teodoro, *La Convenzione intramericana di La Paz del 24 maggio 1984 sui conflitti di legge in materia di adozione dei minori,* in *Riv. dir. civ.,* 1984, p. 672 *et seq*.; A. Beghè Loreti, *La legislazione dell'adozione dei minori nei Paesi dell'America Latina,* Milan, 1984.

reference to the kafala being contained in Article 24 of the Hague Convention of 19 October 1996. This Article deals with international adoption only as a residual and alternative means of care for the child to be used solely "if the child cannot be placed in a foster or an adoptive family or cannot in any suitable manner be cared for in the child's country of origin" where foster family may be read as an implicit reference to kafala of Islamic law. The convention also rules that when deciding among the various forms of childcare listed, states should take into account the need for a certain continuity in the education of the child, as well as the child's ethnic, religious, cultural and linguistic background.

In the 1993 Hague Convention, the preamble explicitly refers to the rights of the child, reaffirming the obligation for public authorities to verify that the adoption procedure corresponds to the interests of the child involved. The need for uniform regulation on adoption and the awareness that only a system agreed upon would have any chance of ensuring the child's best interest prompted states to sign a legally binding document on the issue of child protection, and to address cooperation in international adoption, which currently represents the reference text in this area.[126]

It is important to point out that this text emphasized respect for two basic rights: the rights of the child and the principle of subsidiarity. The latter does not only imply subsidiarity of adoption with respect to other forms of child protection, but also subsidiarity of international adoption with respect to national adoption. It refers to the indispensable priority of the child's stability with regard to his/her family, social and cultural background and the residuality of international adoption as a possible answer to the state of abandonment. The focus here is therefore on balancing the right of the child to family life and respect for his/her identity. However, the text does not mention kafala specifically, but references to it are made clear. The goal of the international community is, in fact, made explicit in Article 26, which outlines the effects of recognizing only the adoption available by legitimate status. Other forms of child protection are excluded, and in the subsequent Article 27 it is specified that when a child moves from one country to another for adoption purposes, the provision of the child's state of origin will be legally converted.

This convention governs basic guidelines and provides precise procedural direction for adoption between different countries. It emphasises the creation

---

[126] A. VACCARO, *L'adozione internazionale e la Convenzione dell'Aja,* in *Dir. fam. e pers.,* 1996 p. 1127 *et seq.*; M. DOGLIOTTI, *L'adozione internazionale e la Convenzione dell'Aja*, in *Dir. fam. pers.,* 1995, p. 262; A. BEGHÈ LORETI, *La tutela internazionale dei diritti del fanciullo,* Padua, 1995.

of a definitive parent/child bond as an essential element of adoption and that this procedure should be administered by a state authority. Direct agreement between natural parents and adoptive couples, typical of the consensual kafala, is thus ruled out since it does not offer sufficient safeguards to protect the rights of the child or his/her identity, on account of the agreement operating outside official channels.

A basic precondition prior to commencing the adoption procedure is a declaration by the foreign authority of the state of origin as to the child's adoptability. This presupposes that consent must have been acquired by the people, institutions and authorities involved. In the case of family members, it is necessary to verify that they have been accurately informed about the legal effects of adoption. It is by seeking full, informed and legitimate consent that the system codified by the Hague Convention of 1993 is able to establish its procedural nature.

There are three basic principles of the convention – namely, to realize the child's best interests; to recognize the subsidiarity of international adoption; and to establish a Central Authority as a means of communication between the authorities of the country of origin and those of the country of destination of the adopted child. The heavily emphasized subsidiarity principle is one which requires that preferential solutions should be sought in the country of origin as an alternative to international adoption when identifying the best interests of the child.[127] It also highlights the issue of whether it might be appropriate to examine what limits should be placed on international adoption policies and which regulatory instruments and schemes should be preferred in order to reach, through different routes, the greatest possible wellbeing of the children and families involved. In the framework of adoption, then, this principle is no longer about identifying and entrusting a child to a couple, but about providing a parentless child with a family. No Islamic country has ratified this convention since its scope is restricted to adoptions that "form a legal parent/child relationship".[128]

The 1996 Hague Convention on Jurisdiction, Applicable Law, Recognition, Enforcement and Co-operation in respect of Parental Responsibility and Measures for the Protection of Children, also lay the

---

[127] N. MEYER-FABRE, *La Convention de La Haye du 29 mai 1993 sur la protection des enfants et la coopération en matière d'adoption internationale,* in *Rev. crit. dr. int. privé,* 1994; C.L. SANTILI, *Sussidiarietà e residualità nell'adozione internazionale,* in *Le nuove regole delle adozioni,* edited by P. Morozzo Della Rocca, Naples, 2002.

[128] M.Y. MATTAR, *Trafficking in Persons, Especially Women and Children,* in *Countries of the Middle East: the Scope of the Problem and the Appropriate Legislative Responses,* in *Fordham Int. Law Journal,* 721, 2003.

foundations for the principle of the best interests of the child and perfected the evolutionary process in this matter.[129] At an international level, what emerges is the desire to make the concept of international adoption unique and to bind it to the principles of residuality and subsidiarity. Numerous articles deal with private international law, regulating the identification of applicable law on the protection of children along the lines of two distinct hypotheses, with particular attention to both the child and the parents. The approval of this document removed many doubts and broadened the child's protection, including, *inter alia*, the principle of parental responsibility in the classification of a series of cases concerning parent/child relations and altering their subjective effectiveness.

For the first time in an international convention, Article 3, paragraph (e), variously included the placement of the child in a foster family or institutional care, the provision of care by kafala, or a similar institution. Clearly, these measures cannot be taken in a state whose domestic law does not provide for it. In this sense, the convention represents a decisive step in the recognition of cultural diversity, and explicitly mentions for the first time a principle which has essentially a strong religious connotation, despite this principle being denoted by civil law formulations in many countries as well.

Though the recognition and inclusion of this fundamental principle of the Islamic world represents a step towards recognising cultural rights also at an international level, it does raise important issues among jurists, who fear that it may restrict the equally fundamental and inalienable rights of freedom of conscience and religion. Allowing religiously-orientated child protection systems to enter into the international debate could threaten the recognition of the rights so painstakingly attributed to children – not only the freedom of conscience and religion, but above all the rights that modern democratic states recognize in a legal parent/child relationship. In this regard, a re-reading of regulatory institutions is therefore required outside any limitation of individual rights recognized in liberal political contexts, and fully abides by the notion of diversity.

As regards the attribution or extinction *ex lege* of parental responsibility, the reference is to Article 16, which identifies the criterion of the child's habitual residence through standardization of this type of discipline. Article 20 is an interesting one in that it states that the law applicable may also be that of a state that is not party to the convention. It also provides for the elimination of any direct competence on the part of

---

[129] L. SANDRINI, *Protezione dei minori (dir. int. priv.), Matrimonio, (dir. int. priv.),* in *Dizionario giuridico* edited by N. IRTI, Milan, 2010.

the authorities of the state of which the child holds citizenship, and implies, by virtue of forum and *ius*, that the role of the national law of the country to which the child belongs is no less relevant for the discipline of parental responsibility. The most important international organizations have stressed that this last principle protects the child in the cultural context of reference, and must work to preserve the core of relationships that characterize the child's existence in his/her original context, keeping in mind the child's best interests.[130]

4. Protecting the Child in Europe Alongside Family Life and Cultural Diversity

Countless articles in the European Convention cover the relationship between the child and the family. In particular, the convention specifies that the state must take into account the parents' rights and duties when ensuring the child's protection; a child cannot be separated from his or her parents against their will, except when the appropriate authorities deem it necessary (and for the best interests of the child); and a child who is separated from one or both parents has the right to maintain personal relations and direct contact with both parents. It also states that family reunion should be encouraged when a family member lives in a different state; both parents have common responsibilities for the upbringing of the child; and the state is obliged to assist parents in the performance of their child-rearing responsibilities.[131]

---

[130] E. BARTHOLET, *International Adoption: a Way Forward,* in *New York Law School Rev.,* 2010-2011, p. 687 *et seq.*

[131] G. CAROBENE, *Sulla protezione internazionale della libertà religiosa,* in *Il Diritto Ecclesiastico,* 1998, 2, pp. 363-383; G. SERGIO, *La convenzione europea sull'esercizio dei diritti dei fanciulli: una tappa decisiva verso il riconoscimento della soggettività dei minori,* in *Cittadini in crescita,* 1, 2003, p. 11 *et seq.*; F. MILANESE, *Il Garante per l'infanzia nella promozione di una cultura dei diritti dei bambini,* in *Il garante dell'infanzia e dell'adolescenza, un sistema di garanzia nazionale nella prospettiva europea,* edited by L. Strumendo, Milan, 2007; G. CAMPANATO, *Dirittti del bambino e ruolo del giudice. Spunti di riflessione sulla Convenzione di Strasburgo,* and P. DE STEFANI, *Adattamento alla Convenzione di Strasburgo: lo spirito e la legge,* both in *I diritti del bambino tra protezione e garanzie. La ratifica della Convenzione di Strasburgo sull'esercizio dei diritti dei fanciulli,* edited by L. Strumendo, P. De Stefani, Padua, 2004, pp. 61-74 e pp. 135-144.

The European Convention, though not expressly referring to the status of a child,[132] deals with the child's best interests by way of interpretation, in particular by recognizing private and family life.[133] In this vein, it is considered that the provision may include the guarantee of the pursuit of those interests against possible interference by public authorities in the exercise of those rights, permitted to protect "the rights and freedoms of others".

The interpretation of the law makes it possible to highlight the shift, fundamental to the issue of supporting children, from the concept of parental authority to parental responsibility. In other words, the rights and duties of parents with regard to their offspring are attributed in order to encourage the child's psycho-physical development, emphasizing personality and its central role in affecting choices regarding how the child should be managed.[134] The decision to employ the term parental responsibility, unusual in most European national legal systems, highlights the need to place parental responsibility and the rights of children within one single concept.[135]

The convention provides for the possibility of limiting the principle of equality and to take "such measures as are necessary in the interests of the children", where the child's needs coincide with the demands of a democratic society. Thus, interference with the parent's subjective position may be based on an imperative social need that is proportionate to the aim of pursuing the child's interest, an assessment of which is left to the states. These states, however, do not have unlimited discretionary power in the matter since the motivation behind any interference must be "relevant and pertinent".

---

[132] C. BREEN, *The standard of the best interest of the child. A Western Tradition in International and Comparative* Law, The Hague, 2002, p. 249 *et seq*.

[133] C. RAVERA, *Art. 5, Uguaglianza degli sposi,* in *La Convenzione Europea dei Diritti dell'uomo e delle libertà fondamentali commentata ed annotata,* edited by C. Defilippi, D. Bosi, R. Harvey, Naples, 2006; A.O. COZZI, *Parità fra coniugi,* in *Commentario breve alla Convenzione Europea dei diritti dell'uomo,* edited by S. Bartole, P. De Sena, V. Zagrebelsky, Padua, 2012, pp. 905-908.

[134] A. ADINOLFI, *Il diritto alla vita familiare nella giurisprudenza della Corte di giustizia dell'Unione europea,* in *Rivista di diritto internazionale,* n. 1, 2011; M. FINOCCHIARO, *Responsabilità genitoriale: dal 1 marzo 2005 va in soffitta l'istituto della patria potestà,* in *Guida al Diritto (Diritto Comunitario e Internazionale)*, 2005, n. 1.

[135] S. GILMORE, *The Limits of Parental Responsibility,* in *Responsible Parents and Parental Responsibility,* R. PROBERT, S. GILMORE, J. HERRING. (eds.), Oxford, 2000, pp. 63-83.

Europe has gradually established itself on the basis of a genuine and long-standing acknowledgment of cultural diversity and, in this sense, aims to create universal values. One of the main effects of globalization is to weaken the link between cultural phenomena and geographic location, while also bearing upon European cultural traditions. Severing this link can, at times be experienced as an opportunity, at others, a loss of reference and identity.

Adherence to the multicultural principle – formally codified in some legal systems, such as Article 22 of the Charter of Fundamental Rights of the European Union, which requires respect for cultural, religious and linguistic differences – does not in itself determine specific rights attributable to cultural identity, but rather identifies an interpretative criterion along with a principle of relationship. The former requires interpretation of the provisions to be consistent and compatible with respect for cultural pluralism. The latter suggests that a legal system qualifies as multicultural not so much on the basis of pre-existing legal elements – such as the coexistence of different languages, races, religions, ethical, social or sociological concepts, or globalization or increased migration – but by virtue of the (dual) relationship that is established within society and between this and the state. The state approach to the religious phenomenon has experienced significant change over time – so much so that an analysis from a historical perspective points to a multifaceted polyhedron. At times, religious precepts have been identified as a qualifying element of the state (as is currently the case in Islamic States). At others, the law has gained its independence from religious rule (as is currently the case in many European countries). In addition, the indifference and extraneousness of the public sphere with respect to religion has been theorised upon (as enshrined by the Constitutional Court of Italy). Neutrality as an instrument of public authority has been identified as the most suitable for promoting the coexistence between different faiths and between those and non-believers.

Perhaps one of the best ways to understand cultural diversity as it pertains to children's rights is to consider the concept of margin of appreciation. This concept is a corollary of the principle of subsidiarity and allows international judges to leave the final decision to national authorities since they are practically closer to the real case and are able to assess the social impact of their decisions. Though with certain limits, this flexibility allows for respect of the cultural, ideological and legal variety and diversity that are held to be characteristic of Europe. One of the principles behind the doctrine of the margin of appreciation is that where there is consensus among Member States as to a solution to a particular problem, the margin of discretion left to national authorities will be narrowed in scope.

With regard to kafala, however, it appears that this institution has not received equal assessment by the Member States of the Council of Europe. In fact, national authorities have a wide margin of appreciation and the European Court can only verify whether the grounds examined are sufficient and relevant to justify the decision.

The European Convention on the Adoption of Children of 1967, as amended in 2008, was wholly devoted to childhood. This text, however, does seem to perpetuate the private law negotiating stance to the principles of adoption, which are ultimately outdated. It pays less attention to the overriding right of the child to a 'good, loving family', and completely ignores the need for a strong presence of public authorities with regard to the prevention and detection of family difficulties and the provision of support. In other texts, especially those emanated after 2008, there are some innovations that considerably ease access – though without adequate motivation – to so-called open adoption, which still raises many doubts and perplexities among legal theorists.

In order to safeguard the practical aspects of the promotion of children's rights and facilitate their full exercise under the Council of Europe, the 1996 Strasbourg Convention on the Exercise of Children's Rights promoted the child's best interests from the Preamble onwards, so that they may "have the opportunity to exercise their rights, in particular in family proceedings affecting them". This is a very significant text, which is likely to introduce some very clear-cut innovations into the laws of the ratifying states. Often pre-empting customs, these innovations are symptomatic of the profound changes that are taking place in the family model.

In this convention, priority was given to broadening procedural areas involving children, based on the consideration that unimplemented rights are basically non-existent, and that the implementation of denied or contested rights should be defined procedurally. With this text, the Council of Europe made up for the weaknesses in the convention, where references to the child were few. Its aim was to develop instrumental regulations to facilitate implementation of the substantive rights of children through the creation of new procedural rights that could also be exercised personally by children capable of judgement.[136]

---

[136] G. SCIANCALEPORE, P. STANZIONE, *Minori e diritti fondamentali,* Milan, 2006; M. MARCHEGIANI, *Diritti dei minori,* in *Codice della Famiglia,* edited by M. Sesta, vol. II, Milan, 2007; F. TOMMASEO, *Il processo civile familiare e minorile italiano nel contesto dei principi europei,* in *Dir. fam. pers.,* 3, 2012, pp. 1265-1280.

In this sense, this convention represents one of the most significant advancements of child law, and marks the birth of the notion of the rights of the child replacing the traditional best interests of the child. In this regard, the most significant innovations concern the recognition of rights which may be exercised directly by the child (through his/her representatives) and the structuring of the "right to be heard".[137] This saw a shift from formal to substantive protection, the main purpose of which was to promote the rights of children in the judicial field. In this way, in the European context, the child became a procedural subject vested with legal capacity and recognized as an independent party that may act and be heard to exercise his/her rights through the introduction of effective instruments that offer a substantive guarantee.[138]

In the European system, a further guarantee closely linked to family relationships lies in Article 14 of the EU Charter of Fundamental Rights of 2000, which in particular provides that "the right of parents to ensure the education and teaching of their children in conformity with their religious, philosophical and pedagogical convictions shall be respected, in accordance with the national laws governing the exercise of such freedom and right". This provision, though, does not allow the state to derogate to the right of parents, nor does it impose any positive obligations as to performance on the state.

Partially reproducing Article 3 of the 1989 Convention on the Rights of the Child, Article 24 of the Charter,[139] through its binding character as envisaged by the Lisbon Treaty,[140] reaffirms the child's best interest as a

---

[137] G. MAGNO, *Il minore come soggetto processuale. Commento alla Convenzione Europea sull'esercizio dei diritti dei fanciulli,* Milan, 2001; C. FIORAVANTI, *I diritti del bambino tra protezione garanzie: l'entrata in vigore, per la Repubblica Italiana della Convenzione di Strasburgo,* in *Le nuove leggi civili commentate,* n. 3, 2003, pp. 561-568.

[138] G. CAMPANATO, V. ROSSI, S. ROSSI, *La tutela giuridica del minore,* Padua, 2005, p. 712 *et seq*.

[139] L. FERRARI BRAVO, M. DI MAJO, A. RIZZO, *Carta dei diritti fondamentali dell'Unione Europea,* Milan, 2001; P. MARTINELLI, F. MAZZA GALANTI, *Diritto del bambino,* in *la Carta dei diritti dell'Unione Europea. Casi e materiali,* edited by G. Bisogni, G. Bronzini, V. Piccone, Taranto, 2009, pp 303-319.

[140] J.L. MURRAY, *The Influence of the European Convention of Fundamental Rights on Community Law,* in *Fordham International Law Journal,* 33, n. 5, 2011, pp. 1388-1422; S. GRATALOUP, *L'enfant et sa famille dans les normes europennes,* Paris, 1998; M.C. BARUFFI, *La cittadinanza dell'Unione e i diritti dei minori nello spazio giudiziario europeo,* in *Cittadinanza e diversità culturale nello spazio giuridico europeo,* edited by M.C. Baruffi, Milan, 2010, p. 69 *et seq*; C. NOVI, *La tutela dei diritti dei minori nell'ordinamento comunitario,* in *Diritto pubblico*

primary consideration. What is significant here is the decision to place the rights of children in the chapter on equality. This completes the principle expressed in Article 21 and thus also defines the subjectivity of the child in the European context and the right not to be discriminated against by virtue of age.[141] In this sense, through the provisions of Article 24, the European system explicitly recognizes that the child, *inter alia*, has the right to the protection and care necessary for his/her well-being and to have a personal relationship and direct contact with his/her parents. These rights are acquired by children at an early age and in the pursuit of these rights they must be able to contribute themselves, also by expressing their opinion on issues that involve them and consistent with their age and degree of maturity.

Particular importance is also given to the right of the child to maintain a personal relationship and direct contact with both parents, which is expressed separately from the provisions of the Charter relating to the protection of the family. Here, once again, emphasis is placed on how this responds to a fundamental need of the child and, at the same time, how it mirrors the right of parents to maintain family unity. This concept is taken up and specified in the Explanations Relating to the Charter, which expressly refers to the requirements arising from the establishment of an area of freedom, security and justice, and affirms the EU's legislative competence in civil matters with cross-border implications.

By complying with the principle of subsidiarity, the EU is thus committed to supporting Member States by promoting exchange of good practices, cooperation and communication with and between national authorities responsible for the protection and promotion of children's rights. To this end, the definition contained in the 2003 Regulation works to facilitate the circulation of decisions concerning children and their non-discrimination within individual Member States. Parental responsibility is defined in the same text as "all rights and duties relating to the person or the property of a child which are given to a natural or legal person by judgment, by operation of law or by an agreement having legal effect. The term shall include rights of custody and rights of access" and means "any

---

comparato ed europeo, n. 1, 2007, pp. 186-216; G. TURRI, *I grandi principi europei di tutela dei minori,* in *Minorigiustizia,* n. 2, 2008, pp. 7-12; S.M CARBONE, C. TUO, *Gli strumenti di diritto dell'Unione europea in materia di famiglia e il Trattato di Lisbona,* in *Studi sull'integrazione europea,* n. 2, 2010, pp. 301-324.

[141] A. FURIA, *L'Unione europea,* in *Promozione, protezione ed attuazione dei diritti dei minori,* edited by C. CARLETTI, Turin, 2009, pp. 112-134.

person having parental responsibility over a child".[142] Among the rights included in parental responsibility, then, emphasis is now placed on the reference to the right of custody, which is defined by the Court of Justice as an independent notion of national law.

It is interesting to note the omitted reference to a legal or natural parent/child relationship between which a fundamental difference is still retained in Islamic law. This distinction seems to have been surpassed in Europe by virtue of a reading of the provisions of Article 8 of the European Convention designed to ensure the protection of "family life". According to this, in the name of the child's best interests, equality between a parent/child relationship based on marriage and one established outside a 'traditional' family is promoted, while any national provisions that do not guarantee this should be discouraged. The reference here is obviously to religiously-oriented legal systems that impose a strict family structure but pay little respect to individual rights and freedoms.

It would be a mistake, however, to make a mere formal comparison of legal systems or to impose a certain cultural and legal model. It is better to build a model that reveals the substantive aspect of the parent/child relationship by virtue of the combined provisions of the principles of best interests, non-discrimination, the protection of religious freedoms and the neutrality of legal rules.

Viewed this way, family relationships are also governed by European sources, and this also attests to an increased competence in family law by the EU, resulting in a residual application of the domestic laws relating to private international law and international conventions.[143] The universal principle of the best interests of the child applied to family relationships constitutes the limit to exercising the rights-duties that characterize parental responsibility. The use of this notion, albeit widespread in international law, is progressively replacing the legal language of parental responsibility even within individual states, with this responsibility/authority heavily pointing to a traditional and conservative view of the relationship between parents and children based on disciplinary control, or to a set of prerogatives and faculties recognized to the person who acts as a parent in the interests of the child.

---

[142] I. QUEIROLO, *La disciplina della responsabilità genitoriale:il Regolamento CE 2201/2003,* in *Lezioni di diritto dell'Unione Europea e relazioni familiari,* edited by I. Queirolo, L. Schiano di Pepe, Turin, 2014, pp. 288-289.

[143] C. HONORATI, *Verso una competenza della Comunità Europea in materia di diritto di famiglia?* in *La famiglia nel diritto internazionale privato e comunitario,* edited by S. Boriatti, Milan, 2007, p. 3 *et seq.*

The term 'parental responsibility', on the other hand, reflects a view of the child as holding fundamental rights, embedded in a complex system of rights-duties of the parent. Going beyond the authoritarian concept of parenthood has meant setting duties before rights, and resulted in such rights now being in place in order to fulfil those duties.

The most recent and innovative doctrinal positions underline the need for a substantial revision of the concept of the total subjection of the child to the authority of the parents as a key to understanding the general lack of legal capacity of the child in private law.[144] Fundamental to this is a further development of the child's right to be heard, which falls within the framework of those fundamental principles which the Juvenile Court should take into account when assessing the adoption or custody measures in place in the foreign state concerned.[145] This has led to the progressive affirmation of the subjectivity of the child, and consequently to an extension of the protection of the child, with a shift of focus from the interests – a juridical category prone to approximation – to the rights of the child which best define the effectiveness of the protection. What is taking shape, then, is a limitation on the discretion of the interpreter to identify the best interests of the child and the emergence of a new mode of parent/child relationship, where the best interests of the child may also mean sacrificing the parents' position by creating different equilibriums. It makes it possible, among other things, to focus more attention on the principle of parental responsibility framed in a context of child protection, that is, when family ties break down.[146] The move from a traditional view of the patriarchal family to a modern approach of marital parity in domestic law has progressively affected international law as well. Thus, in this context too, the primacy of the child has also been recognized, irrespective of the different parental roles. The discipline of international adoptions has now been enhanced and largely determined by a shift in interpretation with a constant mind to protecting the child's right to a family.

Kafala could be included in this framework, resulting from the need for a proper balance between the universalisation of human rights and the

---

[144] E. MOSCATI, *Il minore nel diritto privato, da soggetto da proteggere a persona da valorizzare (contributo allo studio dell'interesse del minore"),* in *Dir. fam. pers.,* 2014, p. 1151 *et seq*.

[145] L. MOLLICA, *Osservazioni a Cass. 23 luglio 1997, n. 6899,* in *Dir. fam. pers.,* 1998, p. 54 *et seq*.

[146] E. AL MUREDEN, *La responsabilità genitoriale tra condizione unica del figlio e pluralità dei modelli familiari,* in *Fam dir., 2014*, p. 471 *et seq*.

protection of different cultural identities.[147] It represents an open dialogue inserted in a dynamic process. It is well known that the principle of equal rights does not necessarily mean the right to equality and that a difference of treatment, based on cultural diversity, can meet the conditions of objectivity and substantial equality. Conversely, any difference in treatment resulting in direct or indirect discrimination cannot be accepted because it is based on subjective criteria, such religious affiliation.

Respect for cultural diversity may not undermine the principle of the universality of human rights as long as cultural practices do not undermine respect for public order. But a religiously-motivated ban on adoption is different, and may lead to discriminating between abandoned children solely on the basis of their country of origin. This appeared to be the orientation of the European Court, which stated the principle that no difference in treatment can be objectively justified on the basis of the origin of a person in a democratic society based on pluralism.[148] Other principles to be properly balanced are the relationship between formal and substantive equality that does not tend towards equal treatment through texts at hand but to equality of fact.

The problem should be correctly placed within the setting of *accomodement raisonnable* to arrive at a better assessment of the legal status of children placed in custody under kafala and allow "*aux individus qui, en raison de leur pratique religieuse, sont pénalisés par une mesure ou une clause contractuelle pourtant justifiée par un objectif légitime, d'obtenir un aménagement de celle-ci, à condition que cet aménagement reste raisonnable, c'est-à- dire qu'il ne porte pas atteinte aux droits d'autrui et n'entraîne pas d'inconvénients ou de frais démesurés*".[149]

---

[147] Y. DONDERS, *Human Rights: Eye for Cultural Diversity, Inaugural Lecture delivered upon appointment to the chair of Professor of International Human Rights and Cultural Diversity at the University of Amsterdam on 29 June 2012,* Amsterdam, 2012, p. 19 *et seq.*; L.M. CRACIUNEAN, *The European Court of Human Rights' approach to cultural rights and cultural diversity,* in *Rom. J. Comp. L.,* 2, 2013, p. 238 *et seq.*

[148] J. RINGELHEIM, *Diversité culturelle et droits de l'homme – L'émergence de la problématique des minorités dans le droit de la Convention Européenne des droits de l'homme,* Brussels, 2006, pp. 267-275; N. COLAIANNI, *Eguaglianza e diversità culturali e religiose. Un percorso costituzionale,* Bologna, 2006; A. FUCCILLO, *La tutela dei minori e l'identità religiosa,* in *Giustizia e religione,* edited by A. Fuccillo, Turin, 2011, p. 192 *et seq.*

[149] Translation: "individuals who, because of their religious practice, are penalized by a measure or a contractual clause yet justified by a legitimate objective, to obtain an adjustment of it, provided that such an adjustment is reasonable, in other

The European Convention on the Adoption of Children 2008 took this development forward by redrafting the principle of parental responsibility. It deals with conventional adoption but does not exclude different forms. Thus, while stipulating that the adopted child has the same rights and obligations as a legitimate child, there are some exceptions: the child may choose not to take the surname of the adoptive family and may maintain ties with the family of origin. New parents also have a duty to present a realistic plan on how to tackle any problems of integration and racism. Instead, at the time of ratification of the Hague Convention of 1993, Italian legislature opted to defer to the criteria for national adoption when declaring adoptive parents eligible, without providing for any particular rules on the special condition of the future parents of a foreign child bearing a different identity.

In Europe, the growing crystallization of fundamental rights, as enshrined in the European Convention on Human Rights and the Charter of Fundamental Rights of the European Union, does not advance the application of foreign regulations of Islamic origin. The notion of attenuated public order, however, means that some effects on acts that have been pronounced by foreign jurisdictions should be recognised. In Islamic countries, this phrase expresses an absolute religious value and the fundamental values to be defended by the application of this legal structure refer exclusively to Sharia law. Public order will then have a religious foundation allowing the any foreign law that sanctions a legal rule incompatible with the fundamental principles of Islamic law to be disapplied.

There are several sources on coexistence and their coordination is far from easy. In general, it can be stated that the most applicable criterion is that of the child's habitual residence. It has the merit of having a factual and non-legal value and of focusing attention on the best interests of the child. However, critical issues arise when it is not sufficiently clear whether the controversial issue concerns parental responsibility or the protection of children when the judicial level is involved. Another complex issue regards the reconstruction of regulations for the determination of applicable law, which is not regulated by European law, but only by sources of private, international, national and conventional law.

In terms of applicable law, the criterion of citizenship, traditionally used in family law, has maintained a certain relevance despite the fact that

words that it does not infringe the rights of others and does not entail any inconvenience or disproportionate costs".

reference is made to the child's residence. Unlike residence, citizenship has the advantage of stability, but is still a legal criterion and as such can only be assessed on its strictly legal basis, which is not always an easy task. Hence, while it may provide greater certainty in the interpretation of law, it becomes critical when dual, multiple or non-existent citizenship is involved.

It is worth noting that in Italy, the adopted child currently acquires citizenship as a result of the transcript of the adoption order in the civil register. On this basis, a time lapse occurs between the *status filiationis*, which begins when the foreign action becomes definitive in the state of origin, and the *status civitatis*, which is acquired only by its transcription in the host state, at the time of the actual entry of the child into the country. This anomaly could result in statelessness contrary to Articles 2 and 10 of the Italian Constitution, which can be resolved on the basis not of a formal reading of the regulation, but of the *ratio* underlying it, that the adoptive child of Italian citizens acquires or should acquire the citizenship of his/her parents at the same time as he/she acquires the status of legitimate child.[150]

It is also important to point out that, in the area of applicable law, public order will apply with the application of foreign law. In family law, this limit is particularly incisive given its connection to cultural, ethical and religious values that characterize the legal system as a whole. Consequently, it can be stated that in countries with a common cultural matrix the use of the public order limitation has little or virtually no application. But this limitation will be necessary, however, when assessing the possibility of applying the law of a system that falls at some distance from our own cultural *Weltanshauung*, as is the case of Islamic countries. Another controversial issue is related to the procedures for the recognition and enforcement of foreign decisions. Such measures, in fact, are likely to differ according to the origin and the object. Finally, the issue of the applicability of the Hague Convention of 1961 as it relates to recognition is still unresolved since the applicability of Article 3 is not univocally understood.

---

150 R. CLERICI, *La cittadinanza nell'ordinamento giuridico italiano,* Padua, 1993; M. CORSARO, *L'affidamento preadottivo nelle procedure per l'adozione internazionale,* in *Fam. dir.,* 2002, p.78 *et seq*.; P. MAROZZO DELLA ROCCA, *La condizione giuridica del minore straniero,* in *Minori e giust.,* 2002, p. 30 *et seq*.; L. SACCHETTI, *Il nuovo istituto dell'adozione internazionale,* Rimini, 2000, p. 152 *et seq*.

5. Italian Private International Law. Intercultural Translation and Protection of Minors

In Italy, decisive action took place only after the law on the reform of private international law in 1995 had been approved, almost at the same time as the 1961 Hague Convention was being ratified. In the past, Article 20 of the preliminary provisions of the civil code referred to the national law of the *father* while Article 36 of Law no. 218 of 1995 referred to the national law of the *child*, highlighting the continuous change to family relationships that domestic legislation had absorbed from international law.[151] Among the most innovative contents of the reformed law were undoubtedly the rules on filiation and on child/parent relationships. Parental authority, the guiding principle of the civil code of 1942, was definitively replaced by the principle of the primacy of the interests of the

---

[151] Originally, it stated that "relations between parents and children are governed by the father's national law, or by that of the mother if only motherhood is ascertained or if only the mother has legitimized the child. The relations between the adopter and the adopted are regulated by the national law of the adopter at the time of adoption". The rule for the law applicable to the constitution, assessment and disavowal of legitimate, natural and adoptive filiation was Article 17 of the preliminary provisions to the Civil Code which considered the national law of the interested parties as the principle factor: cf. *Manuale di diritto internazionale privato*, G.CONETTI, S. TONOLO, F. VISMARA (eds.), Turin, Giappichelli, 2013 esp. on Article 20, esp. p. 112 *et seq.*; cf. A. GIARDINA, Art, 17, in *Commentario del nuovo diritto internazionale privato*, F. POCAR, T. TREVES, S.M. CARBONE, A. GIARDINA, R. LUZZATTO, F. MOSCONI, R. CLERICI (eds.), Padua, Cedam, 1996, p. 95 *et seq*. The Constitutional Court intervened in 1987 with two judgments, March 5 n. 71 and December 10 n. 477 emphasizing in the first "a clear contrast with Article 3, para. 1 of the Constitution, which prohibits discrimination between the sexes, and Article 29 para. 2, of the Constitution, which specifies equality of spouses" and declaring, in the second, the illegitimacy of Article 20, para. 1 of the preliminary provisions of the Civil Code "where it states that if both parents are known and they do not share the same nationality then the father's national law will take precedence". The Court also specified that national parental law would remain valid in preference to any other: Constitutional Court, December 10 1987, n. 477, in *Foro It.,* 1988, vol. II, col. 2831 *et seq.* with comments by E. PAGANO, *La legge regolatrice dei rapporti personali tra coniugi e dei rapporti tra genitori e figli dopo la declaratoria di incostituzionalità degli artt. 18 e 20 delle preleggi*, and Constitutional Court March 5 1987, n.71, in *Foro It*, 1987, vol. I, col. 2316 *et seq*. With comments by B. POLETTI DI TEODORO, *Una svolta storica nel diritto internazionale privato italiano: il primo intervento "abrogativo" della Corte Costituzionale.*

child compared to those of the parents (no longer only of the father).[152] While maintaining the criterion of citizenship, this was no longer bound to the parents but to the child. It was up to the national law of the child to establish his/her status, regulate the legitimacy and recognition of the natural child as well as the patrimonial and personal relations between parents and children, including parental authority.

Italy took several years to ratify the Hague Convention of 1961 as regards jurisdiction of the authorities and the law applicable to the protection of minors. It was not until 1995 that it came into force because of the need to set up a system of private international law that could be integrated with the discipline of the convention itself.[153] As regards the material scope of the 1961 Hague Convention, a distinction must be made between the area of efficacy established by the convention and the considerably broader scope dictated by Article 42 of Law no. 218/1995.[154]

In view of the object of its protection it would seem to refer to the protection of both the person and the property of the child.[155] Interestingly,

---

[152] Cf. Law no. 218 of 1995, in http://www.gazzettaufficiale.it/atto/serie_generale/caricaDettaglioAtto/originario?atto.dataPubblicazioneGazzetta=1995-0603&atto.codiceRedazionale=095G0256&elenco30giorni=false.

Cf. esp. Article 33, Filiation, Article 34, Legitimation, Article 35, Recognising a natural son or daughter, Article 36, Relations between parents and children, Article 37, Jurisdiction in matters of filiation.

[153] After the reform of Italian private international law, the 1961 Hague Convention was ratified in addition to two other conventions on juvenile law: the 1980 Hague Convention on the Civil Aspects of International Child Abduction and, in the area that interests us most, the 1980 Luxembourg Convention on the European Treaty Series-No. 105European Convention on Recognition and Enforcement of Decisions concerning Custody of Children and on Restoration of Custody of Children. Cf. on this point R.L. JONES, *Council of Europe Convention on Recognition and Enforcement of Decisions relating to the Custody of Children*, in *Intern. Comparative Law Quarterly*, 1981, p. 467 *et seq.*; L. SACCHETTI, *Le convenzioni internazionali di Lussemburgo e dell'Aja del 1980. Confronto e problematiche giuridiche*, in *Dir. fam. pers.*, 1997, p. 1496 *et seq.*

[154] Pursuant to Article 12 of the Convention, it applies only to those who are considered minors both by national law and by the law of the country in which they habitually reside. This limits its scope since the protection of minors, considered as such only by one of the countries, continues to be regulated by common law. It is further limited by Article 13 which provides for the application only for minors who habitually reside in a Contracting State.

[155] Article 3, originating from the compromise between the jurisdiction of the authority and the law of habitual residence and the principle of nationality, establishes that the relationships of authority established according to the national law of the minor are recognized by the Contracting States.

the convention mentioned relations between the child and the persons or institutions responsible for the child's care but made no specific mention of adoption. Instead, this was included in specific measures and *in primis* in the 1993 Hague Convention on Protection of Children and Co-operation in Respect of Intercountry Adoption.

The doctrine posed the problem of whether legal institutions which are functionally different from, but structurally similar to adoption, should be excluded from international provisions, with explicit reference to the Islamic kafala. This problem does not relate so much to its qualification in the field of international private law as to its legal provisions (a complex problem because it cannot be assimilated to the measures of fostering or adoption without distorting its nature or rationale), or to the protection measures of the minor (preferable because it is more generic and would not leave legislative gaps).

The issue concerns compliance with the fideistic options of the subjects concerned – parents and children – and the possibility that they may receive protection in multicultural systems. This problem was solved with the 1996 Hague Convention, which finally envisaged "provision of care by kafala" among the institutions included in its scope of application in Article 3 and, in Article 33, explicitly included a procedure for the recognition of the same within the laws of individual Contracting States. Again, with respect to the 1961 convention, it should be noted that reference to the same, contained in Article 42 of Law no. 218, with the use of the phrase "in every case" involves an extension of its scope of application from an objective, subjective and spatial point of view.[156]

Legal issues also arise with the interpretation of Article 7 regarding the recognition and execution of measures adopted by the competent authorities of another state. According to some legal theorists, the scope of application of the 1961 Hague Convention would have been limited only to the jurisdiction and the applicable rules based on a literal interpretation of the name of the law itself. A more correct and preferable substantial reading would lean towards an obligation to recognizing these measures internationally in the interest of the child.[157] To seek a harmonious

---

[156] Thus, the scope of application is extended, exceeding the limits set out in Articles 12-13 of the Hague Convention, which thus completely replaces the law on internal conflict.

[157] Cf. A. BONOMI, *La Convenzione dell'Aja del 1961 sulla protezione dei minori: un riesame dopo la ratifica italiana e l'avvio dei lavori di revisione*, in *Riv. dir. int. priv. e process.*, 2006, p. 608 *et seq.*, *contra*, the classic work by F. MOSCONI, *La tutela dei minori in diritto internazionale privato*, Milan, Giuffré, 1965, esp., pp . 63-65. The 1961 Hague Convention actually followed this dogmatic approach by

solution generally to the tools available for child protection, parental authority must also be considered as a fully-fledged relationship of authority, pursuant to Article 3 of the convention of 1961.[158]

Article 36 of Law no. 218/1995 also provides that "[t]he national law of the child governs personal and property relations between parents and children, including parental responsibility." With reference to personal relationships, the transmission of the name, the obligation of cohabitation, that of the parents to educate and care for the child as well as parental authority are certainly included. The latter can be defined as a set of powers that the law assigns to parents for the fulfilment of their duties towards their children, first and formemost, welfare and education – which ceases when the child comes of age or applies for emancipation, based on national law.[159]

Article 37 provides that in matters of filiation and parent/child relationships, Italian jurisdiction also applies when one of the parents is an Italian citizen or resides in Italy.[160] It thus extends Italian jurisdiction considerably in matters of filiation and parent/child relationships as it takes into account the residence and citizenship of both parties when considering jurisdiction. Protection measures means any jurisdictional or administrative measures aimed at protecting the child, who is naturally

---

including specific norms on the recognition of judgments in order to regulate the matters within its scope – parental responsibility and the protection of minors – uniformly and completely.

[158] Part of the doctrine has interpreted the relationships of authority in a restrictive way, excluding parental authority, which is so rooted in family law that it could not be considered as a measure of child protection: cf. F. MOSCONI, op. cit, p. 359 *et seq*.

[159] Cf. Article 36 Law no. 218/1995. Cf. F. RUSCELLO, *Potestà dei genitori e rapporti con i figli*, in *Il nuovo diritto di famiglia*, G. FERRANDO (ed.), vol. III, *Filiazione e Adozione*, Bologna, il Mulino, 2007, pp. 75-199. In Italian law parental authority comes under Chapter IX, Book I of the Italian Civil Code, as well as Article 147 of the Civil Code obliging both parents to be responsible for the welfare and education of their children.

[160] In addition to the cases provided for in Articles 3 and 9 of Law no. 218/1995, Article 3 states that Italian jurisdiction applies when the defendant is domiciled or resident in Italy. Article 9, with reference to jurisdiction in non-adversarial proceedings, states that jurisdiction applies when the relief sought concerns an Italian citizen or resident, or when such relief relates to situations or relations to which Italian law is applicable, as well as where the present law specifically so provides, or where venue is proper before the Italian judge to whom the matter is brought so as to have correspondence between *forum* and *ius*. Cf. R. LUZZATTO, Article 9, in Cf. *Commentario del nuovo diritto internazionale privato*, cit., p. 49 *et seq*.

fragile and immature from a psycho-physical point of view.[161] In summary, private international law, as structured by the 1995 reform law, considers parental authority within parent/child relationships and child protection measures, though without referring to parental responsibility, which would come later with the 1996 Hague Convention and 2003 EC Regulation.[162]

If, as repeatedly stated, the general criterion of international regulations is based on the principle of the child's best interest, this means that every jurisdictional measure concerning a child in difficulty should respond to standards of immediacy and effectiveness. Jurisdiction is generally attributed on the basis of the child's habitual residence, but exceptionally the nationality of the child may be applied as an alternative.[163]

In terms of application of the law, the principle of respect for public order as an expression of the foundation of the legal system at any given historical moment is fundamental and is the only criterion that may act as a barrier to the application of foreign legislation. It works to defend the internal coherence of the legal system, precluding the entry of extraneous legal values that may violate the fundamental and inalienable principles of the system itself. It is a tool for protecting coherence and is thus made up of each and every fundamental principle of the law itself.[164] The judge's discretionary margins remain rather broad to allow for adaptation to changes in social sentiment. This limit is functional and relative in space

---

[161] For Italian law, protection, including its establishment and forfeiture (Articles 343, 346, 361, 371, 384 of the Civil Code) may fall into this category as well as public administration intervention measures supporting abandoned minors (Article 403 of the Civil Code), the provisions relating to the custody of the minor (Articles 2 - 5 of Law no. 184/1983), the measures for exercising parental authority referred to the tutelary judge (Article 337 of the Civil Code) and those referred to the Juvenile Court (Article 336 of the Civil Code).

[162] Cf. P. PICONE, *La nuova Convenzione dell'Aia sulla protezione dei minori*, in *Rivista di diritto internazionale privato e processuale*, 1996, p. 705 *et seq.*

[163] Cf. M. FRANCHI, *Protezione dei minori e diritto internazionale privato*, Milan, Giuffré, 1998 esp. p. 22.

[164] Cf. G. BADIALI, *Ordine pubblico internazionale*, in *Enc. Giur.*, vol. XXII, Roma, 1990; *L'ordre public à la fin du XXème siècle*, T. REVET (ed.), Paris, Dalloz, 1996; L. FUMAGALLI, *EC Private International Law and the Public Policy Exception*, in *Yearbook of Priv. Int. Law*, vol. 6, 2004, p. 171 *et seq.*; F. ANGELINI, *Ordine pubblico e integrazione costituzionale europea*, Padua, Cedam, 2007; *La famiglia nel diritto internazionale privato comunitario*, S. BARIATTI, (ed.), Milan, Giuffré, 2007; *The External Dimension of EC Private International Law in Family and Succession Matters*, A. MALATESTA, S. BARIATTI, F. POCAR (eds.), Padua, Cedam, 2008.

and time, requiring the determination of the content case by case and is relative since it must always be contextualized.[165]

The protection of the child in family life, relevant in terms of violating the limit of public order, is not a horizontal relationship but the enhancement of the protection of the vertical parent/child relationship. It can thus no longer be based on an exclusively traditional and homogeneous family model from the point of view of religious identity. On the one hand, the social reality does give us a family pluralism protected by the system but, on the other, the perspective has shifted from the couple to the parent/child relationship, to whose protection the institution of the family is preordained. In this perspective, the pursuit of the best interests of the child is fundamental to the notion of public order in the family context.

Of frequent concern are conflicts with countries of different cultural origins, especially where it regards the application of Islamic law, of deep-rooted religious influence and with a strong impact on matters of personal status and family relationships. The contrast is particularly evident where kafala is concerned, which involves problems of recognition rather than applicable law. On the other hand, in terms of parental authority, there are cases in which public order operates as a limit to applicable law, especially when it concerns the law of an Islamic country that attributes parental authority exclusively to the father.[166]

Relativity and the inherent ductility of the area allow us to draw on solutions capable of adhering to and enhancing the principles that lie at the basis of our legal system. The advent of the Republican Constitution, as an expression of legislation based on principles with a preceptive value, hierarchically overarching ordinary law, greatly influenced the reconstruction of the limit of public order by contemporary doctrine. Bound to this concept are the general principles which derive from the Constitutional Charter, among which of primary importance is the protection of the person and individual and collective freedoms. The notion of public order

---

[165] While in some international Conventions and EU Regulations the formulation of public order is restrictive, by contrast, Articles 16 and 64 of Law no. 218/1995 would seem to indicate a much broader relevance. This interpretation cannot be sustained because such a limit must work to defend the the system, which must remain exceptional. In the matter of parental responsibility, the interpretation of the limit of public order must also always be oriented towards the protection of the best interests of the child.

[166] Cf. in general *Le leggi del diritto di famiglia negli stati arabi del Nord-Africa,* Dossier Mondo Islamico 4, R. ALUFFI BECK-PECCOZ (ed.), Turin, Fondazione G. Agnelli, 1997, in http://www.fga.it/uploads/media/Dossier_Mondo_Islamico_4.pdf.

cannot, however, be reduced to a synthesis of constitutional values or principles that can be derived exclusively from an exegesis of the rules of domestic law. The Constitution itself recognizes the "constraints deriving from EU legislation and international obligations", so that these sources – and the supranational jurisprudence that interprets them – contribute significantly to shaping a unitary and enriched concept of public order.

By virtue of European law cross-references made by constitutional rules, the principles inferable from the European Convention, as interpreted by the Court of Strasbourg, are thus elevated to interposed constitutional parameters that may strongly influence the interpreter, who is called upon to deal with notions and institutions that are largely permeable to European law. The concept of public order must therefore be identified on the basis of principles both internal and external to the Italian legal system, based on the need to protect the fundamental and expressive rights of a shared heritage of values on an international level.

In light of the progressive evolution of the concept of family, in identifying the limit of public order, the interest of the child in the stability of the family relationship must be paramount. In support of the centrality of the role of the child are significant regulatory norms of domestic law. Among these is the recent reform of filiation implemented in our legal system, which has significantly replaced the expression parental authority with parental responsibility.[167] In this way, the functional profile of the role of the parents is emphasized, owing to the powers granted to them in the exclusive interest of the child rather than to satisfy their own desires. At the same time, the child was recognized as having a single status, independent of any different expressions of the relationship between the spouses. Moreover, the reform constitutes a clarification of the principles already enucleated in the international sphere beginning with the 1989 Hague Convention and the 2003 EU Regulation, where it is expressly stated that any evaluation of non-opposition to public order must be made taking into account the best interests of the child.

---

[167] Parental responsibility was introduced with Law no. 154/2013, in http://www.gazzettaufficiale.it/eli/id/2014/1/8/14G00001/sg, which rewrote Article 316 and subsequent articles of the Italian Civil Code. On the one hand, it better identified the duties of parents towards their children, and on the other, clarified the duties of children towards their parents. Parental responsibility exists in all cases where there are children, regardless of whether they were born inside or outside of marriage.

More complex problems arise in cases of children with dual citizenship increasingly present in our social fabric.[168] According to Law no. 218, in the event of dual citizenship the judge must decide to which of the two states the child has the closest connection, applying a criterion that could be defined as neutrality. However, the use of this principle of 'effective' citizenship could be understood in more than one way: it could indicate the intention of an individual to bind him or herself to one state, preferring one to the other, or it might be an indication of an objective localization resulting from the child's ties with one of the states where s/he has citizenship.[169] Where it gets increasingly complicated is if the choice of citizenship also implies specific religious affiliation.

In the Italian legal system, the best interest of the minor is a general clause based on positive law in order to allow the judge to evaluate the peculiarity of the situation under scrutiny, possibly even departing from the substantive and procedural guarantees abstractly provided by legislation.[170]

In the 2003 EU Regulation the problem of a change of citizenship subsequent, for example, to recognition as a legitimate child, was not addressed. In this case each state may decide independently as long as the purpose of the legislation – the interest of the minor – is kept firmly in mind. The procedure for the recognition of foreign decisions pursuant to this Regulation has a monitory character and is used both for obtaining the exequatur for decisions on parental responsibility, and for ascertaining the

---

[168] It is worth remembering that until the 'sixties, in most European legal systems the wife acquired the citizenship of her husband and, if she kept it, she could not pass it on to her offspring. In 1963 the Council of Europe Convention on the Reduction of Cases of Multiple Nationality was approved, amended with the Second Protocol of 1993. Currently, there is a favorable attitude towards dual citizenship, preferred by parents as the best tool to protect their children. In Italy Law no.91 of 1992 applies which considers different situations in which dual citizenship is allowed. Cf. A. BEGHÈ LORETI, *I figli delle coppie plurinazionali*, in *Giust. Civ.*, 1989, p. 303 *et seq*.

[169] Cf. P. LAGARDE, *La nouvelle Convention de La Haye sur la protection des mineurs*, in *Revue critique de droit international privé*, 1997 p. 217 *et seq*. The second criterion is naturally more objective. Article 19 of Law no. 218/1995, however, states that if a person has more than one nationality, Italian law applies if he/she is an Italian citizen.

[170] This principle is also made clear in the 1961 Hague Convention on the habitual residence of the minor as a criterion of jurisdiction. In the 1993 Hague Convention, before continuing with the adoption process, the authorities are required to verify that the procedure complies with the minimum standards of the Convention and that adoption is in the best interests of the child.

recognition or otherwise of the decision.[171] To identify jurisdiction and the law applicable to disputes concerning parental responsibility with a third party (but not the area of recognition and execution of foreign judgments), it is necessary to use the rules of international law on parent/child relationships and those on child protection.[172]

Though provided for by the New York Convention on the Rights of the Child and assimilated to Western measures of child protection, Islamic kafala is one of the institutions related to parental responsibility which encounters greater obstacles in terms of its recognition. With reference to family reunification, the problem in terms of parental responsibility often arises due to public order, aimed at protecting the child's best interest. As to the problem of recognizing kafala in a non-Islamic legal system, three different solutions have been proposed: full recognition, partial acceptance or no legal relevance since it is contrary to public order.

However, it is first necessary to assess whether the principles of national family law can be invoked to define the semantic field of application of the right to family reunification by preventing legal cultures based on religious orientation and thus in violation of the principle of legislative neutrality, as well as restricting the rights of individuals, from entering into the fray. This question translates into a hermeneutical issue since the reference to kafala involves multiple affiliations and the basic rights of the individual. In the domestic law of Islamic countries kafala is a translation of a religious command in accordance with the civil law applicable to all Muslims, based on automatically belonging to the national and religious community. In considering the family, however, we must note the presence of a triad that includes and involves the two parents and the child. In Islamic countries the presence of a Muslim parent means the application of Islamic law with automatic non-recognition of the right of religious freedom for the second adult or the minor, who is automatically included in the *Umma* / community of the faithful.

In Italy, the application of Sharia law in marriage matters, in a mixed union or in immigrant families, is therefore particularly complex. Among the demands put forward by Muslim communities, both in Italy and in other European countries, is the submission of family relationships and relationships between heirs to Islamic law. In this regard, it should be

---

[171] The exequatur is primarily the responsibility of the court where the child or the other party habitually resides; recognition normally takes place with reference to domestic law.

[172] In these cases, Articles 64 - 67 of Law no. 218/1995 apply. For recognition of judgments made in an EU member state, Article 21 *et seq*. of Council Regulation 2201/2003 applies.

clarified that foreign Muslims on Italian soil are subject to Islamic law, as codified in the laws in force in the respective states to which they belong. The conflicts that may arise between the different national variants of Sharia law and Italian law must be resolved in Italy according to the rules laid down by private international law. As far as Italian citizens of the Islamic faith are concerned, it is difficult to imagine their being subjected to a matrimonial, family or inheritance law that is different from the law established by our system or contrary to the principles enshrined in the Constitution.

Particular problems arise when it comes to international adoption which, when pronounced abroad, produces legitimating effects at home after verification by the proper authorities. In some cases, adoption may be pronounced before arriving in the new host country. In this case, having verified compliance with the requirements established by the 1993 Hague Convention (and in Italy with the recommendations of the Commission for Intercountry Adoption), the courts authorize entry and transcription in the civil status registers.[173] It is important to emphasize that the child has already acquired the rights of a legitimate child and after entry needs only obtain citizenship of the host country and transcription in the public register.

If, on the other hand, the country of origin issues a provision to be implemented subsequently in the receiving state, in Italy this is equated with pre-adoption foster care, if not contrary to the principles of our system or with the interest of the minor. In countries that have not ratified the 1993 Hague Convention (nor signed bilateral agreements) any adoption or pre-adoption foster care can only be declared effective in our own system following proceedings with the Juvenile Court,[174] which must verify independently that all requirements have been met.[175]

---

[173] The juvenile division of Rome's Court of Appeal, 17 May 2005, in *Fam. Pers. Succ.*, 2006, p. 465 *et seq.* stressed that the adoption order may still be declared valid in Italy even if the procedure of the foreign country is not based on a formal provision for adoption but relies on other kinds of checks and precautions.

[174] However, this situation can be remedied if the natural parents have made their consent to this effect explicit (Article 32, para., letter b) of Law no. 184 which implemented Article 27 of the Hague Convention of 1993.

[175] Article 36 of Law no. 184: "2. Adoption or foster care prior to adoption pronounced in a country not party to the Convention or signatory of bilateral agreements, may be declared valid in Italy provided that: a) abandonment of the foreign minor is ascertained or consent has been given by the natural parents to an adoption that determines acquisition of the status of legitimate child of the adopters and the termination of the legal relationship between the minor and the family of origin; b) the adopting parents have obtained the decree of eligibility provided for

The next stage involves the Commission for Intercountry Adoption, tasked with authorizing entry and permanent residence in Italy. First, the Commission must, among other things, verify the state of abandonment of the minor, if the adoption pronounced in the country of origin does not produce legitimating effects and the acquisition of the status of a legitimate child with the breaking of legal ties with biological parents. In the event of parental consent, the Juvenile Court can convert the foreign provision into legitimising adoption, as long as it is in accordance with the Hague Convention.

In general, a foreign deed can be recognized in Italy only if it has certain requirements which depend on both the content and the legal nature of the foreign provision. Adoption through the institution of kafala does not have the same effects as Italian adoption but, since the foreign provision produces the same effects in Italy as it generates in the state from which the child comes, it remains to be seen how it can be implemented. Adoptions of minors from Islamic states could fall under adoptions outside the convention (Article 36, paragraph 2 of Law no. 184/1983). This is a direct consequence of the fact that no Islamic country has ratified the Hague Convention on international adoption which, in Article 2, defines its scope of application only to adoptions that "create a permanent parent-child relationship", thus excluding the institution of kafala.

Although there is a sort of functional equivalence between Italian adoption and kafala, for the provision to be declared effective in this country the legal act must be qualified as adoption or fostering for purposes of adoption. The Juvenile Court then needs to verify, pursuant to Article 36 of Law no. 184/1983, the condition of abandonment of the child or the consent of the natural parents to the legitimising adoption; whether there is a preventive decree of suitability of the aspiring adoptive parents; the intervention of the Commission for Intercountry Adoption; the intervention of a private body authorized to mediate; compliance with any indications contained in the decree of suitability; and the existence of the authorization for entry and residence in Italy of the minor by the Commission. This might allow a practical legal comparison of the institutions to be made but fails to take into account the underlying religious command that prevents kafala from becoming adoption.

---

in Article 30 and adoption procedures have been carried out with the intervention of the Commission referred to in article 38 and of an authorized body; c) the recommendations contained in the suitability decree have been respected; d) the authorization provided for in Article 39, para. 1, letter h) has been granted".

In the Italian legal system, adoption procedures involving foreign minors are regulated by two different regulatory bodies that are formally independent but, in reality, strictly connected and obviously without any religious ties. On the one hand is Title III on international adoption, governed by Law no. 184 of 1983, which governs the custody and adoption of minors;[176] on the other are the rules of private international law contained in Title III, Chapter V of Law no. 218 of May 31, 1995. From the relationship between these two regulatory systems it emerges that our legal system is less than willing to open up to foreign disciplines in the matter of filiation. Rather, it seeks to guide adoption into the sphere of national law, in order to ensure that foreign minors enjoy the same protection as Italian minors.

The legislative evolution led 1983 legislation to abandon the previously adopted and essentially private-law model of adoption in favour of a strongly public-law discipline bearing an authoritarian model of adoption, a sort of adoptive nationalism, almost.[177] The situation changed with the 1998 reform recognising the 1993 Hague Convention in which the authoritarian model yielded, at least partially, to a personalist-solidarist model where cooperation between the central authorities for adoptions and the organisations that operate in the field of international adoptions was fundamental. The so-called 'adoptive nationalism' thus turned into 'adoptive internationalism' that still did not imply any openness towards other legal systems.[178] Indeed, though the convention provided for the automatic recognition of measures taken in participating countries, Italian legislation still subjected this recognition to a series of formal checks.

All this amounted to the acceptance of laws common to different countries into our own system. The first paragraph of Article 41 of Law no. 218 provides for the automatic entry into our legal system of those provisions that go beyond the application of Law no. 184.[179] The scope of

---

[176] B. POLETTI DI TEODORO, *L 'adozione internazionale*, in *Il nuovo diritto di famiglia*, cit., p. 701 *et seq*.

[177] G. FRANCESCHELLI, *Adozione internazionale e nazionalismo adottivo*, in *Giur.it*., 1982, I, 2, c. 755 *et seq*.

[178] L. ROSSI, *Il diritto del minore ad una famiglia: affidamento e adozione*, in *Seminari di diritto di famiglia*, M. DE TILLA and U. OPERAMOLLA (eds.), Milan, Giuffré, pp. 433-464 and ID., *La filiazione adottiva*, in *Trattato di diritto civile e commerciale*, edited by N. LIPARI and P. RESCIGNO, Milan, Giuffré, 2009, pp. 1005- 1089.

[179] Article 64 of Law no. 218/1995 regulates the recognition of foreign judgments, while Article 65 sets out a simplified regulation for the recognition of foreign

this, however, is considerably limited by the second paragraph of the same article, under which Italian special laws regarding the adoption of minors remain valid. Thus, for measures subject to the provisions of Law no. 184, recognition is not automatic. The relative procedures differ according to whether the provision comes from countries adhering to the Hague Convention, or from countries that have stipulated bilateral agreements with Italy in the spirit of the convention, or even third-party states or pronounced abroad at the request of Italian citizens living there. What is particularly significant, then, is that provisions originating from signatory countries are still subject to a complex recognition procedure, despite Article 23 of the convention.[180]

Our legal system further demonstrates its lack of confidence in foreign policies in matters of adoption even in cases where the legal systems are bound to Italy by shared principles established by the convention. Because of this mistrust and in view of strong public intervention to protect the child, for the provisions issued by these countries, before ordering the transcription of the adoption in the registers of civil status the Juvenile Court must verify that the requirements of Article 4 of the convention have been complied with.[181] This includes the circumstances in which the minor is declared as being in a state of adoptability, and, after duly examining the possibility of entrusting the child to the State of origin, that the international adoption corresponds to the child's best interest.[182] In addition, the Court must verify that the adoption provision is not contrary

---

provisions regarding the capacity of persons or the existence of family relations where they are pronounced in the State whose law the present law would apply or produce effects in that State, although pronounced in a third State. The reference to both provisions was interpreted as a legislative need to extend recognition to those foreign provisions that could not enjoy the simplified procedures referred to in Article 65. Article 66, on the other hand, relates to judicial orders in non-adversarial proceedings.

[180] Article 23 states that an adoption certified by the competent authority of the State of the adoption as having been made in accordance with the Convention should be recognised by operation of law in the other Contracting States. www.commissioneadozioni.it/pdf.

[181] Cf. V. GIORGIANNI, *L'adozione internazionale*, in *Trattato di diritto di famiglia,* vol. IV, *La Filiazione e l'adozione*, edited by G. BONILINI, Turin, Utet, 2016, pp. 498-524.

[182] Here, reference is made to adoption measures already completed. If, on the other hand, the adoption has to be perfected after the child's arrival in Italy, the foreign provision will be considered as a source of pre-adoption foster care which must last for a period of one year. At the end of this period, if the minor is suitably integrated within the new family, adoption will be pronounced.

to the fundamental principles governing family law and the rights of the child, assessed in relation to the well-being of the child. This activity overlaps with the activities already carried out by the Commission for Intercountry Adoption which issues the certificate of conformity. If the provision originates from a non-signatory state, the Juvenile Court will have to assess the state of abandonment of the child or the free and informed consent of the parents, as well as ensuring that the adopting parents hold a decree of suitability.

When Law no. 184/1983 was applied in Italy there were cases where the courts converted kafala measures into pre-adoption foster care first, and subsequently into actual adoption.[183] Given its generic nature kafala, intended as an institution of child protection, could easily be converted into pre-adoption care and adoption. Furthermore, it should be added that in the past, jurisprudence often downgraded foreign measures concerning the protection of minors to simple documents attesting the child's suitability.[184] With reference to the current law, it is well known that Articles 31 and 32 of Law no. 184/1983 were repealed and replaced with Law no. 476/1998, so that the jurisprudence developed in its application can no longer be simplistically used to legitimize the recognition of kafala as a legitimising adoption.

The system that emerges from the new text of Law no. 184/1983 provides for three distinct routes to obtaining recognition of adoptions made abroad. The first relates to the adoption of minors from member countries of the Hague Convention; the second relates to adoptions from countries that have not ratified the convention, and the third relates to adoptions in countries where the adoptive parents have resided for at least two years.

[183] The original text of Law no. 184/1983 provided for the Juvenile Court to declare efficacy in the State of the measures "of adoption or pre-adoptive foster care of the minor issued by a foreign authority to Italian citizens resident in Italy or in the foreign State, or other measures regarding protection and other institutions for the protection of minors" (Articles 31 and 32).

[184] Cf. Court of Cassation 22 October 1992 no. 11544, in *Foro it.*, 1993, I, 2637, Article 32 is designed to allow the transposition of those measures which, "although they do not have the typical elements of adoption (because, for example, the State of which they are citizens does not recognise the institution of adoption, or it is provided for in very few specific cases), do respond to identical or similar purposes". Cf. also Court of Cassation 11 January 1988 no. 67, in *Dir. fam. pers.*, 1988, 1212; 4 July 1991 no. 7357, in *Riv. di dir. intern. priv. Proc.*, 1992, 549; M. ORLANDI, *La kafala islamica e la sua riconoscibilità quale adozione*, in *Dir. fam. pers.* 2, 2005, p. 635 *et seq.*

Regular and irregular multicultural families constitute a social phenomenon whose specifics cannot always be translated in legal terms.[185] The critical issues and difficulties typical of multicultural families now more than ever need to be faced. This does, however, require some degree of intercultural competence, which may stand at some distance from the juridical world, but is indispensable in settling conflicts.[186] Alongside globalization, today's jurists find themselves up against what has been lucidly defined as 'axiological relativism'.[187] At the same time, they are faced with the unfolding of these phenomena within open and 'liquid' societies that characterize social relations by affecting the reconstructed and extended family structure,[188] understood as a nucleus formed by children, the natural parent and a third parent.[189] In effect, these are relations that are created regardless of biological ties or legal models of reference. What they require is legal recognition at some distance from traditional areas of law, founded and legitimized by social and emotional relationships which, rather than attesting to an extended family ahead of its time, imply extreme protection of the legitimate family through the inviolable dogma of its unity.[190]

It is clear that a reform is needed. But first it is up to lawmakers to think carefully, to come up with a series of 'mild' actions and with a more open legislation based on principles.[191] It is through this legislation that

---

[185] On the natural 'foreign' family cf. G. GRECO, *Gli accordi di convivenza ed i diritti dei singoli nella giurisprudenza*, in *Rapporti familiari e regolazione: mutamenti e prospettive*, M. FRANCESCA and M. GORGONI (eds.), Naples, ESI, 2009, p. 354 *et seq*.

[186] Cf. A. PORTERA e P. DUSI, *Gestione dei conflitti e mediazione interculturale,* Milan, F. Angeli, 2006.

[187] C. SALVI, *La famiglia tra giusnaturalismo e positivismo giuridico*, in *Studi in onore di Davide Messinetti*; F. RUSCELLO (ed.), I, Naples, ESI, 2008, p. 883 *et seq*.

[188] Cf. Z. BAUMAN, *Modernità liquida*, Roma- Bari, Laterza, 2000, esp. p. 72.

[189] S. MAZZONI, *Nuove costellazioni familiari: le famiglie ricomposte*, Milan, Giuffré, 2002, defines them as "new constellations", which include all the nuclei formed after separation or divorce, acquiring different levels of complexity due to the choices made by adults. By the same author see also *Le famiglie ricomposte: dall'arrivo dei nuovi partners alla costellazione familiare ricomposta*, in *Dir. fam. pers.*, 1999, p. 369 *et seq.*; A. OLIVIERO FERRARIS, *Il terzo genitore. Vivere con i figli dell'altro*, Milan, Raffaello Cortina, 1997.

[190] See also A.L. ZANATTA, *Le nuove famiglie*, Bologna, Il Mulino, 2008; A. DE MAURO, *Le famiglie ricomposte*, in *Familia*, 2005, p. 767 *et seq.*; G. FERRANDO, *Famiglie ricomposte e nuovi genitori*, in *Giur. it.*, 2007, c. 12 *et seq.*

[191] Reference is to G. ZAGREBELSKY, *Il diritto mite. Legge, diritti, giustizia*, Milan, Einaudi, 1992.

personal relationships can acquire legal relevance and the necessary protection, regardless of biological ties or the formal limits of the law. It should be based on emotional and social bonds, where the family is not so much as simply the place to acquire status, but to affirm one's identity, the phenomenological proliferation of emotional existence.

Our jurisprudential path seems to have charted a course which "though theoretical, comes close to intercultural legal translation" in which the key criterion is the evaluation of the minor's interest with the tools of *cross-contextual resonance*.[192] The use of the tools of intercultural translation, fundamental for the modern jurist, allows the correct evaluation of the prevalence of elements in common to be made. As has been correctly emphasized, what generated the change "were the *mute parts*, the apparently extraneous sense indices, at some distance from the morphological configuration of linguistic categories or behaviours directly called into question by the regulations in play".[193] This intercultural connection has highlighted a regulatory hybridization that is now part of the juridical fabric that could find a space for its application.

The most innovative jurisprudential operations on the matter, which have forced the system to allow the entry of kafala into our juridical fabric, have nonetheless highlighted the first stage of a possible legislative path but also, conversely, a transformation of the codes of the Islamic family. For "the immigrant family, assisting a child according to European and Italian standards can greatly change the *mute*, implicit use of kafala, its meaning" emphasizing that "the effects of intercultural transaction are bidirectional".[194]

---

[192] M. Ricca, *Culture interdette. Modernità, migrazioni, diritto interculturale*, Turin, Bollati Boringhieri, 2013 esp. p. 158 *et seq*.
[193] M. Ricca, *op. ult.cit*., p. 159.
[194] M. Ricca, *op. ult. cit.,* p. 164.

CHAPTER THREE

RELIGIOUS IDENTITY AND FILIATION IN THE ITALIAN LEGAL SYSTEM

1. Evolution of the Ethical-Legal Profile of the Italian Family System

Adoption was unknown in Jewish law and legal experts agreed on its prohibition. Simply caring for a child was not sufficient basis for a legal bond of filiation. In Christian law, adoption is not mentioned in the Gospels. While in pre-Islamic societies it was structured as a sort of artificial bond of kinship, codified by a contract, it was expressly prohibited in the Quran. The three great monotheistic religions have therefore never accepted this practice, which called into question the divine organisation of the child/parent bond.

In ancient Rome filiation was patrilinear or agnatic and there were two forms of adoption: *adrogatio* and *adoptio*. The term 'adopt' from the Latin *optare* is thus tied to the inherent faculty of choice; in fact the *pater familias* was completely free to reshape his family lineage and the chosen son would inherit the name, estate and also the religion of the adopter. Adoption in Roman law also had a dual effect, both inclusive and exclusionary, signifying that upon completion of the adoption the adoptee acquired the status and *nomen* of the adopting family, along with the consequent inheritance rights and duties towards the worship of the domestic Gods of the new family. At the same time, though, the adoptee lost the rights of agnation and inheritance as regards the original family and would no longer worship the domestic Gods of the natural family.[195]

---

[195] Cf. C. RUSSO RUGGERI, *La datio in adoptionem, dalla pretesa influenza elleno-cristiana alla riforma giustinianea*, Milan, Giuffré, 1995. The two types of adoption had in common: l) the original purpose of strengthening the family unit with new members; 2) certain effects, whereby the adoptee assumed the faith, name and tribe of the adopter and as well as heir to the male line. Despite their similarities, the two institutions had very different fates. *Adoptio* was the act by which the *pater familias* took on under his own authority an (adopted) person

Justinian distinguished the adoption of a *filius familias* made by an ascendant from that of one outside the family and therefore between *adoptio plena*, in which the adoptee was equivalent in all respects to a natural child and *adoptio minus plena* in which the adoptee remained in the family of origin, did not fall under the power of the adopter, but was allowed the right to inherit the latter's estate. What set it apart from traditional *adoptio* was this possibility of inheritance in the event of the death of the adopter. With Justinian's intervention, adoption therefore placed greater emphasis on natural bonds, theorising the principle of *adoptio natura imitatur*.

As in pre-Islamic societies, the type of adoption practiced in ancient Rome responded to the same needs and brought out similar values on which society and its system of parental relationships were founded. Adoption was in both cases a strategic measure to guarantee hereditary succession, ensuring that the genealogical line of the family survived and keeping tangible and intangible family assets intact.

In the Middle Ages, *de facto* situations related to different forms of elective kinship were recorded across Europe.[196] The Catholic Church, however, imposed marriage as the only tool for family legitimisation and jurists of the fifteenth and sixteenth centuries introduced a series of reservations, especially concerning the adoptee's right to succession.[197] In

belonging to another family. The adoptee thus left his family group and joined the adopter's family as *filius familias* (son or grandson, never a brother). *Adrogatio* was adoption of the subjects *sui juris*, by virtue of which the Roman citizen passed under the parental authority of the adopter with all the others who depended on him and all his estate (a true *successio per universitatem*).

[196] Cf. U. GALAZZINI, *Adozione. Diritto intermedio*, in *Novissimo digesto italiano,* Turin, Utet, 1957, p. 288 *et seq.*; J. P. GUTTON, *L'histoire de l'adoption en France*, Paris, Publisud, 1993, esp. pp. 37 - 43. J. GOODY, *L'évolution de la famille et du mariage en Europe*, Paris, A. Colin, 1985, attributes the disappearance of adoption in its juridical form to the desire to encourage donations to the Church in the absence of direct heirs (cf. p.82 *et seq.*). In agreement also A. FINE, *Adoption et parrainage dand l'Europe ancienne*, in *Adoption et fosterage*, M. CORBIER (ed.), Paris, De Broccard,1999, pp. 339 - 356, who, however, placed greater emphasis on moral responsibilities that the Catholic Church imposed on crimes such as infanticide and the abandonment of minors; he also stressed the importance that the ideology of the 'bloodline' and the will to 'maintain the race' acquired in this historical phase. On legislation in the Middle Ages to this regard cf. also A. BURGUIERE, *Un aussi long refus. Droit et pratiques de l'adoption en France du XV siècle aux temps présent*, in *Adoption et fosterage*, cit., 124.

[197] F. ROUMY, *L'adoption dans le droit savant du XIIe au XVIe siècle*, Paris, LGDJ, 1998, esp. p. 315.

modern Western-style civil codes of the nineteenth century, however, adoption reappeared but only as a tool by which inheritance could be passed on and marriage was explicitly indicated as the only way to establish the family.[198]

In the Napoleonic code of 1804, the first instrument of the so-called modern era, adoption was reserved only for adults while unofficial protection only was provided for minors, both with very limited effects. From 1923 onwards, French law further extended adoption to children, emphasising the social function of the inclusion of the minor within a family unit. It set out two types: one where the minor established a relationship with the adopter but without severing family ties with the biological family and one in which relations with the natural parents ceased altogether.[199] The first type, 'simple adoption', allowed for filial bonds and essentially concerned adults without heirs who adopted their relatives' children to allow them to inherit. Full '*plénière*' or '*ordinaire*' adoption, introduced in 1962, at last allowed the child, *inter alia*, to acquire the status of legitimate child and to take on the surname of the adopted parent.

Yet, in the parliamentary debates of the early Italian state, it was still stressed that adoption no longer had any reason to exist because it was believed that it altered the marital status of individuals.[200] Adoption, however, was introduced into the civil code of 1865 though it did not fulfil the function of assistance towards the adoptee but simply served the purpose of providing continuity to the adopter's family, with simple functions regarding the adopter's property and reserved for adults only. The adopter (man or woman) could adopt only if s/he had no heirs (legitimate or legitimated), had reached fifty years of age and was at least eighteen years older than the adoptee. This code also included requirements for the adoptee whereby "the minor cannot be adopted if s/he has not reached the age of eighteen".

---

[198] J. P. GUTTON, *L'histoire de l'adoption...*, cit., 133.

[199] This was amended with subsequent legislation: the laws of 8th August 1941, 15th April 1943, 23rd April 1949, 17th April 1957, the ordinance of 23rd December 1958, the laws of 1st March 1963, 17th November 1965, the decree of 2nd December 1966, Law no. 76-1179 of 22nd December 1976. Cf. M.P. CHAMPENOIS MARMIER, *L'adoption*, Paris, A. Colin, 1972; M. VISMARD, *L'adoption*, Paris, Librairies Techniques, 1968; J. CHAMPION, *L 'adoption*, Paris, Delamas, 1977.

[200] G. FERRANDO, *L'adozione ordinaria, problemi, prospettive e ipotesi sistematiche*, in *Riv. trim. dir proc. civ.*, 1979, p. 443 which includes Pisanelli's statements during parliamentary debate.

The adoption act had a contractual form meaning that to complete the adoption procedure, consent of the adopter and the adopted child and the parents of the latter, if alive, was required. The adoptee acquired the surname of the adopter (adding it to his/her own) and the new status of son or daughter (in line with his/her status within the natural family). However, completion of the adoption did not involve placing the adoptee within the adopter's family, nor did it create kinship relationships between the former and the latter's family members, in line with the principle that the contract is effective only between the parties. The adoptee acquired the right of succession towards the adopter and the adoptive parents were obliged to raise, support and maintain the adoptee. Finally, it was established that all rights and duties towards the adoptee's natural family continued. What came out of the legal debate surrounding adoption, then, was the need to develop ethical and social principles that would determine the subsequent shift from rigid individualism to solidarity and social integration.[201]

Adoptive legitimacy was progressively formalized in many European countries in the early twentieth century and was soon characterized by the definitive breakdown of ties with the family of origin, the adoption of the surname and the recognition of hereditary rights. It was written in the margin of the birth certificate with definitive assimilation of the adopted child to legitimate children.[202] From that moment on, the minor gradually began to be considered as a legal subject, both at home and in the

---

[201] In the same vein, many laws subsequently followed. Cf. Royal Decree 13th July 1919 no. 1357, converted into Law no.2137, 6th December 1925 and the law of 18th July 1917 no. 1143 amended into Law no. 1397 of 26th July 1929, which set up the *Opera Nazionale Orfani di Guerra* allowing war orphans to be adopted notwithstanding the age limit; this was extended with the law of 24th September 1940, no. 1458. Cf. I. BAVIERA, *Diritto minorile*, Milan, Giuffré, 1976, vol. I, esp. p. 288 *et seq*. The 1942 Civil Code abolished the minimum age limit of eighteen for the adopted subject (Article 206 Civil Code 1865) and replaced approval with a decree declaring adoption.

[202] It was introduced in the civil code of 1804 in France, Austria in 1811, Italy in 1865, Spain in 1889, Germany in 1890, Switzerland in 1907, England in 1929, the Netherlands in 1956, Portugal in 1966. In the second half of the century some western states, such as France, also made a regulatory distinction between simple and full adoption: the first was additive and did not entail severing ties with the family of origin, which did, however, lose its parental authority; in the new family the minor was fully included as a legitimate child, acquiring the name of the adopters and the rights of succession; it could only be revoked for serious reasons. Full adoption, on the other hand, led to the irrevocable replacement of filiation and could, at times, also be carried out by a single person or an unmarried couple.

international community, and was no longer seen as simply a son or daughter connected to the parent. In actual fact, children were in the past subject to regulations only insofar as they were holders of the *status filiationis*. This new direction came about through the social and legal development of a plurality of family models, with a change of roles in parental authority being no longer entrusted to the father alone as *pater familias* but shared with the mother in an equal relationship.

In the area of social psychology, the family was studied as a paradigmatic model of the small group in which the behaviour of the subject is the result of the interaction between personal and environmental factors. Around the middle of the last century the specific characteristics of the family began to be studied, with interaction being based on reciprocity and face-to-face relationships. Since then, it has been considered as the symbol of the natural or primary group characterised by a specific history, structure and purpose. Systemic relational analyses focused their attention on family relationships, that is, on what emerges from the present but was linked to the subjectivity of the individuals and the history they shared.[203]

At the beginning of the last century, the traditional family was still based on the perfect combination of love and marriage, with a strong consideration of children, structured in our country according to the canonical view of the union between a man and a woman ordained for the procreation and upbringing of offspring (Canon 1013 CIC 1917). From the '70s onwards, however, society witnessed the development of the so-called postmodern family and the emergence of a plurality of family types. According to the systemic perspective, it is an open system interacting constantly with the environment with which it comes into contact and by which it is conditioned. The arrival of a new member within the family, through the natural process of filiation, through fostering, adoption or kafala, therefore necessarily entails the reorganization of the internal balance that the world of law must also understand in order to regulate it.

As well as these considerations, it is worth adding a premise, according to which the body of law cannot be identified in the law itself and it would

---

[203] A first significant definition of the concept of family was structured within the relational-symbolic model and proposed by E. SCABINI, *Psicologia sociale della famiglia. Sviluppo dei legami e trasformazioni sociali*, Turin, Bollati Boringhieri, 1995 who considered the family as a specific and unique organization binding and holding together the original and fundamental differences of the human being, between genders, between generations and between bloodlines whose objective and intrinsic project was generativity (a family can be procreative even if they adopt or foster a child).

be an oversimplification to consider the law as coinciding not with the whole *ius*, inclusive of every single manifestation of legality but only with one area: the law of the state. This would prevent us from highlighting that the law is older and broader than its specific historical expression, represented by the law produced by nation-states. Here, legislative power represents one of the most significant manifestations of state sovereignty, sanctioning the transition of legal particularity to the apex of the law, but conversely, taking the geographic boundaries of states as extremely reductive in the current phase of fluidity of borders and openness to multicultural societies.[204] The result is a profound crisis in the systematic nature of the sources, with a firm downsizing of the role of custom, determining a vision of the reductive legal experience, uprooted from the wealth of the social, expression of a single culture with the tendential risk of a separation between the legal dimension and the civilization behind it and current culture.[205]

This condition may cause a dichotomous rift between official law and the demands, interests, needs and values expressed by society. It would therefore be necessary to recover the plurality of regulatory customs such as to allow the law to truly represent the social fabric, values, facts and interests that must emerge from the legal situation and highlight both the positive and negative aspects. This requirement, bound to the recovery of the historical dimension of law, should lead to a change in the method of legal studies and to the adoption of a relative method which requires the cultural mediation of jurists.[206] It is necessary, then, to ensure that the formation of this new open legal system is not entrusted to those operating in the practical sphere alone, without the support of the historical-systemic framework which, conversely, is the specific task of the doctrine to develop.

---

[204] On relations between state law and its jurisdiction and on the need, imposed by globalization, to go beyond the boundaries of state law cf. esp. N. IRTI, *Norma e luogo. Problemi di geodiritto*, Rome-Bari, Laterza, 2002; M.R. FERRARESE, *Diritto sconfinato-inventiva giuridica e spazi nel mondo globale*, Rome-Bari, Laterza, 2006 stresses that "it goes beyond fixed boundaries...exceeding traditional, established borders" (p. 24).

[205] P. GROSSI, *Società, Diritto, Stato. Un recupero per il diritto*, Milan, Giuffrè, 2006, esp.p.15.

[206] As underlined by P. GROSSI, *Società,...* cit. this new figure should not be "a jurist turned politician (ruined to some extent), but a jurist who can exploit the full potential of a weapon ... that of interpretation ... irreplaceable mediator between the immobility of the text and the mobility of society" (p. 53).

The application of these theoretical developments is evident in the structuring of certain juridical concepts – such as that of family and child – which stem from natural, religious and cultural law and which define the positions and statuses of subjects. Filiation represents the social and legal recognition of the bonds existing between individuals who descend from each other. All cultures recognise filiation, and each has assigned it a more or less important role. In today's Western societies, however, social groups are less structured according to family ties and ever-changing forms and new models of cohabitation and sharing of nuclei or groups are being built.

It is also important to reiterate that the family is not by law a collective body, endowed with legal subjectivity, nor could it become one. Rather, it is considered as a social formation necessary for the realization of the deepest and most essential individual needs and, as such, worthy of legal protection. The traditional concept of the family as a legitimate union founded on marriage, led by two parents of opposite sex and with the presence of legitimate children of the couple, born after the celebration of the bond and only within this bond has, for some time now, been unable to capture the social reality. What is needed is a reworking of what may be defined in line with a more modern terminology, the 'stable family coexistence'. This phrase is better able to outline the complexity and heterogeneity of the relationships that are established in a specific social context, and which can be found, above all, by a careful reading of the constitutional dictate.[207]

Broadly speaking, the ethical-juridical profile of the family system has undergone profound transformation in recent years, with several extraordinary and specific changes having a substantial impact especially in the delicate context of the break-up of relationships, child abandonment and the psychological and social aspects of adoption.[208] The social evolution of this basic family nucleus, from the aftermath of the second world war to the present, is unquestionable and is also reflected in legislation as it attempted to regulate this profound transformation. From a

---

[207] What is interesting is the interpretation of a broader concept of family which may be inferred from Article 572 of the Penal Code, regarding mistreatment in the family or towards children – *Maltrattamenti in famiglia o verso i fanciulli* – which punishes anyone ... who mistreats a member of the family or person cohabiting, or a subject placed under his/her authority or in his/her care for reasons of upbringing, education, welfare, vigilance or custody, or to exercise a profession or skill".

[208] C. CORBEIL, F. DESCARRIES, *La famille: une institution sociale en mouvance*, in *Nouvelles politiques sociales*, vol. 16, no.1, 2003, pp. 16 - 26, and at https://www.erudit.org/revue/nps/2003/v16/n1/009624ar.pdf.

traditionalist structure, centred on the figure of the head of the family, the idea of gender equality has progressively gained ground with the recognition of equal rights to the wife/mother, and a change in power relations between father and son and the abandonment of the anachronistic concept of 'parental authority' replaced in recent times with the more modern principle of 'parental responsibility'. Greater concern for minors and respect for their rights and *identity* today plays a central role in the study of family dynamics and the affirmation of the minor's rights.

For some time now, Italian legislation has been characterised by these changes: consider 'affiliation' before and special adoption at a later date, and the more modern and current modes of fostering and legitimising or full adoption, reworked more recently with the introduction of the innovative principle of continuity of emotional ties.[209] In the spirit and in the letter of Article 30 of the Constitution – together with a critical comparison with the correlating norms of the code – the family was conceived not only as a group of people linked by a collective and reciprocal bond, resulting from marriage or kinship, and a source of ties of kinship and affinity, but mainly as a nucleus that should constitute the natural habitat in which parents must fulfil their basic right and duty to raise, educate and support their children.[210] The evolution of the structure and purpose of the family unit obviously have immediate repercussions on the parent-child relationship, both socially and legally.

The subsequent shift was, again, characterized by the progressive transformation of the concept of 'authority' into 'responsibility': in the changing structure of interests, the father and mother no longer exercised power over the minor, but took on the responsibility to raise, educate and support their child in its growth as an independent subject.[211] This

---

[209] Law no. 431 of 1967 states that "children below eight years of age lacking the material and moral support of their parents or their relatives charged with their care are to be considered eligible for adoption, as long as the lack of support does not depend on circumstances beyond their control". The 1983 law removed any reference to age, put moral support before material support and added 'of a temporary nature' to 'circumstances beyond their control'.

[210] Article 261 of the Civil Code stated, "Recognition entails the assumption by the parent of all duties and rights that apply to legitimate children". The article was replaced by Article 110 of Law no. 151, 19th May 1975 and finally revoked by Legislative Decree no. 154 of 28th December 2013. Italian legislation embraced the principle of equal status for all children.

[211] This idea is enshrined in Council Regulation (EC) no. 2201/2003 of 27th November 2003. A system of principles of European family law, developed during the years 2006-2007 by the Commission on European Family Law (CEFL) conceived parental responsibilities as "a collection of rights and duties aimed at

centralization of the rights of the child represented an important step in the recognition and respect of the child's identity, religious and non-religious.

The socio-legal model of the family, of the parent-child relationship and, consequently, of adoption has changed. While in the past it was conceived as a tool to pass on the name and the estate (sometimes for humanitarian purposes), it is now definitively linked to the interests of the minor, as an institution for the protection of childhood.[212] Reforms of family law, which characterized democratic legislation in the 'seventies of the last century, also gave juridical importance to the minor not only within marriage, but also in the legal recognition by parents. The notion of multi-parenthood is now part of the ethnographic debate of the modern Western world, and is the subject of sociological analysis, though still awaiting a legal definition.[213]

With reference to adoption, it is currently highlighted that it "*met en jeu la capacité des individus de décider eux-memes des usages légitimes de la parenté, in un mouvance de libéralisation des modes de vie familiaux*".[214] The Western model is therefore also undergoing changes due also to the introduction of 'open' adoption, recently introduced in some countries, that allows for contact between biological and adoptive parents.[215]

---

promoting and safeguarding the welfare of the child. They encompass in particular: (a) care, protection and education; (b) maintenance of personal relationships; (c) determination of residence; (d) administration of property, and (e) legal representation".

[212] C. FOCARELLI, *La Convenzione di New York sui diritti del fanciullo e il concetto di "best interests of the child"*, in *Riv. Dir. Int.*, 2010, attempts to define the concept of best interests of the child interpreting the New York Convention according to the criteria sanctioned by the Convention on the Law of Treaties. Likewise, Article 24, Paragraph 2 of the EU Charter of Fundamental Rights states: "In all actions relating to children … the child's best interests must be a primary consideration" (p. 981). This expression was first used in the UN's Declaration of the Rights of the Child in 1959.

[213] Cf. *La Pluriparentalité*, D. LE GALL, Y. BETTAHAR (eds.), Paris, Puf, 2001.

[214] F. R. OUELLETIE, *L'adoption. Les acteur et les enjeux autour de l'enfant*, Québec, Les presses de l'Université de Laval, 1996, esp. p. 24 and by the same author, *L'intérêt de l'enfant adopté et la protection de ses droits*, in *Éthique publique*, vol. 3, no. l, 2001, and at www.ethiquepublique.revues.org/2645.

[215] They were introduced in the US, Canada, Germany and England and Wales. Cf. *Adoption Law and Practice*, J. H. HOLLINGER (ed.), New York, M. Bender, 1998; F. LAROCHE-GISSEROT, *L 'adoption ouverte (Open Adoption) aux Etats-Unis: Règles, pratiques, avenir en Europe*, in *Rév. de droit comparé*, 50, no.4, 1998, pp. 1095 - 1123. Cf. il volume *Parents de sang. Parents adoptif*, A. FINE, C. NEIRINCK (eds.), Paris, LGDJ, 2000 and esp. in the same volume: D. GOUBAU, *Open*

Western laws have traditionally constructed modern rules of adoption on the principle of transferring filiation. In 'full' adoption, the minor breaks all prior ties and receives a new birth certificate. In a not too distant past, even in Europe, children perceived as objects owned by their parents could be exchanged and sold without fear of scandal or social reprobation even though they were not legally protected. It is worth remembering that full adoption, defined as special adoption, was only introduced into our legal system in 1967.[216]

2. Protection of the Religious Identity of the Minor in the Family Unit

The issue of raising the minor in compliance with the norms of the family unit and articulated within the same constitute a codified right not only in the 'domestic' sphere but also at a European level, including the 1989 UN Convention on the rights of the child. Legislation, as mentioned, is currently concerned with the concept of responsibility and no longer simply with parental authority.[217]

The transmission of one's own set of values, even with a religious connotation, has always been one of the cardinal points by which the role of parents is structured at a social rather than a legal level. The family is, of course, the place where physical, psychological and moral growth take shape and it is unthinkable that the education of a child might exclude such an important area of its essence such as the adherence to a specific faith. Religious cultures claim legal recognition which, in the case of family relationships, touch upon the protection of religious freedom

---

adoption au Canada, pp. 63 - 85; E. WENNER, *Nouvelles formes d'adoption ouverte en Allemagne*, pp. 87 - 102; L. BAQUE, *Le role des services et agences d'adoption en Angleterre*, pp. 103 - 116.

216 On the issue of the sale of children by their natural parents cf. I. BAVIERA, *L'adozione speciale²,* Milan, Giuffré, 1982, which reports the case of a minor, sold by the biological mother, which was subject to an astonishing 22 court provisions shifting back and forth between regular and special adoption, highlighting the inherent legal complications: esp. p. 350. Cf. also M. BESSONE - G. FERRANDO, *Adozione ordinaria*, in *Nss. Dig.It. (Appendix),* Turin, Utet, 1980, p. 72 *et seq*.; M. DOGLIOTTI - G. FERRANDO, *Giurisprudenza dell'adozione*, Milan, Giuffré, 1981.

217 Cf. G. CAROBENE, *Affidamento condiviso, multi religiosità ed educazione (religiosa) dei minori*, at·www.statoechiese.it, no. 26, 2013; R. DE MEO; *La tutela del minore e del suo interesse nella cultura giuridica italiana ed europea*, in *Dir. fam. pers*., l, 2012, pp.461 - 477.

recognized by individuals and the educational relationship/function that parents must carry out towards their children.

These problems also have a particular significance within democratic and largely secularized, state structures that are increasingly characterized by 'secular' religious pluralism and social multiculturalism. Secularism may have several meanings which refer to *values* that are ethically shared in/by a given social structure over and above any legal significance. The *principle* of secularism represents a legislative archetype, taking on different meanings in line with the constitutional framework that outlines and distinguishes it, such as the protection of freedom of conscience and the private nature of religious feeling. It is thus normal for young people to face up to realities that are no longer traditional but open and fluid, even within their own family context. Such openness cannot and must not be precluded, but rather encouraged to reach a fuller and freer shaping of a 'mature' awareness.

The need to protect this fundamental right, especially with individuals growing up within the delicate systems of interpersonal relationships which develop in the family environment, requires particular legal instruments especially in the event of different cultural origins, both between parents (mixed couples, for instance) and between parents and children from different cultural contexts. It also applies to the case of migrating homogeneous families coming up against a social and legal fabric that is profoundly different from their own.[218] Faced with conflicts that cannot be resolved through peaceful settlement, the judge will be forced to play a crucial and incisive role within the delicate family environment, but still placing the interests of the minor at the forefront.

In Italy, the issue of the protection of the religious freedom of the child within the family unit has created religious contrast between parents, especially where the relationship breaks down. In a recent decision by the Court of Cassation on the question of joint custody, the issue was the difficult relationship between the right/duty of parents to raise their children and the exercise of their religious freedom in carrying out this delicate task.[219] With reference to intercountry adoption, however, the Juvenile Court's decision to refuse the application for eligibility of a

---

[218] Cf. E. QUADRI, *L'interesse del minore nel sistema della legge civile*, in *Fam. e dir.*, 1999, l, p. 82 *et seq.*; P. FLORIS, *Appartenenza confessionale e diritti dei minori. Esperienze giudiziarie e modelli di intervento*, in *Quad. dir. pol eccl.*, 1, 2000, pp. 191 - 216.

[219] Court of Cassation, Civil Section I, 12th June 2012, no. 4596, at http://www.olir.it/documenti/?documento=5895.

couple who were unwilling to adopt a child of a different religious faith was upheld.[220]

An analysis of case law has highlighted the difficulties of the judging body, which should normally be the institution where any new questions of law are immediately answered in line with principles already existing in the legal system. The question that arises, therefore, is whether it is legitimate to impose a 'negative' obligation on a parent with respect to the fulfilment of a religious practice and whether or not this constitutes undue interference in the very personal sphere of religious freedom of the parent and his/her duties as educator of the child. This implies, among other things, the possibility of publicly exercising one's religion, also from the point of view of an inner, spiritual growth. The risk is that a line of conduct may be adopted that widens the discretion of the judge.

Under these circumstances, then, rights that are in themselves personal and constitutionally guaranteed may be crushed easily from religious freedom to the task of parents in raising their children alongside the secularism of our legal system. There is no doubt that any intervention in such a delicate sector may appear as an imposition or, conversely, highly discriminatory towards a religious faith.

Generally speaking, it is evident that the judge plays an active role within the conflictual process of separation, an area which has expanded in the face of current multifarious and changing family realities. An important area where clashes may occur is where parents do not share the same religious faith in 'mixed' marriages, or when the faith of one or the other changes over the course of time. And this is especially true where deeply rooted sentiments of religious belonging may result in forms of intolerance almost towards different attitudes, both religious and secular.

Several interesting theoretical considerations also arise here as far as kafala is concerned. Kafala is a legal instrument of clear religious origin and has a profound effect on the construction of parental bonds, but does not allow for the application of a wide range of rights protected by our legislation, even within the family unit. In the future, cases may arise in which, following separation, one of the spouses, who is not bound or is no longer bound to the *Umma*/community of believers, could request the transformation of the legal relationship with the minor appealing to the institutions of 'Western', secular law.

It is interesting to note that in one Italian judgment the judge decided to take an active part in the proceedings, rejecting the agreement of the

[220] Court of Cassation, Civil Section VI, 28th December 2011, no. 29424, at http://www.stranieriinitalia.it/briguglio/immigrazione-e-asilo/2011/dicembre/sent-cass-29424-2011.pdf.

two spouses in which the mother agreed not to indoctrinate the minors in their religious faith. It was argued that it was impossible to accept this private agreement as the commitment of the same would have to be considered as "an obligation not to do something of an infungible nature", and it was stressed that, consequently, it was not a civil obligation, but "purely moral between the two spouses", and could not "enter into an act of settlement of interests between the spouses, which, being contained in a judgment", remained substantially and formally "the result of hetero-determination".[221]

The problem is, therefore, that of identifying and circumscribing the role of the judge and his/her powers of intervention, in the light of the established secularism of our system. From the right to education, including religious education of the minor, derives the related right/duty of parents to impart the teaching they prefer within the framework of the general protection of religious freedom. A secularised state cannot intervene in this choice, nor can it allow an external body to opt for one or another ethical or religious choice. It can take action only in cases of parental disagreement, assessing options for the best interests of the child. In secular systems, the religious education of one's offspring is a right of freedom. This, however, translates into an ethical imperative if viewed from the point of view of different religious denominations which, in different ways, always encourage parents to direct their children to their own way of thinking.[222]

Codifying a principle which had been followed for some time in the doctrine and jurisprudence, pursuant to Article 155 of the Civil Code, the family law reform of 1975 gave the judge the power to adopt any provision relating to offspring with exclusive reference to the moral and material interest of the child. On evaluation of the norm, any mention of the interests of the family or parents alongside the interests of the minor were rejected. Where parental conflicts regarding the upbringing of the minor could not be resolved in the family environment, they were referred to the Juvenile Court, which must always decide on the basis of the

---

[221] Published in *Dir. fam. pers*, 1997, with comments by Roberta SANTORO, *Condizioni della separazione ed educazione religiosa della prole*, in *Dir. fam, pers*. 1998, 3, p. 979 *et seq*.; and by the same author, *Diritti ed educazione religiosa del minore*, Jovene, Naples, 2004. Cf. also M. DOGLIOTTI, *Separazione dei coniugi, educazione religiosa della prole, controllo del giudice*. On the case in question, cf. also V. PALOMBO, *Brevi chiose in tema di educazione religiosa dei figli*, in *Dir. eccl*., 1998, no. l, II, 62 *et seq*.

[222] Cf. e.g., Canon 226, §2 Code of Canon Law and Canon 1366 Code of Canon Law.

minor's interests alone, with a case-by-case evaluation, pursuant to Article 316 of the Civil Code.[223]

The constitutionally structured neutrality option therefore constitutes the major point of departure from an 'ethical' conception of the role of the state, which translates into authoritarian imposition on citizens of certain 'values'. Consider, by way of example, that from an authoritarian and public law conception of the upbringing of minors (for whom the parents themselves appeared almost as executors of a task concerning the public authority) we have moved to a personalistic vision, where respect for the human person has a determining role, especially considering that we are dealing with a subject who is still growing up.

In a democratic regime and a pluralist society, parents may not coerce the will of their children, but preordained educational content cannot be imposed. This in accordance with the principles expressed by Articles 3 and 30 of the Constitution. The strict neutrality of the judge with respect to the opposing systems of values in which the educational conduct of the parents may be grounded must be affirmed. From the combined provisions of the constitutional laws with Article 147 of the Civil Code the obligation to educate children may be deduced, but no educational content is indicated (or even suggested) above another. Any content must remain free and unconditional with the only limit being that of protecting the personality of the minor.

The core idea of the family, which began to take shape in the Italian legal system with the reform of the 1970s, was therefore based on the specific desire to go beyond the classic Christian approach. The family was considered as the meeting point of single individuals, all equally deserving of legal protection. With the reform of joint custody in 2006, the right to have both parents became a subjective right of the minor, falling within the broader genus of personality rights.[224] Any intervention by the authorities would be considered an extreme measure, when the tools of mediation failed to reach an agreement between the parties. The new regulation provided for the right of the child, even in the event of separation of the parents, to maintain a balanced and continuous relationship with each, to be raised, educated and supported by both and to maintain significant relationships with the ascendants and relatives of each

---

[223] Cf. M. DOGLIOTTI, *L'interesse del minore nella separazione tra coniugi*, in *Dir. fam. pers.*, 1986, esp. pp. 1231 - 32.

[224] Law no. 54, 8th February 2006, regulating separation and joint custody of children at http://www.camera.it/parlam/leggi/06054l.htm.
Concerning jurisprudence cf. Appeal Court, Rome, 4th April 2007, at https://www.jstor.org/stable/23203734?seq=l#page_scan_tab_contents.

parent. It is also interesting to note that these rules were directly included in the Civil Code, rather than being external to it, as a measure of their importance.

Article 155 of the Civil Code in its new formulation establishes that among the duties of the judge is to take note, if it does not go against the interests of the minor, of the agreements made between the parents also on the subject of the religious education of minors. It also specifies that in issuing provisions on the custody, the judge should consider the agreement of the parties but can take steps beyond this – even if this may contrast with the requests of the parties themselves. There is a twofold need that the judge must reconcile: to protect the autonomy of the family and to guarantee the interests of the child.

In the past, jurisprudence did not generally consider the religious faith of parents as a relevant criterion for the choice of the custodial parent, nor political ideas or a change of religious faith. It also highlighted that decisions relating to the religious education of the minor should preferably be taken by mutual agreement by both parents and, only in the event of irreconcilable conflict should the intervention of the judge be sought.[225] The prevailing jurisprudence, however, privileges the interests of the minor, regardless of the content of the religious education imparted to the children, underlining that the faith professed by the parents is not among the factors that determine judgement on the greater aptitude to take care of the interests of the child and therefore cannot have any relevance.

If a change of faith is not shared or still less appreciated by the other spouse, due to the constitutional value that this very personal choice has, it cannot in itself have relevance in the public sphere. In the greater respect for the right to religious freedom, combined with that of non-discrimination, it must be legally protected as long as it does not translate into a violation of the duties of spouse and parent. Furthermore, it cannot present an obstacle to custody since both parents have the right to make their religion known to their children without imposing it upon them, as long as it does not translate into practices contrary to morals and public order.

---

[225] Cf. Court of Cassation 27th February 1985, no. 1714, in *Dir. fam. pers.*, 1985, p. 537 *et seq*. Court of Cassation Civil Section I, 27th October 1999, no. 12077, in *Fam. e dir.*, 2000, p. 77 *et seq.*; Court of Cassation, 23rd August 1985, no. 4498, in *Nuova giurisprudenza civile commentata*, 1986, l, p. 125 with note by F. MANTOVANI; Court of Cassation 8th August 1990, no. 8013, in *Dir. fam. pers.*, 1991, p. 511 *et seq.*; recently, e.g., cf. Court of Cassation 6th August 2004, no. 15241; cf. E. MATTU, *Libertà religiosa e diritto di famiglia: una sintetica rassegna di giurisprudenza*, in *Dir. fam. pers.*, 1998, p. 430 *et seq.*

Even the Supreme Court, referring to Article 19 of the Constitution, found that a change of religious faith of one of the spouses cannot affect the custody of the children, if and insofar as it does not exceed the limits of compatibility with the competing duties of spouse or parent. According to the Court of Cassation, the child must be provided with a series of values free from excesses of fideism, compatible with a balanced growth integrated with the surrounding environment.[226] While this may be acceptable to protect the religious identity of the family unit, the transposition of these precise regulatory cornerstones is of particular interest when considering the possibility of introducing kafala into our legal fabric.

Legislative decisions must be able to evaluate the relationship and influence that the choices parents make in terms of ideology and values can have, in concrete terms, in the growth and education of the child but above all in the recognition of his/her fundamental rights. This because the right to profess one's own religious faith in any form, in addition to the common limit of respect for morality provided by the Constitution, also comes up against the limit of constitutional public order in respecting the principle of equality and non-discrimination, that is, the set of ethical and social values on which our constitutional charter is founded. The role of law – as a link between the values and behaviours of subjects – therefore requires careful consideration to be made on the ways in which personal relationships evolve in the family context as a paradigmatic criterion for an effective declination of the principle of secularism in a democratic social structure.[227]

---

[226] Court of Cassation, 7th February 1995, no. 1401, in *Giur. it.*, 1996, I, l, 538, with note by A. GABRIELLI, *Mutamento di fede religiosa, separazione personale dei coniugi e affidamento della prole a terzi*, c. 537 *et seq.*; *Dir. eccl.*, 1996, II, p.18 *et seq.*, *Corriere giuridico*, 1995, p. 707 *et seq.*; *Dir. fam pers.*, 1995, p. 1383 *et seq.*; *Famiglia e dir.*, 1995, p. 351 *et seq.*; S. DOMINELLO, *Osservazioni sulla laicità quale tecnica metodologica di produzione del "diritto giurisprudenziale"*, at *www.statoechiese.it*, March, 2011.

[227] On intercultural issues cf. M. RICCA, *Culture interdette. Modernità, migrazioni, diritto interculturale*, Turin, Bollati Boringhieri, 2013; cf. also V. TOZZI, *Brevi riflessioni su appartenenza e rappresentanza. L'attenzione dell'ordinamento statale al rapporto tra individui e soggetti collettivi religiosi di appartenenza*, at *www.statoechiese.it*, 27, 2012; G. ANELLO, *'Fratture culturali' e 'terapie giuridiche'. Un percorso giurisprudenziale tra multiculturalità e soluzioni interculturali*; at *www.statoechiese.it*, November 2009 emphasised that "the mobilisation of Islamic communities concerning the plan to create separate jurisdictions and that of using arbitration to give relevance to religious law seems to have shaken and challenged the multiculturalist approach to cultural differences

The fluidity of multicultural societies is such that further problems may arise when one or both parents move to another country. These problems can become particularly complex when attempting to anchor legal norms to religious parameters, as in the case of kafala. A Muslim couple from an Islamic country, but permanently resident in the west will, in the name of the rules of 'personal status', request the application of their own (Islamic) legislation. This option will also involve the minor who has been or will be placed in that specific family context. The automatic application of the religious command (transformed into a juridical norm in the Islamic country of origin) not only determines the disavowal of the religious freedom of the child, but above all the rights that our secularized system recognizes to all children present in the territory in the event of non-biological filiation, that is, first and foremost the right to a surname and to inheritance.

This disfunction becomes even more evident in the case of the legitimate children of a Muslim couple who will enjoy, by virtue of the Islamic norm favouring them, the recognition of all the rights that secularized cultures recognize to all minors, regardless of their faith. These rules will also apply in the case of dual citizenship by virtue of the particular extension of Islamic rules to all members of the *Umma*/community of believers.

A further difficulty arises when citizens of secularized countries decide, in the name of religious freedom, to convert to Islam. In such cases they will not be able to make use of kafala or respect the precise religious command since the only normative reference must be national legislation, regardless of private religious faith.

The semantic field of the kafala is, therefore, strictly connected to the meaning of the family and to the institutions of child protection set up in each legal system. It highlights a contrast with the value structures that characterize Italian family law and the status of the non-biological child within the family, especially considering the important legislative developments achieved by our country, particularly in recent times.[228] The

---

both in general terms and in relation to the specific consequences that this system ensures in these cases" (p.19); *Gestire i conflitti interculturali ed interreligiosi. Approcci a confronto*, P. CONSORTI, A. VALDAMBRINI (eds.), Pisa, Plus, 2009; on Islam cf. *Islam in Europa/Islam in Italia tra diritto e società*, A. FERRARI (ed.), Bologna, il Mulino, 2008, 129 *et seq*. in general on various issues cf. *Multireligiosità e reazione giuridica*, A. FUCCILLO (ed.), Turin, Giappichelli, 2008.

[228] On the basis of recent reforms regarding filiation – Law no. 219, 2012 – kinship relations derive from the status of son/daughter regardless of whether the parents are married.

principle of equating the legitimate child with the adoptive child is wide in scope and impacts heavily on the Italian family system. It represents one of those concepts of domestic law, elevated to the rank of principles of public order, theoretical or axiomatic values that largely constitute the identity of the legal system.

3. The Legal Institution of 'Affiliation' and its Affinities with Kafala

In the study of kafala and the legal problems that it entails when coming up against western legal systems, what is particularly interesting is the theoretical confrontation with an institution of our legal system, which has now definitively disappeared: 'affiliation' or simple adoption. This was introduced with a royal decree during the fascist period in 1938 and survived the reforms of 1967 and 1975. It was also governed by the civil code of 1942 and was definitively suppressed by Article 77 of Law no. 184/1983.[229] As a legal instrument, it was an original creation by Italian legislation and was hard to find elsewhere. It demonstrated a particular sensitivity to the current issue and may be considered as very modern by the standards of the time.

In the traditional structure of adoption as was set out in that historical period, a childless couple would make use of this artificial tool to continue the family line. With 'affiliation', on the other hand, the state "recognizing the highly educational action of the family, entrusts it with the task of educating and supporting an element extraneous to it, so that the subject may find a home and a guide for work; it follows that the family, this time, is simply a means, fulfilling the political function entrusted to it by the state, while who needs it the most is the child".[230]

The affinities identifiable with the institution of the same name that arose in the Middle Ages can only be related to the identical spirit of solidarity, nor can it be associated with so-called private adoption or Germanic, as opposed to the classical adoption regulated by Roman law.[231]

---

[229] Significant among the developments in Book I of the new Civil Code was Title XI (Articles 398- 408) concerning minors placed in public or private care or 'affiliation'.

[230] F. SALVI, *L'affiliazione*, Milan, Giuffré, 1946, esp. p. 9; cf. also F. A. MARINA, *L'istituto della affiliazione. Storia-Dogmatica- Questioni pratiche*, Florence, ed. R. Giusti, 1948.

[231] H. LINDSAY, *Adoption in the Roman World*, Cambridge, Cambridge University Press, 2009. The *Pflgekindschaft* or family care of abandoned children under Prussian law was limited to regulating the rights / duties of the adult without

It is true that the first atypical forms of kinship had already been built through the institution of *adoptio*, known since ancient Roman times but this legal instrument was, unlike its possible historical references, strongly inspired by the value of social solidarity. The institution of 'affiliation' was, in actual fact, tied once more to welfare and framed in the code as a commitment to protect the child considering that the recovery, care, protection and upbringing of children could no longer be "conceived as the expression of a simple administrative charitable function", but constituted "normal forms of intervention by the state authority in the discipline of 'affiliation'".[232]

The doctrine of the period warned of the need to fill a gap drew the attention of society to the condition of abandoned children. Legislation sought to create an institution other than adoption by excluding its definition as 'small-scale adoption' even at a semantic level.[233] The two systems had in common the material fact of bringing an outsider into the family but with very different purposes, methods and effects. The main purpose of 'affiliation' was actually to give children the moral and material support they needed – with an essentially charitable purpose – where adoption was impossible due to the lack of age requirements, the presence of children or when they wished to avoid the effects of adoption

attributing any stability to the bond. Similarly, the *Die Übernahme in die Pflege* system of placement of pupils in the Austrian code was limited only to excluding the effects of adoption of these so-called pupils. The unofficial protection of French law was, however, allowed only to those who had no legitimate descendants and had reached the age of 50; moreover, it concerned all minors under 15 years of age, regardless of the state of abandonment (Articles 361 - 370). More similar was the protection of mistreated or morally abandoned children, introduced in France with a law of 1889, which involved the obligation to nourish, bring up and help put the child in a position to earn but required only the ability to protect without the consent of the judge. It was a simple placement of the child without parental authority. Cf. C. RUPERTO, *Dalla legge al diritto (1950-2010)*, edited and introduced by di G. Alpa, Milan, Giuffré, 2010, esp. pp. 105 - 106.

[232] Acts of the Commission, p. 824. Cf. C. RUPERTO, *Dalla legge al diritto*, cit., p. 104 *et seq*.; M. KORNITZER, *Child Adoption in the Modern World*, New York, Philosophical Library, 1952. Interesting to note the jurisprudential analysis underlining the essentially welfare purpose: Naples Court of Appeal, 17th February 1958, in *Giust. Civ. Mass*., 1958, p. 31ss. and the Magistrate's Court of Potenza, 20th January 1942, in *Riv.dir. matrim*., 1942, which stressed that "it does not mean that the subject acquires status in the family but is simply bound in terms of support and recognition" (p. 103).

[233] Cf. Ministerial report to the king no. 182.

on inheritance especially.[234] The rationale underlying 'affiliation' as a form of guarantee of childhood should have led to the establishment of a status of a family nature, albeit attenuated compared to adoption but still permanent with long-term effects. In a positive sense, it can be observed that, for example, it persisted after reaching the child achieved the age of majority of the affiliate and the death of the adopting parent.

Although the reform appeared to concern more administrative law, it was positively evaluated by the jurists because it reorganized an institution in the system of law which was used extensively in practice: the care (raising children according to the system used by the doctrine of the time) and upbringing of abandoned children by third parties and private individuals. A not so distant precedent was found in legislation in favour of war orphans.[235] A further legal precursor of the institution of adoption was constituted by Royal Legislative Decree No. 798/1927 entitled "Regulations governing the support of children who are illegitimate, abandoned or exposed to abandonment", which provided for the possibility of accommodating the minor in a suitable institution or another family if the mother was not able to support her child.[236] It was an act in which public law contributed almost exclusively, as evidenced also by the specification of the purposes to be pursued.

The creation of a stable guardian/minor bond was linked to the institution of adoption, at times free from rigid traditional forms and

---

[234] Cf. C. GRASSETTI, C. CATTANEO, *Affiliazione*, in *Nss. Dg. Italiano*, Turin, Utet, 1957, p. 365 *et seq*.

[235] The peculiarities of adoption under Law no. 2137/1925 were the following: a) the adopter must be over the age of forty (Article 1, Law cit.); b) consent for the adoptee without either parent is given by the provincial committee, based on the report of the tutelary judge, who must hear the opinion of those who exercise protection and ascertain whether the adoption is morally non-prejudicial to the minor; the latter will be heard by the Court if he is over ten years old (Articles 2 and 4); c) the adopter is given special protection over the minor who has lost both parents, similar to the legal protection of the repealed code and subject to the supervision and controls provided for by the law on aid to war orphans (Articles 5 and 6); d) the adoption can be revoked at the request of the provincial committee, where the adopter incurs any infringement that could give rise to measures against the parent or guardian in accordance with the special law; but the revocation does not affect child support or inheritance rights (Article 7).

[236] C. SCHUPPER, *Per la piccola adozione*, in *Foro It.*, 1937, IV, col.89; G. SCHERILLO, *Affiliazione e adozione*, in *Foro It.*, 1939, pp. 259 *et seq*.

essentially appertaining to the public law sphere.[237] 'Affiliation' represented "the latest result in the evolution of an idea that wishes to recognize a different kind of relationship, stronger than adoption, when the legal relationship of kinship is created for the benefit of those without a natural family".[238] The special laws had entrusted public assistance institutions with the faculty to entrust the minor to trusted subjects for their care and support.

Part of the doctrine of the time defined it as an institution whereby minors entrusted to public or private assistance or raised by persons previously unknown to them, by means of a specific procedure or at the request of a party, and by virtue of a provision of the judicial authority could obtain a new family status. As a result of this act, they were linked by a civil parental bond, producing limited effects in the family and patrimonial sphere and different from the blood ties with the people to whom they had been entrusted or by whom they had been raised.[239] Others instead preferred to emphasise that this institution aimed to complete and more fully outline the legal discipline of the voluntary external raising of children. In this way, the state expropriated the parental authority of unsuitable parents and transformed it into a right to be granted, through the tutelary judge, to those who had successfully raised the abandoned child for three years and had applied for the granting of powers inherent in parental authority and the faculty to give the child one's surname.

This system, which the law wished to implement, was born out of the peasant society and had spread to the extended and patriarchal family, meeting the productive needs of agriculture. It was therefore conceived as an opportunity for the child to receive support and find a job, according to a still strongly adult-centric approach to family relationships and the idea of parental authority, which was preserved until recently. This institution also responded to the logic of fascist ethics with the aim of satisfying "a duel individual legal need, the need, or rather the right, of illegitimates to expect the state to intervene to erase family and social inferiority that inflicts on them the fault of their parents and the spiritual, moral and sometimes economic need, especially in the agricultural field, of childless or almost childless couples to have a home cheered by the child's smile

[237] In England and Wales, the Adoption of Children Act 1926 was for minors only. Legitimising adoption was introduced in France with Articles 368 - 370 of the Civil Code.

[238] It should be noted that the actual English term *affiliation* simply refers to recognising a natural child.

[239] Cf. L. MOSCO, *Dei minori affidati alla pubblica o alla privata assistenza e dell'affiliazione*, Rome, Signorelli, 1940.

and to recruit new help to complete the forces of the family economic community".[240] It was feared that the underlying rationale for the law might at times appear to take children away from poor families, as parents were only heard by the tutelary judge and 'affiliation' could also be ordered against their will. A more correct evaluation, however, is that this tool was mainly used by parents, when recognition of children born as a result of adultery was forbidden, to give the children their surname, to obtain family allowances and benefits.[241]

This kind of institution functioned in a system which recognized the right to support to the child without a family but which, in the pre-constitutional regulatory framework, did not recognize the child's right to a family. The institution of 'affiliation' could therefore aid fascist legislation to find a solution to the practical problems that the pre-existing juridical institutions were unable to solve and drew elements both from the legislation to protect abandoned children and from the laws regarding adoption itself. In addition to contingent and economic needs, the institution in question had a clear purpose of solidarity, anchored in the Italian Catholic tradition. In this structure, the affinity with Islamic kafala is evident, subject as it is to the same purpose and connected to an identical traditional vision of the legitimate family.

It was these concrete needs that allowed its legal configuration and characterised its rationale among the measures to protect children. In this way, the attribution of a family status was allowed, with a minor accommodated in a public institution entrusted to a private individual or the raising of the minor directly by a private individual. It was thus a legal act under those who, for at least three years, had raised an abandoned or

[240] Report presented on 4th June 1937 by Piola Caselli, Di Marzo and Costamagna regarding the bill on 'affiliation', defined at the time as 'mini-adoption'. During the Fascist period with Law no. 2277 of 12th December 1925 on the protection and support of motherhood and childhood, a semi-public organisation named Onmi – National Organisation for Motherhood and Childhood – was set up to provide for the vital needs of childhood, and survived until 1975. It aimed to provide medical-social support to mothers and children up to the age of majority who found themselves in temporary or permanent need. Cf. A. BRESCI, *L'Opera Nazionale Maternità e Infanzia nel ventennio fascista*, in *Italia Contemporanea*, 192, 1993, pp. 421 - 442 e in http://www.italia-resistenza.it/wp-content/uploads/ic/RAV 0053532_1993_190-193_30.pdf; M.S. QUINE, *Population politics in the Twentieth Century Europe: fascist dictatorship and liberal democracy*, New York-London, Routledge, 1996.

[241] Article 330 of the Civil Code was amended with the purpose of continuing to allow the judge to intervene only in the event that the conduct of the parents – not the welfare organisation or institution – might be damaging to the child.

exposed child, would be granted indefinitely the powers inherent to parental authority and the power to attribute their surname. However, unlike adoption, it did not create family ties, even though some, evaluating the aims of the institution, came to a different conclusion.[242] It was extinguished, among other things, when the state, which exercised its power/duty of control throughout the 'affiliation' felt that it had to reintegrate the parent who had lost his parental authority.[243] 'Affiliation' was thus implemented at the request of the latter and with the consent of the spouse, by a decree issued by the tutelary judge that was to be approved by the court, subject to the opinion of the public prosecutor, which attributed the surname of the parent to the child.

This legal provision was subsequently taken up and inserted into the norms of the Civil Code of 1942 in which there was the provision that in the event of moral and material abandonment of the minor, s/he would be placed in an institution of protection by order of authority. From there the child could be fostered by a trusted person, who after three years could make a request to the tutelary judge (of the place of residence) to adopt the child. This measure, which accepted the request, could also attribute the surname of the adopter, if requested, to the child if s/he was of unknown parents or recognized by a single parent or could add the surname to his own, if a legitimate child or recognized by both biological parents. If the minor already had a family name, he did not lose it, but the second was added to the original. 'Affiliation' was of an eminently welfare nature and ended with the reaching of the age of majority, except for the preservation of the surname adopted or added. The new surname transmitted to the descendants was not necessarily lost with the termination of the bond or with the revocation of 'affiliation'.[244]

The judicial provision also attributed to the adopting parent the powers inherent to parental authority, as well as the duties to raise, educate and support the minor. The adult had to be a suitable subject even if the code was limited to establishing that he should not be unfit; provided that he was of age, he could be of any age, unmarried, single, widowed or married.[245] If married, as for adoption, only the consent of the spouse was

---

[242] Cf. F. SALVI, *L'affiliazione*, Milan, Giuffré, 1946, esp. p. 50.

[243] Cf. R. BEVILACQUA, *Sulla natura giuridica dell'affiliazione*, in *Giur. it.*, 1941, p. 153.

[244] This was different for those whose prior status had been that of a natural child recognised by one parent only. Cf. also G. SCHERILLO, *Di nuovo sui rapporti tra affiliazione e adozione*, in *Giur.It.*, 1948, l, 2, p. 503 *et seq*.

[245] The jurisprudence would not allow an Italian child to be placed in 'affiliation' with a foreign national: Court of Rome, 15 July 1942, in *Riv. dir. pen.*, 1942 p.

required, free to 'affiliate' the minor or not; the code, however, provided for the possibility for the tutelary judge to issue the measure in two possible cases: when the spouse was unable to manifest her will and in the event of legal separation. Article 403 of the Civil Code introduced an exception from the common discipline on the exercise of parental authority and protection. It vested the administrative authority the autonomous power to have recourse to a precautionary and provisional measure to be implemented in the event of moral or material abandonment of the minor, of raising the child on harmful premises that may be dangerous to health or in the event of those responsible for raising the child being unfit.[246]

There were no further effects resulting from 'affiliation' in the code. In particular, the doctrine excluded inheritance rights (just as maintenance was also excluded).[247] In consideration of the particular bond that bound the adoptive parent to the child, and the possibility that the latter could contribute to the formation of the estate of the former, there was only a reduction of the inheritance tax in the event that the parent made out his will to the child.[248] From 'affiliation', however, arose marriage impediments pursuant to Article 87 of the Italian Civil Code.

Unlike adoption, a lack of legitimate descendants was not required, moreover, there were no age limits. An indispensable condition to attain 'affiliation' was the three-year waiting period, considered as an indispensable requirement for both parties to gain better knowledge and for the adopting parent to understand his responsibilities, defined as taking custody for educational purposes.[249] This period could be interrupted by the child's biological parents at any time, unless otherwise decided by the judicial authority; furthermore, revocation was feasible in the event of late

---

657; nor could a foreign minor be placed in 'affiliation' if this was not provided for in his/her own country: Court of Milan, 13th February 1956, in *Riv. dir. int.*, 1956, p. 193 *et seq*.

[246] M. STELLA RICHTER, V. SGROI, *Delle persone e della famiglia*, in *Commentario del codice civile*, Turin, Utet, 1967, p. 587.

[247] Cf. M. BIANCA, *Diritto civile, 2, La famiglia. Le successioni*, Milan, Giuffré, 2005, p. 468; A. DELL'ORO, *Dell'emancipazione dei minori affidati alla pubblica o privata assistenza e dell'affiliazione*, in *Commentario del codice civile*, edited by A. SCIALOJA- G. BRANCA, Bologna-Rome, Zanichelli, 1972, p.286.

[248] Article 9, Law no. 23, 19th January 1942, and Article l, paragraph 2, Decree no. 90 8th March 1945.

[249] While Law no. 184/1983 confirmed the incompatibility between fostering and adoption, prior to this the situation was exactly the opposite. Cf. P. LARICCIA, *L'affiliazione nella riforma degli istituti di diritto familiare*, in *Studi in tema di diritto di famiglia*, Milan, Giuffré, 1967; S. PUGLIATTI, *Scritti giuridici*, II, 1937-1947, Milan, Giuffré, 2010 (on 'affiliation' p. 299 *et seq*.).

recognition by one of the parents. Attention was therefore still essentially centred on the rights of the adults, of the biological parents rather than the real interests of the minor.

The procedure was carried out in three phases: provision of the tutelary judge, approval of the court and annotation in the margin of the birth certificate. The judge's task was to gather information on the applicant's financial and family circumstances, on the treatment of the minor in the last three years and on the physical, moral and intellectual conditions of the child. A decree was issued against which an appeal was possible. Arising from 'affiliation' was the duty for the minor to carry out work, housekeeping or collaboration in the activities (normally agricultural) of the adopting parent as a sort of consideration for the support offered, thus granted *affectionis vel benevolentiae causa* with no compensation.[250]

'Affiliation' would cease for various reasons: if the minor 'went astray', continually backsliding; if the adopting parent was no longer in a position to adopt (not only in terms of being financially able to provide support); for serious reasons, to be assessed by the judge. It could be extinguished in two cases: if the adopting parent married the adopted child, subject to a necessary dispensation or for the conferral of parental authority on the biological parent of the adopted child; following recognition of natural filiation. In Articles 410 and 411 of the Civil Code, revocation and extinction occurred if the parent who had failed or been prevented from exercising parental authority and whose conduct had thus set in motion child protection measures by the social services, was reinstated in the exercise of power.[251] It should be noted that at the time the minor did not acquire full rights to the family, considering that family status took into account the complex set of relationships that bound not only parent and child but also the child with all the relatives of both parents.[252]

In the civil code of 1942, many elements were therefore transfused by the Pisanelli code of 1865 – those regarding absence of descendants; age of fifty years for the adopter; minimum difference of eighteen years between adopted party and adopter; consent of the parties; addition of the surname of the adopter to that of the adoptee and succession to the estate of the adopter to the same degree as the legitimate child. However, the

---

[250] Cf. M. PASCASIO, *Il lavoro familiare dell'affiliato*, in *Riv. giur. lav.*, 1942, p. 1391 *et seq*.

[251] Articles 404 - 413 of the Civil Code were revoked with Article 77, Law no. 184/1983.

[252] C. GRASSETTI, *La struttura giuridica dell'affiliazione*, Parma, Studi Parmensi, 1950, stressed that "filiation is one thing, family status another" (p. 508).

legislative innovations of the fascist period also brought changes to the discipline of adoption. In the first place, the institution acquired a public law relevance: homologation was replaced with a decree that pronounced the adoption. By letting the effects of the adoption begin with the judicial ruling, rather than from the moment consensus was expressed, the effect of creating a legal relationship was obtained. The second innovation occurred with reference to the age of the adoptee: the minimum limit of eighteen years to be adopted was lost. However, the adopter was not yet expected to acquire parental authority over the child. The possibility of revocation of the adoption had been introduced for causes expressly foreseen – the unworthiness of the adoptee or the adopter, and for reasons of morality. Despite these innovations the primary purpose of adoption was still to ensure inheritance and the continuation of the family line rather than helping a child in difficulty to find a family.

It is now clear that an analysis of this legal institution is particularly interesting when studying particular forms of protection of children, such as kafala, as structured in the Islamic world. In both types, we start from the consideration of the desire to balance two opposing interests: respect and protection of blood ties, and thus the natural, traditional type of the family, and the opposing need to protect abandoned children. Besides war orphans, in the last century abandoning children who were the "fruit of sin" was very frequently associated with conditions of extreme social and economic degradation also in the west. The institution of Italian 'affiliation' therefore acted as a regulatory bridge to the most modern development of adoption, such as to allow Italian doctrine a more refined and accurate conceptual elaboration of these issues. The studies of the time do allow the modern jurist interested in the practices of protection of minors, interesting food for thought, with reference in particular to the Islamic kafala institution with which 'affiliation' shared many similarities.

Since this mode of protection of the minor has been surpassed, it is worth reflecting on the relationship and adaptation of the Islamic institution in our own system, which has done away with 'affiliation' since it no longer functioned and especially in light of the principles and rights recognized by our Constitutional Charter. While 'affiliation' did have the undoubted merit of definitively disengaging the concept of the adoptive parental relationship from a mere economic interest and reaffirming its welfare role, it was still the result of a very traditionalist doctrinal elaboration. Subsequent analyses, more focused on the rights, interests and needs of the minor, highlighted the inadequacy of this methodological approach and the need to impose a *quid pluris* on the new adoptive institution, partially implemented with the introduction of special adoption in our system. and fully accomplished only with the full and complete affirmation of legitimising adoption.

Any real consideration of the adopted child, not just from the point of view of family succession, would only come about with the enactment of the Italian Constitution. Article 30 states that "[i]t is the duty and right of parents to raise, educate and support their children, even if born out of wedlock. In case of incapacity of the parents, the law shall provide for the fulfilment of their duties". Another fundamental legislative step was made with the introduction of special adoption, sanctioned in Italy with Law no. 431/1967, which was added to the so-called ordinary adoption, the application of which remained intact with regards to adults or minors over the age of eight.[253] The priority of natural parents to provide for their offspring was reconfirmed, but it was also specified that in cases of total material and moral abandonment, minors had the right to have a family complete.

These legislative innovations made it possible to shift attention from the interests of the adopter to the needs of the adoptee, implementing the constitutional principles enshrined in articles 2 and 30 of the Constitution and allowing the child to become an authentic subject with rights. In essence, the right to the development of one's personality began to prevail over the alleged right of the biological parents, who did not provide for their own, and it was established that legitimate parents and legitimate children may not necessarily have a 'blood' relationship between them. This regulation also followed the recommendations of the Strasbourg Convention and began to lay the foundations for an adoption that dealt exclusively with minors, with a discipline that was distinctly different from the adoption of adults. The Convention established that an abandoned child should become the child of the adoptive parents in his/her own right, excluding any ties with the family of origin.

This last approach, defined as special adoption, as opposed to the traditional, ordinary form, applied only to children under eight years of age and radically affected the relationship of the child with the family of origin because it definitively severed any biological ties. The child acquired legitimate status and the parents had to meet certain requirements

---

[253] Law no. 431 of 5th June 1967 amending Title VIII of Book I of the Civil Code on adoption with the inclusion of a new Chapter III on special adoption. Special adoption did not change under family law reform, despite the presence of a draft law filed since March 1973 and despite the fact that Parliament had already approved the ratification of the European Convention on adoption, according to which the maximum age of minors adoptable with special adoption was to shift from 8 to 18 years old.

(age, reliability, educational competence) in order to demonstrate that they were able to support and educate the child. A necessary condition was the lack of any material or moral support, as long as this was not due to circumstances outside their control. From this moment on, a new concept of abandonment began to emerge, attributable to the absolute and irreversible unsuitability of the parents to raise and support their child or indeed anyone capable of replacing them in the extended family circle.

The introduction of special adoption was thus undoubtedly the real innovation of the law: it aimed to place the minor within a family and for this purpose the adopters were required to be couple united by marriage bond for at least five years; that the relationship was not affected by a personal separation and that the couple's moral and material conditions were such that they could raise, educate and support the child. The age of the adoptive parents had to be at least twenty and not more than forty-five years older than the adopted child's age, to avoid any generational conflicts at least between the child and the adoptive parents. To guarantee, then, the exclusivity of the relationship between parents and children, which characterises the biological family, the law in question truncated any relationship or legal bond between the adopted child and the family of origin.

The two basic concepts were very simple, but at the same time decidedly revolutionary: the child without a family had the right to a new one; the adoption served to give a family to the child in a state of abandonment – not to give a child to a childless couple. This last point is clearly fundamental because for the first time the minor was recognized, though not expressly, as a subject with needs and fundamental rights – that had already emerged in considerations at an international level – which the legal system had the task and duty to respect and guarantee, in line with the standards of other countries. For the first time in our legal system this laid down the principle that institutionalisation (entrusting to an institution) of the minor might not be the most suitable instrument for the child's growth but was only a further cause of pain and marginalisation. It clarified that the duty/function of educating represented the logical consideration of the child's right to education and was primarily and directly up to the parents, whether they be natural or adoptive.

With this law it was also forbidden for the biological parent to give their child directly to a third party (in practice to 'sell'), for adoption or 'affiliation' purposes, but it was clarified that this transfer must be referred to the Juvenile Court functioning as a guarantee. Unlike the past, pursuant to Article 318, no parent could give his child freely to have him raised by others or entrusted to an institution unless under unavoidable circumstances.

The introduction of these regulations and the consequent recognition of the right of the minor to a family, securely guaranteed, also profoundly changed the way the Civil Code was read as it no longer referred to questions of property and inheritance alone. With this law the minor was no longer an object but a person in his/her own right, with the expression 'born to …' being replaced by 'child of …'. The parental relationship was no longer centred on the biological profile but on the emotional ties being created. This profile was what psychologists explained through the elaboration of the concepts of *maternité/paternité* (procreative act), *maternage/paternage* (material, emotional and educational care), *maternisation/paternisation* (processes by which children make mother and father their natural or adoptive parents).[254]

Subsequently, though, social developments associated with the disappearance of the extended family brought several issues and difficulties to the fore, often no longer manageable within the family unit. In the past, it tended to be very young children who were abandoned but an increasingly larger number of older children in Italy were affected but could not be adopted since they were over eight years of age. Nevertheless, attention was still focused not on the minor, but on the future parents who, after seeing the child, would declare him/her to their 'liking'. With reference to natural relatives, a declaration of abandonment could be pronounced only if the lack of support did not depend on uncontrollable events, but the judge was prevented from assessing its timescale. The rationale behind this approach was to prioritise parental interests. In the 'seventies jurisprudence still exalted the role and function of the 'natural' family, the "right of the minor to have a true and not a false mother" for which "the ordinary legislator may regulate the family within the natural community from which it is formed but may not definitively sever any relationship that derives from the inalienable and imprescriptible character of the family bond."[255]

One of the most important points of divergence between traditional adoption, special adoption and 'affiliation' is that the former had the characteristic of a negotiating act even though it was the judicial provision that determined the desired effects, as it presupposed the consent and the manifestation of the will of all concerned. The rationale for legitimising adoption was, instead, an assessment of the situation of abandonment with

---

[254] Cf. N. QUEMADA, *Maternage et adoption*, Paris, Foulon, 1963.

[255] Cf. Florence court, 12th May 1972 and Palermo Court of Appeal, 29th November 1973. Cf. F. SCADUTO, *Filiazione naturale, famiglia legittima e adozione*, in *Justitia*, 1965, 1, p. 62 *et seq.*; A.C. MORO, *L'adozione speciale*, Milan, Giuffré, 1978.

the doctrine of the time thus hoping for a reform that would harmonise the disciplines in the exclusive interests of the child.

4. Non-Biological Family Relationships in a Secular Legal System. The Custody of Minors

The Italian Civil Code did not provide for the minor's independent rights – the right to be raised, educated and supported, for instance – but pursuant to Article 147 of the Italian Civil Code, the parents do have a duty to provide this.[256] Until the family law reform of 1975, illegitimate children did not enjoy a series of rights; there were restrictive rules for the recognition of paternity, to prohibit the recognition of adulterous children, or to prevent the adoption of a child born out of wedlock. The only rights expressly granted to the minor were property rights.

The law also made a clear division between legal subjectivity, recognized to all, and legal capacity, only to some. A decisive prospective change occurred with a full understanding of the constitutional dictate and the broad protection recognized by Article 2 of the Constitution, which included the minor within the family unit. At the outset it was stressed that the child's right to being raised and educated should be considered an authentic right, constitutionally recognised, since the natural incapacity of the child cannot constitute an obstacle to this recognition. It is a right that belongs to the child, a still undeveloped adult as yet, though this aspect should not mean that the child owes his/her rights to third parties, the family or the state.[257] The family structure was progressively disengaged from the traditional Catholic setting and, with the introduction of the 1970 law on the cessation of the civil effects of marriage, the Italian legal system shifted towards a secularised family structure, in which it recognised rights to freedom, including religious freedom.

---

[256] Article 147 of the Civil Code – Duties towards children: "Marriage imposes upon both parents the obligation of providing maintenance, upbringing, education and moral assistance to their children while respecting their capacities, natural inclinations and aspirations, according to the provisions of article 315-bis of the Civil Code". This article was replaced first by Article 29 of Law No. 151 of 19th May1975, and subsequently by Article 3 of Legislative Decree no. 154 of 28th December 2013. In absence of parents, relatives are bound solely to provide material support (Article 433), the guardian solely to care for the child and represent the child in legal matters and to manage his/her property (Article 357).

[257] Cf. Declaration by the Right Honourable Aldo Moro in his report to the Constituent Assembly.

It was only with Law no. 184 of 1983 on the regulation of the adoption and foster care of minors that the uniform regulation of national and intercountry adoption was finally introduced, filling gaps in previous legislation.[258] It made changes to Title VIII of the first book of the Civil Code, taking steps to: distinguish between adult adoptions and child adoptions (removing the limit of eight years of age imposed by special adoption); regulate foster placement intended as a means to help families in temporary difficulty and / or inability to provide for their children; regulate the adoption of minors in special cases when other forms of support for the family of origin were not sufficient (so-called subsidiarity of adoption); regulate the intercountry adoption of both foreign minors by Italian citizens (residing in Italy or abroad) or foreign couples residing in Italy and Italian minors by couples (foreign or Italian) residing abroad. What was significant was the focus on the recognition of the child's right to a family, which made it possible to identify foster placement as the most suitable means to cater for the needs of both the minor and his/her family in case of temporary difficulties.

This law moved previous legislation forward by placing a specific regulation alongside domestic norms to coordinate the international and national aspects of adoption more fully.[259] First of all, it reaffirmed and recognized the centrality of the interests and needs of the child, who was increasingly becoming the subject of rights to defend and encourage on an equal footing with adults. The relationship between child and family no

---

[258] Law no. 184, 4th May 1983, published in the *Gazzetta Ufficiale*, 17th May 1983, issue no. 133 and at http://www.regione.abruzzo.it/procuraminori/docs/legislazione/Adozioni_L_04051983.pdf.

[259] As far as international adoptions are concerned, the new law was concerned with identifying the jurisdiction of the Italian judge and the functional jurisdiction of the Juvenile Court for all the measures concerning foreign minors (Article 29); determine the necessary requirements for applicants through a preventive assessment of their existence through a special procedure that ends with the declaration (or not) of suitability (Article 30); strictly regulate the entry into Italy of foreign minors for adoption purposes (Articles 31, 34 and 36); subordinate the declaration of effectiveness of the foreign adoption provision to the existence of a decree of suitability (Articles 32, 33); decree the applicability and competence of the Italian law on the adoption of foreign minors in a state of abandonment in Italy (Article 37); provision and ruling of the possibility for specific bodies to carry out intermediation activities in international adoptions (Article 38). Before the law in question, the legislation on international adoption was somewhat lacking in substance: the only references were Articles 17 and 20 of the preliminary provisions of the Civil Code.

longer took on an exclusively private connotation but a social dimension as well.[260]

The law established that parents could entrust their child to relatives up to the fourth degree with no intervention necessary by the local authorities or the Juvenile Court. However, there were cases in which the intervention of the Juvenile Court was sought regarding placement with relatives when, for various reasons, the child's parents were unable to guarantee acceptable conditions for raising their child. This is what is known as intrafamily placement. Alternatively, a child without a suitable family environment, until s/he reaches adulthood, may be entrusted to a another family in order to ensure: that the child is raised, educated and supported in the best way possible and with the emotional relationships that the child needs (with the natural family, the child's own self and the new surrounding context); that ties with the biological family are not severed; to allow the natural parents to be able to welcome their child back into the family. It may be consensual or, as in most cases, judicial.[261]

---

[260] M. ORLANDI, *Le adozioni internazionali in Italia: realtà e disciplina giuridica*, Milan, Giuffré, 2006 stresses that "Italian legislation chose to create a strong adoption model, placing the adopted child fully into the new family, thus affirming social parenting based on love and no longer exclusively on consanguinity. Indeed, one of the most significant innovations introduced with the reform was the greater emphasis placed on the role of the social services, called upon to interact more closely with the Juvenile Court at every stage of the procedure". Law no. 149, 28th March 2001, regulated two actions: the first to adapt the legislative system in relation to the changes introduced with the ratification of the Hague Convention and the second to review some aspects of the adoption institution. Cf. Law no. 149, 28th March 2001, amending Law no. 184, 4th May 1983, on adoption and foster care as well as Title VIII of Book I of the Civil Code, published in the *Gazzetta Ufficiale*, 26th April 2001, no. 96 and at www.minori.it.pdf.

[261] Consensual family custody is carried out with the consent of the family of origin; the parents acknowledge their difficulties and discomforts that the children experience, independently or with the help and support of the social services, and agree to entrust the child to another family, in agreement with the social services, for the necessary time. The difficulties declared and recognized by the family of origin become the starting point of a foster care path that provides guarantees to the minor and at the same time allows the family of origin to recoup. Consensual custody is a measure of support and help to parents and the minor and aims to allow the minor to return to his/her home, returning the minor to his/her family when difficulties have been overcome. The provision of custody is ordered by the social services of the municipality (which must therefore obtain the consent of the parents and listen to the minor if the child is over 12 years old) and is enforced with a decree by the Tutelary Judge who checks their regularity. The social services are responsible for an assistance program (custody project) which must

This type of placement is one of the most innovative in Italy's child protection system. Taking its starting point as the principle according to which every child has the right to a family and that it is within that family that the child will build his/her own identity, it is one of the possible aids available in difficult situations (illness of a parent, problems generated by addiction, alcoholism, social isolation, neglect, physical and/or psychological violence, dysfunctional relationships) – situations that can easily hinder the child's upbringing and the parent-child coexistence. Minors are often entrusted to an institution where primary needs like meals, accommodation and school support are met. If possible, however, family placement is the preferred option, a form of hospitality almost that the minor receives from a family, which is not the one of origin and has no legal obligations towards the child but acts in a spirit of solidarity and altruism.

The key feature of the placement is its temporary nature with this provision lasting from a few months to a year or two at the most. The estimated length of the placement must be noted in the provision prepared by the social services and confirmed by the magistrate and refers to the needs of the minor and the recovery time of the child's family. Once the child has been placed with another family, the child's natural parents are temporarily relieved of their parental function to allow them to restructure their family and regain the ability to manage their role, reorganize their resources and remove the obstacles that make the child's upbringing difficult. This relationship may evolve in different ways: it may cease once the minor has reached the age of majority or, with recent developments, it may also turn into adoption.

---

include activities for the minor (educational and psychological support), action for the family of origin (aimed at removing difficulties and improving parenting skills, as well as maintaining relationships with the child in the most suitable way) and help for the foster parents (support and financial aid measures). Every six months, as for judicial custody, the social services report to the Tutelary Judge on the progress of the placement. In most cases, however, judicial family custody is sought when, due to the serious deficiencies in the responsibilities of care by the parents, and the consequent situation detrimental to the child, it is essential to proceed with removal and placement of the children in a more suitable environment for growth. This is often ordered by the Juvenile Court, following the outcome of a civil proceeding during which the parents, though not completely absent, oppose, deny or underestimate the risks, failing to understand the reasons for the concern of judges and social services. Custody is ordered by the Juvenile Court and carried out by the social services of the municipality, normally when the consent of the family of origin to foster care is not forthcoming. There must be an underlying condition of serious difficulties and risk to the child.

This mechanism is therefore structured as a help and support facility, created with a view to protecting children's rights, to guarantee the minor the right to grow up in an environment that can meet the child's educational and emotional demands. It should also be an environment where the child's needs are respected as regards personal and family characteristics and the child's specific situation of difficulty, with the proposal of another parenting couple and the creation of new relational experiences. Not only do the new caregivers need to take care of the children they welcome, but they also need to help them find the best direction to take. There are no special rules in terms of religious freedom but normally there is a tendency to place children with a family structure that is as close as possible to the culture of origin of the child, to encourage the development of the child's identity.

The greater or lesser presence of the natural family, however, does make the scene extremely complex. It is peculiar in that it places the child in the middle – between biological and 'social' parents – and its success depends largely on the ability of both families and the local community to take on responsibility for citizenship rights, with particular concern for those of the child. The institution's standardization, as encouraged by regulatory developments, provides for the hierarchical division of priorities between support for the child's natural family, foster placement and institutional care.

Nevertheless, a very strong cultural resistance to fostering as a form of parenting support is still widespread. The culture of foster care should be centred not only on the concept of hospitality, but also on a solid community principle to become, in addition to being an opportunity for the peaceful growth of the child, a moment of expansion and strengthening of ties with the family of origin. The concept of foster care must thus extend to that of mutual acceptance – natural family and foster parents – to optimise this fundamental instrument of social solidarity.[262]

The most recent legislative action taken in the field of foster care in Italy was the new law passed in 2015, which considered the critical elements of the system and aimed to go beyond the barrier of temporariness, codifying the principle of continuity of relationships where the interests of

---

[262] National and regional legislation on foster care provided for the establishment of SAT – local foster care service – to promote a culture of foster care, identifying, selecting and training the people and couples available for foster care, to compile a registry, match minors with foster families and provide support to the family of origin.

the child were concerned.[263] This new theoretical approach was clearly a Copernican revolution that allowed the rigid barrier put up by previous legislation to come down. This barrier effectively prevented temporary foster care from becoming permanent adoption, even when emotional bonds were stable, contrary to the provisions of Fascist legislation with the institution of 'affiliation'. In the event of the child being placed within another family, transfer was often sine die due to the inability of the family of origin to recover their parenting skills.

With the introduction of this last law, legislation thus intervened to protect a factual situation, that of the continuity of the emotional ties created with the passage of time between the minor and the alternate family members, essential for the harmonious development of the child's personality.[264]

5. Full Adoption Pursuant to Law no. 184 and Subsequent Amendments

When adoption was inscribed in the civil code in the 19th century, it served to organize a wide range of support activities for children, but above all to comfort the childless couple or combat the solitude of an unmarried bachelor. The purpose of adoption was "to provide the comfort of a child to those who had none of their own (or no longer had), by placing a person from outside the family within the family; it may also be that in addition to the preservation of the lineage or to the continuity of the family, the institution of adoption may pursue other purposes of a civil order or concerning the person of the adopter; but there is no doubt that these purposes are merely reflections or accessories with respect to the main objective now described".[265]

---

[263] The new paragraph 5 *bis* Article 4 of Law no. 184/1983 states that if "during prolonged foster care the minor is declared adoptable … [and] the foster family asks to adopt, in deciding on adoption the court will take into account emotional bonds formed and the stable and lasting relationship established between the minor and the foster family". The next added paragraph also establishes that "the socio-affective relationships consolidated during foster care" should continue even if the child is returned to his/her family of origin.

[264] These emotional ties were protected – for the first time since 1983 – by Law no. 173, 9th October 2015, amending Law no. 184, 4th May 1983, on the right to continuity of relationships with foster parents, at http://www.gazzettaufficiale.it/eli/id/2015/10/29/15G00187/lsg.

[265] F. SALVI, *Adozione (diritto civile),* in *Nss. Digesto It.*, Turin, Utet, 1957, vol. I, p. 291 *et seq.*; C. RUPERTO, *Adozione (diritto civile)*, in *Enc. Dir.*, vol. I, Milan

In addition to detecting the diminished spread of the abandonment of minors, the law of 1983 represented a decisive change in perspective as regards the recognition of the equal dignity afforded to children, whether they be natural, legitimate or adoptive.[266] The law prescribes that in addition to meeting certain objective requirements (age, married for at least three years), the aspiring adoptive parents must be able to raise, educate and support the child. The law brought about the definitive transition from a traditional concept of adoption to a more modern approach. Firstly, the provision of the "declaration of willingness to adopt" instead of the classic "application" presented to the Juvenile Court highlighted a clear and decisive change in point of view, shifting the focus from the parents to the child.

In the field of adoption, the parent-child relationship is created by the relational bonds that are formed, the care, affection and willingness, more than biological procreation. With the introduction of this legislation, the child was recognized for the first time not only as an object, but as a subject of law. The child thus became a subject with basic needs that the legal system must respect and guarantee with the aim of providing the child with a family responsible for his/her upbringing and care.[267]

Through a series of investigation measures carried out by the social services, the Juvenile Court assesses the couple's stability and educational ability (understood as willingness and aptitude to help the child express his/her potential). It also evaluates the emotional capacity of the couple to

---

Giuffré, 1958; A. and M. FINOCCHIARO, *Disciplina dell'adozione e dell'affidamento dei minori*, Milan, Giuffré, 1983; B. DE FILIPPIS, Il diritto di famiglia. *Leggi prassi e giurisprudenza*, Padua, Cedam, (esp. Cap. IX, Adozioni e adozioni internazionali, pp. 711 - 880).

[266] Law no. 219, l0th December 2012 replaced the text of Article 315 of the Civil Code (legal status of filiation), with a new, simple and exemplary text, according to which "all children have the same legal status" and sanctioned that in the Civil Code 'legitimate children and natural children', wherever they occurred, should be replaced by 'children' thus achieving not only equality of the legal status of all children born in or out of wedlock or adopted, but reducing to a single concept the *status filiationis*: cf. G. FERRANDO, *La filiazione: problemi attuali e prospettive di riforma*, in *Famiglia e diritto*, 2008, p. 235 *et seq*.; G. BONILINI, *Lo status o gli status di filiazione*, in *Fam pers. e succ*., 2006, p. 681 *et seq*.

[267] Cf. G. COLLURA, *L'adozione legittimante dei minori*, in *Trattato di famiglia*, II, Milan, Giuffré, p.821 *et seq*. This law partially brought about a sort of 'Copernican revolution', because from that moment on the interests of the minor began to take priority over the interests of the biological or adoptive parents: the focus of attention shifted from the adopters to the adopted; also L. FADIGA, *L'adozione*, Bologna, Il Mulino, 1999.

welcome the child into their family, the social and cultural situation of the family, the state of health, family environment, motivation and financial resources. Though not rigidly codified, the Court also considers other criteria such as the ability to adapt – meaning the willingness to fit one's own pace of life around the child, the ability to accept reality and to relate to different cultures in a welcoming spirit.

The first step of the lengthy legal process leading to adoption is for the Juvenile Court to ascertain that the minor has been abandoned, listening to anyone who may have information to this regard. If this assessment, carried out with the necessary technical support of social workers and psychologists, reveals that the child has been morally or materially abandoned, the court declares that the minor is adoptable and appoints a guardian, whose authority over the child replaces parental authority until the adoption process is completed.[268] From this moment on, the child is removed from his/her family of origin and placed with either a foster family, a family-type community or in a public or private care institution. At the same time, the Juvenile Court examines the applications for adoption submitted by the couples in which they declared their 'availability'.[269] This request must not contain any type of discriminatory

---

[268] On the concept of state of abandonment, which legislation preferred not to codify: cf. Court of Cassation, April 12th 2006, no. 8527; Court of Cassation, 28th March 2002, no. 4503, Court of Cassation, 4th April 2000, no. 5580; Court of Cassation, February 5th 1998, no. 1265, in Jur. it., 1989, l, l, p. 534 *et seq.* Judgment no. 8527 of 2006 stated that "in order for the state of abandonment justifying the declaration of adoptability of a minor, extensive assessment must reveal material and emotional deficiencies of such importance as to be taken in themselves as detrimental to the child, also taking into account the simple inadequacy of assistance or the psychological and / or educational attitudes of the parents, with the consequence that, for the purposes of the declaration of adoptability, it is not enough that there are insufficiencies on the part of the parents or that they are mentally ill, even permanently, since it is in any case necessary to ascertain whether, for reasons of these pathologies, the parent is really unsuitable to take on and maintain full awareness of his / her duties and responsibilities and to provide less than the minimum of material care, emotional warmth and psychological support essential for balanced and healthy psycho-physical growth".

[269] Naturally accompanied by a certification that certifies the personal, family and social situation. Through the social services and fact-finding interviews, the Court decides on the suitability of the couples and prepares a ranking according to availability and capacity. In the original text of Law no. 184/1983, physical and moral fitness was also mentioned, now included respectively in the ability to support and educate, and in the ability to bring up a child. Indeed, the concept of moral suitability was quite reductive, not quite capturing the dynamic aspect of today's parent-child relationship, which has nothing to do with subjecting the

foreclosure, under penalty of non-recognition by the social services of the suitability of the couple. Any orientation towards a certain religious faith or country will manifest themselves only when choosing the country in which to apply in the event of intercountry adoption but should not be taken into account when considering domestic adoption.

The next step is the hearing in which the Juvenile Court evaluates and decides which of the applicants appears the most suitable and carries out an interview. The last stage is pre-adoptive foster care, which lasts twelve months and serves to encourage mutual knowledge-building and the construction of the parent-child relationship that is defined at the official moment of adoption.

Currently, then, the adoption of minors is governed by Law no. 184/1983 and subsequent amendments. In the Civil Code, however, the adoption of adults has remained, an institution that replaced the earlier ordinary adoption, which was completed as a sort of 'family law contract' with the agreement between the adopter and the adopted. Jurisdiction on the adoption of adults falls to the court in whose neighbourhood the adopter resides, while with the adoption of minors, it belongs to the Juvenile Court.

Pre-adoptive custody takes place when the declaration of adaptability has become definitive and when the spouses have been identified who not only have the characteristics required by law, but who are considered the most suitable to meet the needs of the minor, in light of their specific characteristics, as ascertained by the social services.[270] This phase, however, takes shape only with the pre-adoptive placement order, with which the first personal relationship between adopters and adopted is established, also called "adoptive relationship" and the second phase of the adoption procedure begins, which ends with the issue of the adoption order.

Over the years, several questions as to constitutional legitimacy have been raised concerning the severing of ties with the child's natural parents as well as in relation to the child's acquiring the surname of the adoptive parents, but all have been rejected. However, numerous rulings attributed the right of the adopted child under full adoption to maintain a bond with his/her biological family. This was based either on the grounds that termination of relations with the family of origin meant legal relations or

---

minor to another's will. Cf. F. ERAMO, *Manuale pratico della nuova adozione. Commento alla legge 28 March 2001, no. 149*, Padua, Cedam, 2002.

[270] Cf. L. SAPORITO, *L'affidamento preadottivo*, in *Le adozioni nella nuova disciplina*, Milan, Giuffré, 2001, p. 243 *et seq.*

that communication of the placement of the minor in foster care would not impede full adoption.[271]

With Law no. 184/1983, the grounds were also laid for intercountry adoption. In the first place, the requirements that the aspiring adoptive parents must possess were listed. These are the same as those required by national adoption. The adoption procedure is divided into three phases: a preliminary judicial procedure with the Juvenile Court holding jurisdiction, which ends with the declaration of suitability; a second phase abroad before a foreign judicial or administrative authority, necessary for the child to gain entry into Italy, and the third, again jurisdictional, in Italy before the Juvenile Court, aimed at giving effect to the foreign provision, an indispensable prerequisite for any adoption regulated by Italian law.[272]

Law no. 479/1998 extensively reshaped the provisions of Law no. 184/1983 on these points following the ratification and implementation of the Hague Convention of 29 May 1993.[273] In adapting previous legislation on adoption, the law also introduced some new principles or, put differently, theorized axioms that had already been put forward elsewhere. First of all, it clarified the nature of adoption as an instrument of protection and promotion of the minor and his/her fundamental rights. Two important consequences follow from this assumption. The first is that only those children who are in such serious difficulty as to prevent them from growing up healthily should be adopted. Secondly, as well as possessing similar characteristics to biological parents, adopting parents should also have particular skills in dealing with the child's general upbringing and emotional wellbeing.

The second principle put Italian and foreign minors in a state of abandonment in Italy or abroad on the same footing, guaranteeing equal

---

[271] Cf. Juvenile Court of Rome, 5th July 1988, in *Dir. fam.*, 1990, p. 105; Juvenile Court of Rome, 16th Jan 1999, in *Dir. fam.*, 2000, p. 144; Juvenile Court of Bologna, 28th November 2002, in *Minori- giustizia*, I, 2003; Juvenile Court of Milan, 15th November 2004, in *Fam. e dir.*, 2005, p. 653 *et seq.*

[272] The declaration of effectiveness is subject to three conditions: l) that the declaration of suitability has been previously issued; 2) that the foreign provision complies with the legislation of the country of origin; 3) that the provision is not contrary to the fundamental principles that regulate the law of family and minors in the state. In addition, pre-adoptive foster care by the adopters of at least one year is required; if the foreign provision does not provide for pre-adoptive foster care or this has not been carried out, the provision is declared effective as pre-adoptive foster care.

[273] This law was further amended with Presidential Decree no. 492/1999, at http://www.commissioneadozioni.it/it/la-normativa/la-normativa-italiana/decreto-del-presidente-della-repubblica-l-dicembre-1999-n492.aspx.

protection of rights for all, regardless of their nationality or the state in which they reside. The application of this principle therefore considered the religious affiliation of children even more irrelevant. This is because in secularised legal systems, unlike the Islamic system, it is not automatically linked to birth in a specific geographical area but must be the result of a free choice of the minor, not coerced by family or adults or by society, but free to define him or herself with a choice relating to a fundamental right of human beings. Finally, the third principle is the definition of intercountry adoption as an instrument of international social cooperation between rich and poor countries. An attempt was also made to create a mechanism that would ensure – in compliance with the 1993 Hague Convention – automatic recognition of the foreign child's adoption or pre-adoptive foster care in the country of destination. This, however, would be problematic in the event of there being little or no correspondence between the legal institutions of the various countries, as in the case of kafala.

Law no. 183 also introduced special cases of adoption governed by Article 44 and subsequent amendments, which protect the relationship that is created when the minor is placed in a family with which s/he had previously developed emotional ties. The rationale of the discipline is to ensure that where it is not possible or suitable to have a full adoption, the child may be allowed to establish a solid family relationship guaranteeing healthy and balanced growth.

Adoption in special cases is thus a completely different discipline from full adoption, albeit in those limited cases where it is considered appropriate to disregard the subjective and objective characteristics of the aspiring parents and children so that the protection of the minor's best interests can actually be sought. The relationship created between the child and the adoptive parents does not replace but adds to what the child already has with the biological parents. These are cases in which the permanence of a stable and lasting relationship between the adopter/adopters and the adoptee must take precedence over any full adoption starting from scratch. Or there may be cases where the relationships between the natural parent of the minor and the adopted person invite the establishment of an adoptive relationship, or even cases where the minor is in a state of physical, mental or sensorial impairment, or where pre-adoptive care is impossible.

It is a tool with more limited effects because relations with the family of origin are not interrupted, nor is a relationship of kinship established with the adopters. Moreover, it has a very narrow field of application, characterised by much simpler operating procedures and procedural guarantees, which give the Juvenile Court greater discretion to make a practical evaluation of whether or not to resort to adoption.

The absence of a relationship of kinship with the adopting family would seem to be in contrast with the first article of Law no. 219 of 2012 – which modified Article 74 of the Civil Code – according to which a relationship of kinship between those who descend from the same ancestor also applies to adopted children, the only exception being the adoption of an adult – not special adoption. Cases where this type of adoption may be sought are strictly provided for by law and, apart from some exceptions, the adopted child will place the adopted parent's surname before his/her own.[274]

A fundamental prerequisite is that the natural parents of the child give their consent if they are able. Though this consent allows the child to be placed definitively within a new family, the child does not sever ties with his/her natural parents, whose rights and duties of in terms of upbringing and care must be coordinated with those of the adoptive parents, thus giving rise to a duel status. Cases might include: a person bound to the minor by virtue of relations up to the sixth grade, or by a stable and lasting relationship when the minor is an orphan who has lost both parents; a spouse, if the minor is the child (adopted or not) of the other spouse; minors who are in the circumstances indicated in Article 3 of Law no. 104 of 1992 and are orphans of both parents; and finally if pre-adoptive foster care is impossible to provide.[275] Law no. 184 also provides for adoption in special cases by a single parent, provided that there is a relationship with an orphaned child who has lost both parents or when the parent has been regularly looking after a child declared adoptable, or when no other couple is seeking to adopt the same child.

---

[274] The Constitutional Court, 11th May 2001, no. 120, at http://www.giurcost.org/decisioni/2001/0120s-01.html, decreed in favour of the adopted adult, child of unknown persons, the decision whether to adopt the surname of the adopter alone or also keep his/her own, attributed by the registrar: "In the case in question, not only did the interested party always use that surname, transmitting it also to their children, but this distinctive sign is rooted in the social context in which he finds himself living, so precluding the adopted person from keeping it means depriving the subject unfairly of an element of his personality, traditionally defined as the right 'to be oneself'". The court thus recognized that the surname is an instrument for identifying the person, a sign of personal identity.

[275] Law no. 104, 5th February 1992, framework law for the assistance, social integration and rights of handicapped persons, in *Gazzetta Ufficiale* n.39, 17th February 1992 - Suppl. Ordinario no. 30 and at http://www.gazzettaufficiale.it/eli/id/1992/02/17/092G0108/sg.

Ties with the family of origin, as mentioned, remain and in this type of adoption the adoptive parents do not acquire any rights over the property of the adopted child. The child, on the other hand, is equated to any legitimate children and will be in line like any other child to inherit the adopters' estate. Finally, it should be specified that unlike full adoption, special adoption may be revoked at the request of the adopter, the adopted child or his/her relatives and the public prosecutor if the adopted child or adopted parent are deemed unworthy or if the adoptive parent fails in his/her duties to the child. The last aspect that differentiates the two types of adoption, which embodies the essence of this peculiar discipline and which seems to attribute to it the characteristics of a permanent placement, is the possibility of revoking the adoption provision restoring the status *quo ante* – though this eventuality is conceivable only in certain strictly limited cases.[276]

The most vexing question that currently arises in the adoption field concerns the paradox between full adoption, which effectively cancels out the origins of the child, and the demands of multi-parenthood, which is ever increasing in more culturally advanced societies and appears to absorb some forms of traditional societies. The study of adoptive practices does help to clarify and structure the modern system of kinship as a whole. At times, the closed single couple typical of western societies may actually seem less considerate of the child's best interests compared with the greater flexibility offered by the extended family characterising more traditional societies. It is a broad and extensive issue given the multiplicity of actors and interests.

An evaluation of adoption at a jurisprudential level, widely used for the recognition of the Islamic kafala in Italy, should make it possible to re-develop the legal choices available in multicultural disputes in an attempt to identify legal solutions that do not affect the fundamental principles of a democratic legal system. This requires a continuous evolutionary process and a rethinking of these institutions – that cannot be simplistically anchored to decidedly anachronistic, traditional ways of life.

Article 1 of the 2001 law replaced the title of Law no. 184/1983 – "Discipline of the adoption and placement of minors" – with "Right of the child to a family".[277] Since the title change, the law took on a greater consideration towards the child, also providing robust guidelines on who

---

[276] Attempted murder, committing crimes one against the other and / or violation of duties incumbent on adopters pursuant to Articles 51-53.

[277] A. and M. FINOCCHIARO, *Adozione e affidamento dei minori: Commento alla nuova disciplina (L. 28 March 2001, n. 149 e D.L. 24 aprile 2001, n. 150)*, Milan, Giuffré, 2001.

should be heard. Adoption measures should thus respond to two fundamental needs: on the one hand, offering a family to the child who has none and provide a suitable and comfortable environment for the development of his/her personality; on the other, ensuring that the adopted child will inherit the name and the estate of the adoptive parent.[278]

In the name of the principle of equality, of the fundamental principle of dignity and the child's best interests, Italian legislation finally caught up with other EU states with the 2012 law to unify filiation status. This new approach determined the dismantling of theoretical constructions based on the marriage bond to give more importance to the emotional relationships and material contribution offered by the family nucleus or the new family membership in the event of adoption. A new role of the family has emerged – that of the extended family.[279] The use of the regulatory framework for adoption in special cases is particularly suited to the translation of the Islamic kafala in our system, facilitated by the similarity of legal instruments. The tools of an intercultural translation should, however, allow further evaluation to be made, aimed at identifying a new category of laws. Based on the existing judicial framework, fresh, new legal approaches should be sought that are more respectful of the requests for recognition of minority groups, but do not compromise our basic rights.

---

[278] Several changes were introduced: an increase in the age difference between the adopters and the minor from 40 to 45 years; transformation of the adoptability procedure: legislation rejected the traditional model (in chambers, adversarially posteponed process) opting for an adversarial approach between the parties; the obligation to appoint a lawyer to the minor and the parents in the judicial procedures for the declaration of adoptability and in those procedures that limit – or are suitable for establishing the lapse of – parental authority; the creation of a national (electronic) database set up at the Ministry of Justice to facilitate and encourage the matching of aspiring adopters to abandoned minors; the sufficiency of marriage only between the aspiring parents (previously, in addition to marriage, the cohabitation of at least three years was necessary, now instead cohabitation occurring before marriage will also be taken into consideration); a gradual closure of institutions and the placement of children with willing families or a family-type community; the introduction of the right of the minor (foreigners included) to obtain information about their origins.

[279] Article 315 *bis* of the Civil Code states that "the child has the right to grow up in the family and to maintain significant relationships with relatives". Article 74 of Law 219 clarifies that "kinship is the bond that unites people who descend from the same bloodline, regardless of whether filiation took place within marriage, outside marriage or through adoption".

6. The Protection of the Child in Secularized Families and Intercultural Law

Marriage relationships are full of intercultural connections and in this sense the use of the theoretical tools of intercultural translation represent the only hermeneutic way of reading modern transformations in which "tracing intercultural standards is equivalent to providing a grammar of personal freedom, through which individuals can articulate their irreducible individuality, make it visible, recognizable and recognized by the legal system beyond the walls of cultural diversity".[280] The evolution of legislative guidelines, combined with a different social and juridical conception of the family, have placed adoption in a relational sphere at some distance from the traditional-patrimonial one. No longer constructed as a remedy but as an instrument of social policy and no longer definable as simply "a very ancient practice common to many cultures, whose aim is the conservation-continuation of a family with its heritage of values, traditions and myths, and contains individual, family and socio-cultural dimensions".[281] It allows minors to have a family, the best place for the development of the individual, albeit from a solidarity perspective.

It is a type of welfare institution where public authorities play an essential role that is not simply formal but also practical, with an accurate assessment of the child's best interests. With an emphasis on welfare the relational dimension between adults and children within the family unit is renewed, where parenting is no longer tied to the simple biological factor in the context of a legitimate and legal bond. It is attitudes and behaviours that characterize the new nucleus, as it is currently understood, regardless of the formal aspects, whose centre of gravity is the child and his/her needs. This new perspective of the concept of filiation in the western juridical tradition is thus characterized by the diminishing importance of 'blood ties' and the emergence of the emotional relationship, of filiation experienced as a fundamental element for the recognition of the parent-child bond.[282]

---

[280] Cf. M. RICCA, *Pantheon. Agenda della laicità interculturale*, Palermo, Torri del vento, 2012, esp. p. 335 *et seq.*; S. DOMIANELLO, *Il pluralismo in materia religiosa nel settore matrimoniale*, in *Diritto e religione. Rapporto nazionale sulla salvaguardia della libertà religiosa in regime di pluralismo confessionale e culturale*, S. DOMIANELLO (ed.), Bologna, Il Mulino, 2012, pp. 113 - 138.

[281] Cf. R. LOMBARDI, G. VALVO, *Il percorso istituzionale dell'adozione: realtà e prospettive*, Rome, Seam, 1999, esp. p. 7.

[282] In France and Belgium, following recent reforms, they have taken the direction of new functions served by the idea of one's own status. Cf. M. REMOND -

With the current evolution of the concepts of multi-parenthood, the adoption question arises in new terms. Some countries have developed a concept of open adoption,[283] which allows communication between blood relatives and adoptive relatives, unknown in our legal tradition.[284] In our legislative system, in fact, there are only two types of adoption, which have taken on different names from time to time: *adoptio plena*, as opposed *to adoptio minus quam plena*; special adoption as opposed to ordinary adoption and, finally, full adoption as opposed to non-legitimising or special adoption. At the international level, we speak of full adoption as opposed to simple adoption. The first attributes the fullness of the status of son or daughter to the adopted child, completely equal to that of biological filiation. The second, by contrast, may be revoked and gives rise to a weaker relationship of filiation, much less complete than full adoption. In short, this is a precarious adoption.

As a first approximation, by open adoption we mean that the adopted child maintains relations and relationships with significant members of his/her original family in various ways and measures. The term originated in the US, where it has been the subject of lengthy debates and concrete experience. Making a distinction between legal relationships and interpersonal relationships, Italian jurisprudence has also, at times, and in the child's best interests, admitted the possibility of contact between the adopted child and his/her previous family, albeit with certain precautions and after ascertaining the willingness and cooperation of the adoptive family. There is thus no contradiction in terms between open and full, legitimising adoption. On authorising the adoption, the judge may also decide to allow certain interpersonal relationships between the adopted child and significant members of his/her previous family to be maintained.

There is no real definition of an open adoption and it is up to individual state legislation to identify the exact characteristics and level of relationship

---

GOUILLOD, *La possesion d 'état d'enfant (A propos de la loi du 3 jan. 1972),* in *Rev. Trim. dir.civ.*, 1975, p. 459 *et seq.*; C. MECARY, *Réflexions sur le destinées de la possession d'état d'enfant*, in AA.VV., *Mélanges à la mémoire de D. Huet-Weiller. Droit des personnes et famille*, Strasbourg, 1994, p. 319 *et seq.*; N. GALLUS, *Le droit de la filiation. Role de la verité socio-affective et de la volonté en droit belge*, Brussels, Bruylant, 2009.

[283] USA, Canada, Germany partially. Cf. A. FINE, NEIRINCK, *Parents de sang, parents adoptifs: approches juridiqu es et anthropologiques de l'adoption: France, Europe, USA, Canada*, Paris, LGDJ, 2000.

[284] Cf. W. L. PIERCE, *Open Adoption*, in *Adoption Factbook*, C. MARSHNER - W. L. PIERCE (eds.), III, pp. 233 - 238, National Council for Adoption, Washington, DC, 1999; also www.openadoption.org.

that the child may maintain with his/her family of origin. This form of adoption is normally implemented by means of a verbal/informal agreement or written/post adoption contract agreement through which the limits of the relationships between the child and the biological family are defined. The agreement thus concluded will be subsequently examined by the court, which is responsible for verifying whether or not this agreement pursues the best interests of the child.

In Italy there has been much talk over 'soft' or open adoption, that is, a particular type of adoption to resort to if the child is in a situation of 'permanent semi-abandonment'. This might be in those cases where, despite the biological family being unable and/or unwilling to properly provide for the growth and upbringing of the child, it does play an active and positive role for the child, and so it would be inappropriate to sever family ties permanently. In this legal form "the rights of the child are not inferred indirectly from the corresponding duties of the parents, but are stated positively and explicitly … ; what should be emphasised is the child's right to be raised and nurtured in his/her own family and to maintain significant relationships with relatives, which reinforces the meaning of the protection of the minor in the natural need to avoid resorting to an adoption that severs and replaces the original family ties".[285]

Thus defined, the use of open adoption would seem to be the solution to the problem of implementing kafala, though close analysis of its effects does raise some doubts. First of all, it is always worth remembering that the rationale behind kafala binding it to a specific religious orientation is profoundly different. Attempts to compare or assimilate kafala with Italian adoption endeavour to identify practical similarities, leaving aside the fundamental sub-theme that involves the rights of freedom of the members of the family unit with significant repercussions on the interests of the child. In terms of practical feasibility, the first hurdle is the extensive exegesis of Article 44, paragraph l, letter d), Law no. 184/1983: admitting an adoption when placement is legally impossible is equivalent to distorting the residual nature of the article, whose scope of application has historically been considered as marginal. Furthermore, this interpretation does allow the judge excessive discretion in the decision of individual cases. A second critique put forward by the doctrine is of conceptual origin. The term 'permanent semi-abandonment' is actually a contradiction in terms, since it is difficult to see how a minor can be abandoned only in

[285] Cf. T. MONTECCHIARI, *Adozione "mite", una diversa forma di adozione dei minori od un affido senza termine?* in *Dir. fam. pers.*, 2013, p. 1581 *et seq*. esp. on the formulation of Article 315 *bis* of the Civil Code.

part: abandonment implies the cessation of a pre-existing legal situation between two subjects, this means that if a relationship still exists between the child and the parents, albeit weak, the child cannot qualify as 'abandoned'.

In particular, it should be emphasized that an institution of a religious matrix does not always regard abandonment because, as with consensual kafala, it may come about as the result of the free choice of parents who, in compliance with a religious command, decide to entrust their offspring to another. Thirdly, it would seem that this institution was also intended for those minors who have not previously been declared adoptable, while pre-adoptive foster placement may only be ordered by the Juvenile Court if minors have been declared adoptable. In actual fact, allowing more children to be admitted to pre-adoptive foster care would penalize those children who find themselves completely without assistance, but would prove fertile ground for the violation of the obligations towards minors as well.

Jurisprudence has also highlighted a weak point in the application of open adoption: maintaining ties with the biological family risks jeopardizing the child's own interest, since s/he might face the possibility of being raised in two different ways and coming up against two different cultural/religious codes (the adoptive family on one side and the biological family on the other). The last noticeable exception is inherent in the legal qualification of kafala which, given the prohibition set by the Quran, could not qualify as an adoption, especially legitimising adoption.

The regulatory reference could be represented by Article 21 of the UN Convention on the Rights of the Child, which establishes that "States Parties that recognize and/or permit the system of adoption shall ensure that the best interests of the child shall be the paramount consideration", and Article 4 of the Hague Convention reaffirmed this principle by extending its scope to intercountry adoption.[286]

[286] Advocates of open adoption say that for a child with family difficulties there are three different paths in the current system: family support; foster care; adoptability and adoption, which, however, would have the serious limitation of completely neglecting and leaving the so-called grey areas unresolved. Cf. Bill 1007/Senate proposed by Sen. Burani Procaccini, 20th September 2006, presented at the XV legislature to partially modify Law no. 184/1983:
http://www.senato.it/japp/bgt/showdoc/frame.jsp?tipodoc=Ddlpres&leg=15&id=00221948&part=doc_dc-articolato_ddl&parse=no. At the basis of this legislative proposal is the concept of semi-abandonment: by which, in practice, adoption is used in particular cases for minors who are not declared adoptable. This has sometimes been implemented at jurisprudential level starting from semi-

Furthermore, a new form of social parenting emerges at the European and wider international level, alongside and in some ways equivalent to the traditional biological family, which characterizes the typical family structure.[287] The attribution of a meta-legal value to the social family, i.e. the family whose members provide care and moral/material guidance, regardless of any biological or legal ties, may in some ways be likened to solutions adopted by some legal systems for the so-called significant third party – partner of the cohabiting parent – who takes on a legal relevance in the relationship with the offspring. These new forms of non-biological relationships could allow for the acceptance of kafala within our legal systems, building more open and inclusive forms while overlooking its substantive aspect – which compromises the right to religious freedom.

In secularized structures, new family relationships are being increasingly tried out. In this sense what is particularly interesting is an innovative legal figure introduced in France in 2002 and modified in 2010, built around the interests of the minor and which allows shared parental responsibility, through a simplified procedure of the classic parental delegation. With Article 377 of the French Civil Code, French law allows parents, where circumstances require, to delegate all or a part of their authority to a third person, member of the family or trustworthy relative subject to the Juvenile Court's opinion.[288]

---

abandonment: that is, from family groups which, though constituting a reference point for the child, are 'insufficient and inadequate'. Proposal 1007 on open adoption strengthens the concepts of foster care (as present and regulated by current laws) prefiguring an alternative family in support of the family of origin in difficult circumstances. An adoption that "should have all the characteristics of a legitimate adoption, with the exception of maintaining relationships with the family of origin", to use the description of the senator herself, whose outcome as far as the underlying legal institutions are concerned remain unclear.

[287] Cf. F. UCCELLA, *Dalla 'famiglia pluriematica' alla 'famiglia putativa' come soggetto giuridico: prime considerazioni*, in *Familia*, 2005, p. 447 *et seq*., alluding to the loss of importance of the bond of consanguinity. Going beyond the concept of kinship, M.G. STANZIONE, *Filiazione e "genitorialità". Il problema del terzo genitore*, Turin, Giappichelli, 2010, esp. p. 109 *et seq*.

[288] Law no. 769, 9th July 2010 and previously Law no. 305, 4th March 2002. Cf. M.G. STANZIONE, *Rapporti di filiazione e "terzo genitore": le esperienze francese e italiana*, in *Fam.Dir*., 2012, p. 204 *et seq*. which refers to the jurisprudence on the subject, underlining in particular the intervention of the Cour d'appel, Paris, June 16th 2011 where the need for involvement of the third partner with the mother was affirmed through a common parental project that could legally ensure the necessary emotional stability to the minor as realized in practice; also D'ANGELO, *La famiglia nel XX secolo: il fenomeno delle famiglie ricomposte*, in *Riv.dir.civ*.,

This *délegation-partage* does not limit the faculties or duties of the delegating parent but distributes authority between the parties. It aims at sharing care and support through a reorganization of family ties sanctioned by the intervention of the judging body, with the creation of an inclusive group of figures who play different parental roles. In our country, taking on parental responsibility according to new regulatory procedures has only led to the presentation of draft laws.[289]

Comparing experience home and abroad, however, some similar lines may be identified – three approaches to regulation. A first approach might be defined as voluntaristic and leans towards the formalisation of the role of the third parent on condition that the biological parent is excluded and is substantially 'non-interventionist'.[290] A second approach is based on substitution and means replacing one of the two parental figures, where the biological parent is missing to recreate the family nucleus. Finally, an inclusive approach would result from the support of parental figures

---

2011, p. 31 *et seq.*; M. SESTA, *Verso nuove trasformazioni del diritto di famiglia italiano?*, in *Familia*, 2003, p. 158 *et seq.* which examines the possibilities provided by Article 44 paragraph 1, letter b) of Law no. 184/1983 regarding adoption; A. CORDIANO, *Funzioni e ruoli genitoriali nelle famiglie allargate e ricomposte: una comparazione fra modelli normativi e alcune riflessioni evolutive*, at www.comparazionedirittoivile.it. Cf. also G. BILÒ, *I problemi della famiglia ricostruita e le soluzioni dell'ordinamento inglese*, in *Familia*, 2004, which outlines the so-called family rebuilt as a family "consisting of spouses or cohabitants and children of only one of the two partners who share the same home. Since there are no suitable terms in the Italian language to identify the members of these family models ... we also frequently resort to English terminology which defines it as stepfamily, with stepparent being the companion of the foster parent and stepchild the child" (p. 831).

289 Two bills were presented but not debated: delegating parental responsibility proposed by Sen. Manconi and taking on parental responsibility proposed by Sen. Lo Giudice to be included in Article 290 *bis* and 290 *quater* of the Civil Code.

290 Cf. P. SAITTA, *La genitorialità "sociale" e la sua regolazione. Una rassegna europea*, in *Quaderni della Sezione Diritto e Comunicazioni Sociali*, 2006, p. 19 *et seq.*, and at http://www.cirsdig.it/Pubblicazioni/lsaittastepparents.pdf. The 'voluntaristic' model is non-coercive in its approach and thus divorced from legal regulation, between offspring and third parent, promoting the emotional relationship and, possibly, voluntary adoption. Conversely, the 'neo-family' approach, heavily critical of families where one of the parents is absent, as opposed to the traditional family, is a substantially non-interventionist model, which, from the jurist's perspective, turns out to be similar to the 'voluntaristic' model.

through the legal recognition of the care and support provided by the third parent.[291]

The first approach regulating the figure of the third parent and implicitly excluding the biological parent, is characterized by being (almost) always an abstentionist and non-interventionist model, which eschews ad hoc tools recognising the figure and function of the third parent, turning, instead, to the expedient of voluntary adoption. The abstentionist model of our legal system emerges from adoption in special cases. It should be noted, however, that despite the profound diversity of the systems proposed, those countries that have opted for the recognition of the social parental figure also tend to encourage a new, participatory family grounded in emotional ties and relationships.

Widely secularized democratic approaches, then, tend to experiment with new types of family relationships, since they have definitively disengaged the family model from the traditional religious-derived family structure embedded in ancient law. The Islamic religious model, which claims its own space and recognition in the Italian context too, thus risks destabilizing our democratic structures. If, as verified, a formal comparison is possible, and represents the path taken by jurisprudence in the desire to guarantee the rights of minors, it is the substantial profile that highlights the absolute incomparability of these codes of values.

The rights and duties that arise for parents protecting the interests of their children are subject to a legal discipline linked to different sources with regard to the various areas of relevance both at national and international private and procedural level.[292] It is difficult to highlight which institutions are attributable to parent-child relationships and which are simply protection measures for minors since the border between them is extremely blurred. In these dynamics the problem of the religious identity of the entire family comes to the fore, considered in its entirety

---

[291] Cf. A. D'ANGELO, *La famiglia nel XX secolo: il fenomeno delle famiglie ricomposte*, in *La famiglia e il diritto tra diversità nazionali ed iniziative dell'Unione Europea*, in D. AMRAM, A. D'ANGELO (eds.), Padua, Cedam, 2011, pp. 13 - 47, esp., p. 24. For an overview of different legislative approaches, M. SESTA, *Manuale di diritto di famiglia*, Padua, Cedam, 2007, esp. p. 179 *et seq*.

[292] Parental authority is governed by Council Regulation (EC) no. 1347/2000 of 29th May 2000 and Article 36 of Law no. 218 of 1995, parental responsibility by Council Regulation (EC) No 2201/2003 of 27th November 2003 and the 1996 Hague Convention. Child protection is provided for in Hague Conventions 1961 and 1996 and by Article 42 of Law no. 218 of 1995. Cf. M. DOGLIOTTI, *La potestà dei genitori e l'autonomia del minore*, cit.

because it is not possible to break down the individual rights of each subject, especially with regard to children.

The fragmentation of the classic family structure, no longer seen as an intangible principle, derives from the observation of a multiplicity of family types in secular society.[293] In this sense, it is worth reflecting on new mechanisms that may support and guarantee the modern family, with a view to encouraging a family law that does not overlook emotional ties, social bonds and solidarity.[294] Endorsing the emotional relationship, not the act that constitutes it, represents a favourable option that for some time now serious doctrine has emphasised.[295] However, respect for our democratic structures should impose the transformation of this institution into legitimising adoption as it applies to all cases in our legal system, regardless of the religious faith or nationality of the subjects. This should come about, above all, by evaluating the interests of the minor living within his/her own family, but still guaranteeing all the rights that our legal system recognises to children placed in a family context, regardless of whether filiation is legitimate or adoptive and regardless of the religious options of the parents.

---

293 D. MESSINETTI, *Diritti della famiglia e identità della persona*, in *Riv. dir. civ.*, 2005, p. 137.

294 Indicative in this sense the collection of writings by C.M. BIANCA, M. MALAGOLI TOGLIATTI and A.L. MICCI, *Interventi di sostegno alla genitorialità nelle famiglie ricomposte*, Milan, F. Angeli, 2005; C. VAN CUTSEM, *Le famiglie ricomposte. Presa in carico e consulenza*, Milan, Cortina Raffaello, 1999. On social and cultural change and new family types see *Introduzione*, in *Trattato diritto di famiglia*, edited by P. ZATTI, vol. I, *Famiglia e matrimonio²*, edited by G. FERRANDO, M. FORTINO, F. RUSCELLO, Milan, Giuffré, 2011, esp. p. 25 *et seq*. and vol. II, *Filiazione²*, edited by G. COLLURA, L. LENTI, M. MANTOVANI, 2012; as well as S. ALAGNA, *Famiglia e rapporti tra coniugi nel nuovo diritto*, Milan, Giuffré, 1983; L. MENGONI, *La famiglia in una società complessa*, in *Iustitia*, 1990, p. 4 *et seq*.

295 N. LIPARI, *Riflessioni sul matrimonio a trent'anni dalla riforma del diritto di famiglia*, in *Riv. trim. dir. proc. civ.*, 2005, p. 715 *et seq*.

CHAPTER FOUR

CHILD PROTECTION IN RELIGIOUSLY ORIENTED AND SECULARIZED CONTEXTS: EUROPEAN AND ITALIAN JURISPRUDENCE FROM A COMPARATIVE PERSPECTIVE

1. Introductory Considerations. European Courts and the Recognition of Kafala in Secularized Contexts

The semantics of kafala relies on the understanding of a fundamental sub-theme: it constitutes the transfer of a child who is inextricably linked to his/her own origins in terms of nationality, culture, family and therefore also religion and identity – a bond which may not wish to be severed.[296] Being Muslim is an indispensable precondition for access to kafala care. In many countries Islam is a state religion and religious identity is part not only of the structure of the nation, but of the cultural identity of the individual. In this socio-religious context, the abandoned child should then be placed within a family of his/her own religion. It is generally assumed that though orphaned or of unknown parents, the child is still of Islamic faith. Future adoptive parents are therefore required to be Muslim, though in some cases, as in Morocco, prospective parents may be allowed to convert to join the *Umma*/community of believers. The registrar in these countries attributes the name of father and mother as well as a name and patronymic of the Arab-Muslim tradition to the orphaned child, which immediately frames the child's belonging to a nation, a land, a culture and a religious community.

Kafala must thus always be understood as an instrument of a transition, of the transmission and continuity of an identity, a culture and a religion. When a child in kafala care enters into the west, this effectively produces a

---

[296] M. C. LE BOURSICOT, *La kafâla ou recueil lègal des mineurs en droit musulman: une adoption sans filiation*, in *Droit et Culture*, no. 59, 2010, p. 297 *et seq*.

split between two official identities. The legal conflict seems to revolve around the difference between a concrete definition of the concept of the *child's best interests*, based on the real existence of a child-parent relationship, and a more abstract/formal concept according to which protecting this interest should involve rigorous compliance with the national law of the child's country of origin so as not to deprive the child of his/her origins and identity. It is on this legal dualism that the principle issue of validating the institution of kafala between different legal systems unfolds. Greater attention to the best interests of the minor should force a change in the law, such as to allow the transformation of the institution of kafala in most cases in order to provide the child with parents, naturally using the legal framework that is most favourable to the child in the new country. However, it should be noted that even the automatic translation of kafala into adoption would, in the absence of specific regulation, lead to an undoubtedly anomalous situation. In violation of Islamic legislation, the minor would lose his/her membership of the *Umma* and would undergo a change in surname as well as citizenship to become a legitimate child of a 'western' couple. This situation, however, could never be recognized as valid in the Islamic country of origin because it is contrary to public order. Legal uncertainty would arise as both states would consider the minor as their own. Supposing the natural parents of the minor claimed the repatriation of their child, the 'western' judicial authorities would have to refuse as it would be in contrast with the new status of the minor as a legitimate child, according to the parameters of 'western' legislation. Upon returning to his/her homeland, the minor may lose the rights acquired in his/her new country.

It should be stressed, however, that this theoretical approach is based on an assumption – yet to be verified – that a child born in a specific country is part of that country's cultural and religious community as well. In light of the conceptual development of the principle of religious freedom, this too should be evaluated because it does not fully protect one of the fundamental individual rights, that of the freedom of conscience. It is also necessary to distinguish the legal position of orphans who have lost both their parents from children whose own parents place them in kafala care – similar to our own foster care – since, as already happens in other European countries, it would then be possible to convert the measure into adoption.

The failure to assimilate the effects of kafala to those of legitimizing or full adoption means, on the one hand, that the prohibition set in place by the Quran is respected, but on the other it can also entail negative consequences for the child (in terms of inheritance, for instance), and thus go against the child's best interests.[297] Following this legal direction would thus introduce a serious form of discrimination since it would allow cross-cultural adoption for some and not others, without them being informed or having the power to decide, but only on the basis of what is presumed to be their own personal law that applies to them.

It should also be remembered that the goal of adoption is to place a child into a family and to subject the child, *inter alia*, as a minor, to the same legislation as the parents. Adopting this perspective, excessively protective of the domestic jurisdiction of individual states, and anxious to avoid international deadlock, would inevitably produce a generation of 'invisible' individuals – without protection or legal recognition of their status, (particularly serious in the case of children). It may also lead to dangerous forms of discrimination based on the culture of origin of the child who, as a minor, cannot independently defend his/her rights and freedoms.

These observations are compounded by the fear – often underlying this type of operation – that immigration or adoption regulations may be circumvented.[298] Any interpretation that excludes kafala from the right to family reunification should be considered illegitimate and, moreover, "would penalize (against the principle of equality as well) all minors from Arab countries, whether they be illegitimate, orphaned or in a state of

---

[297] Of particular interest here the observations by the Court of Cassation 4th November 2005, no. 21395 in *Guida al dir.*, 2005, *fasc.* 45, 28, according to which "kafala ... aims to task the parents with whom the child is placed with the upbringing of the child, easily comparable to our own foster care from a juridical-formal point of view, but does not transfer protection as well, since that would go against the principle, which is particularly dear to that legislation, that the child's bond to his/her own origins must never be lost". The interest in respecting the prohibition posed by the Quran does not stem, however, exclusively from multicultural issues, but also from the opportunity to maintain good diplomatic relations with foreign states.

[298] Cf. R. GELLI, *Kafalah di diritto islamico ed altri atti stranieri di dismissione della potestà genitoriale: il giudizio di equiparazione ai fini del ricongiungimento familiare*, in *Fam. Dir.*, 2012, p. 472 *et seq*. The author analyses the decision of the Italian Court of Cassation, which, unlike previous rulings, re-dimensioned the abstract scope of the principles affirmed in previous cases that had authorized the family reunification of the foreign minor in kafala care. The court, in fact, limited the scope to minors who came from legal systems where adoption was not envisaged. As regards Italy see also A. LANG, *Le Sezioni Unite chiariscono quando la Kafalah è presupposto per il ricongiungimento familiare del cittadino italiano*, in *Dir. imm. Citt.*, 2013, pp. 91-99.

abandonment, for whom kafala is ... the only institution of protection provided for by Islamic legal systems".[299]

In the delicate balance between the right to family life and the right to family reunification, any form of limitation or denial of the latter is bound to limit the former. It is therefore necessary that the different meaning that it is intended to protect can justify – in terms of axiological identity of the system – the choice to limit or sacrifice in full the exercise of this right.[300] The semantic field of the right to family reunification is closely linked to the meaning of family and family members.[301] In Italy, the Consolidated Immigration Act of 1998 clarified that "for the purpose of reunification ... adopted, fostered or protected minors are treated as legitimate children" (Article 29), highlighting the centrality of the effective parent-child relationship, beyond any possible legal qualification, in order to give concreteness to the minor's right to family unity.

The latter clearly represents one of the primary rights of the individual and reunification can be ascribed to the set of legal guarantees in place to protect the family, understood as the natural and fundamental core of society. It is the means by which family unity is achieved and allows those who regularly reside/stay in one country to be joined by family members

---

[299] On family reunification and the right to family unity, held as fundamental rights of the individual and thus applicable to foreign nationals, cf. Constitutional Court, 12th Jan. 1995, no. 28, in *Foro it.*, 1995, I, 2068.

[300] Cf. 'Whereas' n. 10 of Directive 2003/86, which states that "[i]t is for the Member States to decide whether they wish to authorise family reunification for relatives in the direct ascending line, adult unmarried children, unmarried or registered partners as well as, in the event of a polygamous marriage, minor children of a further spouse" adding that authorisation "is without prejudice of the possibility, for Member States which do not recognise the existence of family ties in the cases covered by this provision, of not granting to the said persons the treatment of family members with regard to the right to reside in another Member State, as defined by the relevant EC legislation".

[301] In accordance with Article 29 of Legislative Decree 286/1998, which includes: a) the spouse not legally separated and under the age of eighteen; b) minors, including those of the spouse or born out of wedlock, unmarried, provided that the other parent, if present, has given consent; c) dependent children over 18 years of age, if for objective reasons they cannot provide for their indispensable life needs due to their state of health which entails total disability; d) dependent parents, if they do not have other children in the country of origin, or parents over sixty-five years of age, if the other children are unable to support them due to serious health reasons. This clearly alludes to the family nucleus made up of spouses, parents and children, despite paragraph 2 of Article 29, Legislative Decree 286/1998, which equates adopted minors as well as minors 'fostered or under guardianship' to actual children.

from other countries. Its legal recognition detracts from the traditional principle according to which, among the sovereign prerogatives of states, is the regulation of entry and residence of foreigners within its borders. In its functional sphere, it also appears to be an important indicator of the qualitative leap in immigration policy, from containment to integration. To this should be added the consideration that it arose as a "strong" right and becomes even stronger since it connects with highly protected subjects, such as the minor, who enjoy special guarantees in international law.

It is governed by European Community Directive 86/2003, which accepts a very narrow notion of the 'nuclear' family, limited to the spouse of the resident and to unmarried minors, which countries may choose to extend to other subjects. The directive also provides that states may revoke or refuse to renew their residence permit for reasons of public order or security, leaving a wide margin of discretion to the sensitivity of the judging bodies.

In case-law, a distinction has been made between whether the person requesting reunification is an EU or non-EU national. In the first case, the judges came to recognize the right to reunification, observing that between protecting borders and protecting the minor, the latter must come first. Others reached different conclusions as regards family reunification with a non-EU child entrusted to Italian subjects under a kafala arrangement.[302] In particular, it is a question of clarifying whether the principles that underpin national family law can be invoked to define the semantic field of the right to family reunification, and therefore its scope of application, preventing the entry of meanings properly belonging to other legal systems. and contrasting with those same principles.

The issue of possible circumvention appears to be central to the non-recognition of family reunification on the assumption that it goes against public order.[303] In this sense, it would certainly be legitimate to reject any entry request on behalf of a child in kafala care to hinder the spread of

[302] In this case the applicable law is Legislative Decree 30/2007, which includes neither the child in kafala care nor, with reference to domestic law, children under foster care.

[303] Law no. 184 of 1983 sanctions the only procedure for placing a foreign child within an Italian family. This conclusion is supported by the different normative data referred to in the Consolidated Immigration Act, which governs the right to family reunification of the foreign national, and Legislative Decree 30/2007, concerning the European citizen. In the first case, the law refers to reunification with 'reunifiable family members', expressly including minors placed within the family. In the second case, it concerns descendants, with the exclusion therefore of fostered children.

semi-adoptive practices that are contrary to the child's best interests. The use of immigration legislation could also lead to the coexistence of two different measures within the same legal system such as to allow entry to foreign minors in kafala care by virtue of the application of the legislation on family reunification in immigration contexts, and not to allow the use of the same legal instrument for 'western' citizens who wish to take a child into kafala care and take him/her to their own country.[304]

It has been argued that the different treatment afforded to 'Western' citizens might be determined by the difference in underlying circumstances. Indeed, for the Islamic foreign national, whose laws prohibit adoption, the only recognizable provision would be kafala, whereas the 'westerner' can turn to an express regulation – international adoption. There are several objections to this approach: the difference in treatment between a 'western' citizen and a 'non-western' national would result in unjustified discrimination based on nationality, since a 'western' citizen, of Muslim faith, would be forced to violate the Quran's prohibition of adoption (with violation of religious freedom) to be able to take care of a minor in a state of total abandonment.[305] Any measure which *effectively* takes into account the religious faith of those applying for the entry of a child in kafala care should differentiate on the basis of their faith and not on their citizenship.

The kafala issue recently came up before the European Court of Human Rights and led to two rulings, in 2012 and 2014. The first case, Harroudj v. France, was based on the appeal of a woman who had taken an Algerian girl into her legal care under the kafala procedure and now

---

[304] Cf. A. VENCHIARUTTI, *No al ricongiungimento familiare del minore affidatario con kafalah: i richiedenti sono cittadini italiani*, in *Dir. fam. pers.*, 4, 2010), p. 1629 *et seq*. Italian doctrine feels that the inclusion of the kafala in the child protection system can be interpreted as proof of compatibility with international public order. Cf. P. MAROZZO DELLA ROCCA, *Cittadino italiano e minore straniero ricevuto in kafalah: una decisione non condivisibile dalla Cassazione*, in *Corr. Giur.*, 2012, p. 3 *et seq*.

[305] The doctrine stated that the jurisprudence of the Court of Cassation would end up endorsing discrimination based on religion and ethnic origin: cf. Y. ROCCHINI, *La kafala marocchina alla prova dell'ordinamento giuridico italiano*, in *Dir. imm. e citt.*, 2, 2011, p. 80 *et seq*.; in jurisprudence the theory of the illegitimacy of discrimination resulting from the application of the citizenship criterion is supported by the Court of Tivoli, 22nd June 2010, in *Quad. dir. e politica ecclesiastica*, 2011, p.805 *et seq.*, which ordered the issue of an entry visa for a child "in order to avoid an unjustified difference in treatment between Italian citizens and non-EU citizens in violation of Article 3 of the Constitution and Article 2 of the Constitution in reference to the child's right to support, care and conservation of emotional bonds within the family".

wished to fully adopt her so that the girl could remain in France and enjoy inheritance rights.[306] In the second, a Moroccan couple wished to adopt their granddaughter after taking her into legal care under kafala with the consent of her parents.[307]

In both cases the Court recalled that Article 8 of the European Convention protects private and family life,[308] but does not recognize a right to adopt.[309] It noted that in this matter the State enjoys a certain

---

[306] European Court of Human Rights, 4th October 2012, *Harroudj v. France*, application no. 43631/09, at hudoc.echr.coe.int/webservices/content/pdf/001-113818?TID; A. DI PASCALE, *La kafala al vaglio della Corte Europea dei diritti dell'uomo: tra tutela dell'interesse del minore e preoccupazioni di ordine pubblico*, in *Dir., imm. citt.*, XIV, vol. 4, 2010, p. 115 *et seq.*; J. LONG, *Corte Europea dei diritti dell'uomo e kafalah: un'esortazione alla flessibilità del diritto civile minorile, sentenza della Corte europea dei diritti dell'uomo 4 ottobre 2012, caso Harroudj c. Francia*, in *Minori e giustizia*, l, 2013, pp. 304-313; *Rapporti tra diritto francese e diritto islamico*, in *Osservatorio della Corte europea dei diritti dell'uomo*, M. PACINI (ed.), in *Giorn. dir. amm.*, l, 2013, p. 67 *et seq.*

[307] European Court of Human Rights, 16th December 2014, *Chbihi Loudoudi and Others v. Belgium*, Second Section, application no. 52265/10, at hudoc.echr.coe.int/app/conversion/docx/pdf?library.

[308] Article 8 of the ECHR imposes on States the negative obligation of non-interference in the [private and] family sphere of individuals, but also the positive duty of adopting measures inherent to respect for family life. Therefore, where there is a family bond, the state must act in order to allow that bond to develop. The concept of 'positive obligation' allowed the Court to broaden the scope of the rights guaranteed by the Convention by requiring, on the one hand, that contracting States also adopt positive measures – providing individuals with the rights and privileges necessary to guarantee the protection of rights enshrined in the Convention – and, on the other, placing an obligation on States to protect the private and family sphere of people from aggression carried out also by private individuals. Since Article 8 of the Convention does not establish an absolute right, regardless of whether the state is under a negative or positive obligation, it is up to the Court to decide to what extent state authorities have correctly balanced the competing interests of the applicant and the community.

[309] "although the right to adopt is not one of the rights specifically guaranteed under the Convention, the relations between an adoptive parent and an adopted child are as a rule the same family relations protected by Article 8 of the Convention".: ECHR, *X. v. France*, 5th October 1982, no. 9993/82, Decision 31, p. 243; (Application X against Belgium, no. 6482/74, 10th July 1975, Decision 7, p. 75. In a more recent case, *E.B. v. France* ([GC], no. 43546/02, ECHR 2008), the Grand Chamber reiterated that Article 8 does not guarantee the right to found a family or to adopt. According to the Court, the right to respect for family life does not protect the simple desire to found a family but presupposes its existence or at

margin of appreciation and thus concluded, in the first case, that the French law of 2001 (which denies the possibility of transforming kafala into adoption) did not contravene the Convention. The point of reference, Article 8, would seem to guarantee exclusively the right to live within one's family understood as a traditional union founded on marriage, sheltered from any interference by the state.

However, in interpreting the notion of family life, at times also applying article 14 – the principle of non-discrimination in the enjoyment of the rights enshrined in the Convention – the Court guarantees protection of a broader family model than the 'traditional' family. The notion of family life is, in fact, an autonomous concept and the Court examines the constraints that *de facto* bind the various interested parties.[310] It also stresses the possibility recognized by French national law of ensuring that the minor may inherit through suitable testamentary clauses and to circumvent the prohibition of adoption by obtaining citizenship for the child of the State in which s/he lives, thus, at that point, clearing the way for the possibility of adoption.

Through similar measures, according to the Court, France established a progressive mechanism for the integration of the foreign minor, avoiding the total severance of ties with the child's homeland and respecting cultural pluralism, seeking just the right balance between all public and private interests. Furthermore, according to the Court, preventing the full adoption of minors in kafala care, or even the assimilation of the legal effects of kafala to those of legitimizing adoption is not, in itself, contrary to the Convention. What will be necessary though is to verify in practice what other tools are available to look after the child's best interests. It should also be noted that the child's best interests are likely to be in held in a delicate balance with the other interests underlying the issue, including public interests, such as regulating the acquisition of child status (including adopted children).

In the French case, the European courts preferred not to mention the notion of the 'child's interest', opting instead to justify their decision in

---

least the fact that a potential relationship could have developed, or the bond arising out of a legal adoption.

310 Cf. ECHR, *Abdulaziz, Cabales and Balkandali v. The United Kingdom*, 28th May 1985, paragraph 62, Series A, no. 94; *Beldjoudi v. France*, 26th March 1992, Series A, no. 234 A; *Berrehab v. The Netherlands,* 21st June 1988, § 21, Series A, no. 138 (inclusion of legitimate children); *Keegan v. Ireland*, 26th May 1994, (inclusion of natural children); *X, Y and Z v. The United Kingdom*, 22nd April 1997, in *Reports of judgments and decisions 1997* (children conceived through artificial insemination).

the name of 'cultural pluralism'. They therefore considered that France did not intend in any way to exclude the existence of a family life between the applicant and the minor entrusted to her in kafala care – an undeniable reality – but excluded the possibility that French law could consider adoption as interference. At the same time, the French state does not deny the possibility of acquiring citizenship in a rather short period of just five years, nor the acquisition of inheritance rights through a regular will and testament or the appointment of a guardian in the event of the death of the parent. This desire not to put Muslim culture in opposition with Western culture can be expressed in the formula "*une tolérance au nom de indifférence*".[311]

In the second case, the European Court chose to follow a similar reasoning, albeit with different outcomes, and stressed that although Belgian law does not recognize the Islamic institution of kafala, it does allow the transfer of a minor from a country that does not allow adoption towards Belgium. In this case, the Court developed an erroneous analysis of the concept of the child's best interests, "allowing a particular conception of international adoption policy to prevail over the concrete interest of the child".[312]

While some authors argue that the notion of the 'child's best interests' in the context of kafala should be interpreted *in abstracto*, and especially in the case of family reunification, this interpretation should not be generalized to all issues affecting kafala. In particular, when it comes to the intrafamily question, where the child/*makful* enters a European country, the possibility of obtaining adoption should be specifically assessed. Indeed, it is hard to defend against not taking into consideration the various negative consequences of this institution, which in 'western' countries may create a series of inequalities incompatible with liberal and democratic constitutional systems.

In Belgium it is well known that some types of kafala may obtain recognition and not others, and that the country's adoption law became

---

311 C. SIFFREIN-BLANC, *Kafala et adaptian vues par la CEDH - Le refus de métamarphoser une Kafala en adoption n'est pas contraire aux droits fondamentaux*, in *Revue des droits et de libertés fondamentaux*, 25, p. 5 *et seq*., and at http://www.revuedlf.com/droit-international/kafala-et-adoption-vues-par-la-cedh-commentaire. Cf. N. HERVIEU, *L'adoption internationale aux prises avec la kafala sous le regard européen*, in *Lettres "Actualités Droits-Libertés" du CREDOF*, 2012, http:/lrevdh.org/2012/10/08/adoptioninternationale-kafala-regard-europeen.

312 ECHR, *Chbihi Loudoudi and Others v. Belgium*, cit. Dissenting opinion of judges KARAKAS, VUČINIĆ and KELLER, par. 11.

rather restrictive after the entry into force of the Hague Convention of 1993. Indeed, from that moment on, the adoption procedure was no longer free, but framed and characterized by cooperation between the various central authorities that match children who have been declared abandoned with possible adoptive parents. As in France, this procedure allows for the adoption of children only from countries which in turn recognize this legal instrument and whose job it is to declare the adoptability of those children. Lobbying by Belgium's Muslim community led to the introduction of a law in 2005 on the implementation of the Hague Convention, mitigated by another law of the same year which recognized the possibility of transforming kafala into adoption but on one condition: the child in kafala care had to be abandoned at birth, orphaned or declared as such by the national authorities.[313] Only extra-family kafala, however, could be recognized and become full adoption.[314]

Belgium adopted a regulatory approach towards cultural diversity that can be defined as "*pragmatisme à géométrie variable*" in which, by using *ad hoc* solutions, the authorities leaned towards a potential unity of the system that could balance the multiple facets present in the country.[315]

The Court therefore held in both cases that there had been no violation of Article 8 of the ECHR and that both France and Belgium acted within the limits of the margin of appreciation granted to them and in compliance with the principle international conventions, opting for non-adoptability. In the second case there was a certain legal evolution since the European Court took into consideration the best interests of the child to analyze a possible violation of Article 8. Despite stressing that its role was to verify whether the best interests of the child had been the main consideration

---

[313] Law modifying certain measures relating to adoption, 6th December 2005, at http://www.etaamb.be/fr/loi-du-06-decembre-2005_n2005009965.html.

[314] Confirmed by the Council of State in its judgment of 28th March 2003, no. 117667, at https://www.legifrance.gouv.fr/affichJuriAdmin.do?idTexte=CETATEXT000008106344. With intrafamily kafala there would be no chance whatsoever of obtaining a permit of stay in Belgium for family reunification.

[315] N. BONBLED, *Les minorités culturelles en droit public belge*, in *Le droit et la diversité culturelle*, J. RINGELHEIM (ed.), Brussels, Bruylant, 2001, p. 125; F. BLANMAILLAND, *Droit familial et diversité culturelle: un point de vue de praticienne*, in *Le droit et la diversité culturelle*, Brussels, Bruylant, 2011, considers that "*le point de vue du refus pur et simple de prise en compte des situations légalement créées à l'étranger, meme lorsqu'elles l'ont été sans léser les droits de l'autre partie, relève d'une forme d'impérialisme juridique peu compatible avec un tant soit peu de prise en compte de la diversité des origines*" (p. 719).

which justified the decision of the national authorities, however, the court reiterated that what counted was the principle of having a single personal status and concluded that the authorities had been able to calculate that the girl's best interests did not lie with adoption, in accordance with Belgian law.

Such premises should have more properly led to a different perspective. The applicants had, in actual fact, requested simple adoption, which differs from full adoption in the sense that it allows legal ties with the biological family of the child to be maintained despite the creation of a parent-child relationship with the adoptive parents. It thus appears that the court exaggerated the impact of the possible coexistence of a dual personal status on the girl since, in the case in question, her relations with her homeland were reduced to summer holidays only and she had no emotional bond with her biological mother. The Court preferred to put the protection of Belgian decisions over and above the creation of a stable environment for the girl. It is also worth considering that while French law allows some loopholes to get around the prohibition of adoption, such as, for example, the possibility of granting French citizenship after five years of residence before setting the adoption procedure in motion, there are no similar mechanisms in Belgian law.

The two decisions are thus not comparable because the starting positions and regulatory contexts are different. Furthermore, in the Belgian case, the wishes of the girl, around fifteen years of age, to remain in Belgium and consider her adoptive parents as her real parents were not taken into consideration. To this stress should be added the length of the procedure, which meant the girl had to wait fifteen years before she could acquire Belgian nationality, with obvious repercussions on her daily life.

As for the indications provided in this regard by the case-law of the European Court, it would appear that the task of each country is mainly to find a fair balance between national security, public order and the concrete interest of minors. Finally, it is important to reiterate that Article 8 of the Convention, as has always been emphasised, cannot and should not be interpreted as meaning a real right to adopt. The choice of a state whether or not to consent to the adoption of a minor, indeed, should be based on the principle of "providing a child with a family, not a family with a child".[316] However, bearing in mind that, in the event that there is already

---

[316] ECHR, 26th February 2002, *Fretté v. France*, application no. 36515/97, at http://www.equalrightstrust.org/ertdocumentbank/frette%20v%20france.pdf, esp. para. 42 and the judgment of 22nd September 2004, *Pini and Others v. Romania*, application no. 78028/01 and 78030/01, at

a family tie with the minor, "the State must act in a manner calculated to enable that tie to be developed and establish legal safeguards that render possible the child's integration in his family".[317]

With the ruling filed on March 26th, 2019, in case C-129/18, the Court of Justice of the European Union established that kafala cannot be equated to adoption because there is no parent-child relationship. Thus, the minor in kafala care, according to Directive 2004/38 on the right of citizens of the Union and their family members to move and reside freely within the territory of the Member States, cannot be included among direct descendants. It also established that the minor may, however, be included in the notion of 'other family member'. Consequently, Member States, who are required to preserve the unity of the family in a broad sense, must facilitate the entry and residence of the minor. The circumstances leading to the request for a preliminary ruling concerned a French couple residing in the United Kingdom, who had taken an Algerian minor into their care under the kafala system. The husband then returned to the United Kingdom, but the minor's subsequent application for entry was rejected by the Entry Clearance Officer. The UK's First-tier Tribunal (Immigration and Asylum Chamber) rejected the appeal as the kafala system was not recognised as adoption under UK law. Thus, the minor was not considered a family member. The Court of Appeal also shared this position on the basis of Directive 2004/38. The Supreme Court of the United Kingdom, however, asked for help from the Euro-judges. First of all, the EU Court ruled that the minor could not be considered as a 'direct descendant' (notion proper to the EU system) of a citizen of the Union according to Article 2. (2) (c) of the directive, because the kafala in Algeria is temporary and revocable and the guardians of the child are not linked by a parent-child relationship or adoption, the latter prohibited in Algeria. Thus, considering that permanent legal protection alone does not make the minor a direct descendant (by adoption) of his/her guardian, the possibility of including the minor among the direct descendants must be excluded. Having said that, however, the EU Court did state that the minor could be considered as one of the 'other family members' according to the directive. It is thus up to national authorities to ascertain whether the minor is another family member who may take advantage of Article 3 of the directive, which requires Member States to facilitate the entry and

---

https://www.crin.org/en/library/legal-database/pini-and-ors-v-romanian, esp. para. 151.

[317] See ECHR decision of 28th June 2007, *Wagner and J. M. W. L. v. Luxembourg*, application no. 76240/01, in *Rev. critique droit internat. privé*, 2007, pp. 807-821, and in *Chbihi Loudoudi and Others v. Belgium*, cit., esp. para. 41.

residence of family members. In their assessment, national courts should focus on the best interests of the child, affirmed in the 1989 New York Convention on the Rights of the Child, and the protection of the right to respect for private and family life guaranteed by Article 7 of the EU Charter of Fundamental Rights which, according to Article 52, paragraph 3, has the same meaning and scope as Article 8 of the European Convention on Human Rights, as interpreted by the Court of Strasbourg.

An imperfect correspondence of legal systems and procedures should not, however, prevent those called upon to interpret the law from recognising kafala so as to ensure that the best interests of the minor prevail. Indeed, the nature of this system attributes a heavy burden on the jurist, responsible for choosing not only which procedural regime to apply, but above all for encouraging a conscientious and rational evolution of the entire system.

2. Analysis of French Legislation and Jurisprudence. Putting the Constitutional Principle of Secularism to the Test

Along its historical, philosophical and juridical path, the French nation has demonstrated that there is a particular bond between the concepts of the Republic, secularism and society.[318] Considering the communitarian tendencies of certain social groups,[319] which might undermine such a highly structured system (in particular Islam), some feel that immediate legislative intervention capable of curbing a dangerous implosion of the social fabric is needed.[320] The neutrality of political power, with reference to the religious factor, does appear to guarantee equal respect for all beliefs and allow for the peaceful coexistence of all faiths. Secularism,

---

[318] Cf. G. CAROBENE, *I nuovi percorsi della laicità, il pluralismo religioso ed il difficile equilibrio con la religione islamica*, in *Dir. fam. pers.*, 2, 2006, pp. 840-862; E. POULAT, *Notre laicité publique*, Paris, Berg International Editeurs, 2003; G. COQ, *Laïcité et République. Le lien nécessaire*, Paris, Editions du Félin, 2003; J. BAUBEROT, *Vers un nouveau pacte laïque?* Paris, Le centurion, 1990; ID., *Histoire de la laïcité en France*, Paris, Seuil, 2004.

[319] On the concept of communitarianism cf. C. TAYLOR, *La politica del riconoscimento*, in C. TAYLOR - J. HABERMAS, *Multiculturalismo. Lotte per il riconoscimento*, Milan, Feltrinelli, 2001, pp. 9-62.

[320] The clash between Islam and the western world, as a phenomenon almost consequential to the cessation of the cold war and to the dichotomous East – West opposition was proposed in a famous work by S. HUNTINGTON, *Lo scontro di civiltà e il nuovo ordine mondiale*, Italian trans., Milan, Rizzoli, 1990.

then, would appear to consist in "*frankir l'ensemble de la sphère publique de toute emprise exercée au nom d'une religion ou d'une idéologie particulière*".[321]

Since the *Déclaration des droits de l'homme et du citoyen* and well-known law on the State-Church separation of 1905, secularism was inscribed among the founding and fundamental principles of the French Republic. Though this legislation has been subject to progressive erosion by the jurisprudence – only two articles remain in force – the fundamental principle for the protection of freedom of conscience remains confirmed,[322] "*la loi établit une double rupture: avec la tradition de l'établissement de l'Eglise catholique dans la société politique; avec la tradition régalienne, du gallicanisme de Louis XIV aux Articles organiques de Napléon Ier, selon laquelle l'Etat régent les choses religieuses ... Cet loi libérale témoigne d'une nouvelle orientation de la pensée laïque*".[323]

Soon after, authoritative comments highlighted the markedly anticlerical and antireligious imprint that a so-called *laïcité de combat* would lead to. Nevertheless, it was pointed out that the changing political climate immediately following the First World War had already greatly mitigated this negative connotation to leave room for a more open secularism.[324] It was thus accepted as a method of peaceful coexistence in the face of a multiplicity of cultural and religious expression present in society. In this sense, the values included in the bedrock of secularism, insofar as they point to a project for opening up society, based on respect for all consciences and on the equal freedom of individuals, may provide the political and legal instruments suitable for the formation of a single collective identity.

---

[321] H. PENA-RUIZ, *Qu'est-ce que la laïcité?*, Paris, Gallimard, p. 24.

[322] In the conclusion of the *Laicità e Repubblica*, drawn up by the Stasi Commission on 11 December 2003, a series of proposals were made, including devising a law on secularism capable of specifying the operating rules in public services and in businesses and to guarantee respect for the country's cultural diversity: COMMISSIONE STASI, *Rapporto sulla laicità. Velo islamico e simboli religiosi nella società europea*, Milan, 2004.

[323] J.P. BURDY-J. MARCOU, *Laïcité/Laiklik: Introduction*, in *Cahier d'études sur la Méditerranée orientale et le monde turco-iranien*, no. 19, 1995, p. 45 *et seq*.

[324] Cf. the famous analyses by E. POULAT, *Liberté, laïcité. La guerre des deux France et le principe de modernité*, Paris, Editions du Cerf, 1987 and by the same author, *La solution laïque et ses problèmes*, Paris, Berg International, 1997. "*En un siècle ou presque, on est passé d'une laïcité de combat à une neutralité armée... La laïcité à la française est donc polymorphe dans l'espace et évolutive dans le temps*": G. BEDOUELLE - J.P. COSTA, *Les laïcités à la française*, preface by R. Rémond, Paris, PUF, 1998, p. 6.

The new demands of society have, however, forced the legislative authority to assess the capacity of current legislation in the face of new social phenomena, coming from deeply different cultural areas and with a profoundly diverse social and political fabric. In many cases regulatory 'short circuits' capable of destabilizing the system and questioning the possible fulfilment of the rights of the child have been recorded.

A fairly frequent legal problem is related to the case in which the adoptive parents are subject to a dual, conflicting regulation on adoption. If they show their willingness to use the kafala tool in their own country, they will not be able to obtain authorization in the 'western' country of residence to apply for a visa. This situation is frequent with citizens coming from the geographic area of the Maghreb but permanently resident in France. They state their willingness to adopt and seek 'suitability', according to French procedure, but plan to adopt in their own country to make use of a series of advantages associated with a low financial investment, geographical proximity, speed of the process and the possibility of adopting under the kafala system with its added bonus of a solid family and social network and knowledge of the language. In these circumstances kafala simultaneously represents a problem (because it hinders adoption in France and may lead to illegality) and a solution (as it facilitates the adoption process).

The jurisprudence is known to have taken different attitudes to kafala and its assimilation to various legal instruments: full or simple adoption, adoption in special circumstances, foster care. The first European country to deal with its recognition was France, mostly because it was linked by its colonial past, especially to the countries of the Maghreb area. Early on, between 1984 and 1997, the position of the various Courts of Appeal differed. In some cases, the effects of kafala corresponded to the same effects as adoption if the national law of the adopter was applied. In others, where countries prohibited full adoption, the French judge would transpose the provision as a simple adoption.[325] In one case the full adoption of a Moroccan child, of unknown parents, was admitted, where it

---

[325] *Cour de Cassation 7 nov. 1984, arrêt Torlet, Iere chambre civ.,* in *Juriclasseur Périodique*, IV, 1985, p. 19 *et seq*. with note by E. POISSON- DROCOURT. *Cour de Cassation, arrêt Pistre, 31 Jan. 1990,* in *Juriclasseur Périodique*, II, 1991, p. 216 *et seq*. with note by H. MUIR WATT. In this last judgment, it was emphasised that if the national law of the adopter prohibits full adoption then only simple adoption may be obtained in France. This approach was confirmed by the same court, *l juill. 1994, arrêt Moreau,* in *Rév. Crit. Droit internat. Privé*, 1994, p. 654 *et seq*. with note by H. MUR WATT.

had been rejected by others, thus highlighting an extremely heterogeneous and contradictory jurisprudential approach.[326]

The international adoption law of 2001 attempted to regulate the phenomenon by resorting to the national laws of the adopter.[327] The adoption of a child under kafala was prohibited in France only when one or both spouses were nationals of a country that expressly prohibited adoption. Instead, if they resided in France and their union was governed by French law, adoption could also be pronounced for a child in kafala care, provided the person was born and resident in France. Despite the introduction of the law, the jurisprudence continued to record strong opposition from the judges,[328] even though it was easy to see which direction the Court of Cassation was taking.[329] The 2001 law was, in fact,

---

[326] *Cour de Cassation civil, I, 10 mai 1995, arrêt Fanthou*, in *Les Petites Affiches*, no. 32, 1996, p. 22 *et seq*. with note by J. MASSIP. According to this ruling, it is sufficient for the child's legal representative to consent to the adoption. This was followed by the *Cour d'Appel de Paris, 19 juin 1997,* which considered kafala and departure from the national territory as an acceptance by the Moroccan judge such as to allow the pronouncement of adoption. *Cour de Cassation civ. I, l juil. 1997, arrêt Lorre*, in *Juriclasseur Périodique*, II, 1997, p. 22916 *et seq*., with note by T. GARÈ.

[327] *Loi n. 2001-111 du 6 févr. 2001* regarding international adoption, at www.legifrance.gouv.fr/affichTexte.do?cidTexte=JORFTEXT000000221699.

[328] The Court of Appeal of Limoges pronounced a full adoption for an Algerian child in October 2007, specifying that "*les autorités algériénnes confient des enfants à des étrangers sachant qu'une adoption sera prononcée*". In Morocco before the 2002 reform, translations used the term 'kafala pending adoption' and the consular visa was granted for adoption. Since 2002 this has changed to 'pending placement or guardianship', even if these States do not legally contest adoptions made in various European countries such as Italy, Spain, Belgium, Switzerland, France but also Canada and the United States.

[329] The Court of Appeal of Reims, 27th September 2001, at www.doctrine.fr/d/CA/Reims/2001/JURITEXT000006938105, stressed that the law of February 6th 2001, concerning international adoption, applicable to judgments in progress when it entered into force, expressly forbid the full adoption of a minor if prohibited by the citizenship law. It may be deduced from the principles established by previous case-law that the law of the adoptee determines the conditions of relations to consent, so that when the law prohibits full adoption, consent must be assigned to the adoptee with full knowledge of the consequences by French law. In the same direction, the Court of Appeal of Versailles, 27th November 2003, no. 03/05159, at https://www.doctrine.fr/d/CA/Versailles/2003/JURITEXT000006944198. *Contra Tribunal de Grande lnstance de Nimes, 9 gen. 2002, TGI de Nimes, n. PR 825 E 70/01* granted full adoption to a Moroccan child observing that the legislation of

a response by French legislation to the presence of children in France from countries that did not recognize adoption and was originally intended to ensure that judicial decisions would be unanimous in a very disharmonious context. It is now clear that kafala can be converted into adoption, but it is important to note that, despite the explicit regulatory ban, some jurisdictions continued to tread a particularly confused and uneven path. In 2005, the Court of Cassation decided not to accept an application for full adoption of a child born in Morocco declaring that the notarial deeds did not amount to consent of the Moroccan authorities to a full adoption and subsequent consequences, and that the certificate produced could only demonstrate that the child had been placed in the care of the applicants but could not be considered as consent.[330]

The Supreme Court intervened in 2006 with two decisions in which, in alignment with the provisions of the 2001 law, it reprimanded the judges who had admitted the simple adoption of two children.[331] However, other, almost contemporary, judicial decisions converted kafala into adoption. Thus, despite explicit legislative prohibition, some children raised in France were actually children originally in kafala care, subsequently translated into adoption, though it may be revoked at any time. Once they become French, these minors will experience a situation almost similar to that of their parents: a dual nationality and belonging to two countries, each of which claims exclusive loyalty to its own laws.

French legislation appears to have been extremely concerned with not violating the sovereignty of the country of origin where it prohibits adoption.

Morocco responded "*à une procédure identique à celle de l'adoption en droit français et avait le même but: donner des parents à un enfant abandonné*". In 2006, with two consecutive rulings – no. 1486 and no. 1487 of 10th October 2006, the Court of Cassation rebuked the judges who had admitted a simple adoption as both Moroccan and Algerian law use kafala, which is not comparable to adoption, as also underlined by the French law of 2001 in *Cass. I civ., 10 oct. 2006, n° 06-15.265, Bull. 2006 l, n. 432* p. 369 and at https://www.doctrine.fr/d/CASS/2006/JURITEXT000007054866. On July 9th 2008, the Civil Chamber of the Court of Cassation reiterated that kafala could not be assimilated to adoption, in *Cass., n. 07-20.279, Bull. 2008, l, n. 198*, at https://www.doctrine.fr/d/CASS/2008/JURITEXT000019165681 and yet again *Cass. l civ., 25 févr. 2009, n. 08-11.033, Bull. 2009, l, n. 41*, at https://www.doctrine.fr/d/CASS/2009/JURITEXT000020321307.

330 *Cass. I civ., 25 janv. 2005, n 02-11.927, Bull. 2005 I n. 34* p. 27, at https://www.doctrine.fr/d/CASS/2005/JURITEXT000007050839.

331 *Arrêt n. 1487, 06-15.264*, and *arrêt n. 1486, 06-15.265*, at www.courdecassation.fr/jurisprudence_publications_documentation_2/actualite_jurisprudence_21/premiere_chambre_civile_568/arrets_569/br_arret_9386.htmlbr.

It has thus seemed intent on defending a logic that is contrary to that of the system of intercountry adoption, which implies the irreversible change of name, filiation and nationality. France normally cancels the biological relationship of origin, the blood ties as well as the original cultural belonging, the bond with the land itself except for the adopted *makful.* This extremely protective attitude has meant that a generation of adopted children has been forced to choose illegality, accumulating level after level of illegitimacy, first as abandoned children and then as adopted children not legally recognizable. Making an exception based on the place of birth generates clear discrimination.

3. Italian Jurisprudence. Kafala in Contexts of Dual Citizenship/Dual Religious Affiliation

In Italy, the issue of international adoption followed a regulatory process that started from Law 184/83, but left a series of problems unresolved, including the possibility of adopting minors from Islamic countries.[332] Kafala is known to share some similarities with our own foster care, but differs in that the latter provides for the temporary placement of the minor. In Italy, before the 1983 reform, part of the jurisprudence had converted kafala measures first into pre-adoptive foster care and then into actual adoption.[333] However, it cannot be simplistically assimilated to pre-adoptive care which, although temporary, is essentially aimed at adoption. It is therefore oriented towards an institution with which kafala shares only the grounds of solidarity but not the legal regulation of interpersonal relationships.

The latter, in fact, can be defined as a subordinate procedure which is not in itself sufficient to acquire a stable or definitive legal position. Foster care – designed to protect the minor who has been temporarily deprived of the family environment – is different. It does not determine any filial bond, acquisition of the name, or hereditary rights. It imposes only the obligation of support, care and upbringing, taking into account the wishes of the parents and shares with kafala the idea of solidarity and non-definitiveness, as well as the obligations towards the minor.

---

332 Amended by Law no. 476/98 and no. 149/01, cit.

333 According to Articles 31 and 32, it is up to the Juvenile Court to declare the efficacy in the State of the "measures of adoption or pre-adoptive care of the minor issued by a foreign authority regarding Italian citizens residing in Italy or in the foreign State, or other measures on protection and other institutions for the protection of minors".

The law of 1983 identified three distinct routes to obtain the recognition of adoptions pronounced abroad and to ensure that the Italian provision was not such as to change the legal nature of the original.[334] Acknowledging that states are free to adopt systems of protection for minors other than adoption, Italian legislation concerned itself with ensuring that Italian judges would not distort a foreign provision by transforming it into adoption, thus avoiding international friction as well. In this sense, the legal perspective is similar to the one taken by French legislation.

There are thus several judgments by Italian judges who, in compliance with this principle, excluded the possibility for kafala parents/guardians to obtain legitimising adoption of the *makful*,[335] likening the institution to adoption 'in special circumstances' or foster care.[336] The risk of this

---

[334] The first related to the adoption of minors from the member countries of the Hague Convention: in this case adoptions were 'recognized' in our country. The second related to adoptions from countries that had not ratified the Convention which could be recognized in Italy, as long as they complied with the conditions set out in Article 36, paragraph 2. The third related to adoptions made in countries where the adoptive parents had resided for at least two years. Article 36, paragraph 2, of Law no. n. 184, allowed the recognition of the adoptions of minors from countries not members of the Hague Convention, recognizing only the adoption measures or pre-adoptive care. Article 36, paragraph 4, recognized adoptions pronounced in the countries where the adoptive parents had resided for at least two years, and was still formulated differently from the two previous cases, referring to adoption measures alone.

[335] In first place the Juvenile Court of Trento, 11th March 2002, in *Riv. dir. intern. priv. e proc.*, 2002, p. 1056 *et seq.*; in *Dir. Fam. Pers.*, 2004, p. 135 *et seq.*, with note by A. GALOPPINI, *L'adozione del piccolo marocchino, ovvero gli scherzi dell'eurocentrismo*; in *Nuova giur. civ. comm.*, l, 2003, p. 149 *et seq.*, with note by J. LONG, *Adozione extraconvenzionale di minori provenienti da Paesi islamici*; in *Dir. imm. e citt.*, 2, 2004, p. 178 *et seq.*, with note by A. VANZAN, L. MIAZZI, *Kafala e protezione del minore in Italia*.

[336] This was the solution accepted by the Trento Court of 11 March 2002, cit.; however, it does seem above all to have been dictated by practical reasons. The judge, in fact, unable to accept the request for adoption by the kafala parents, took into consideration the fact that the minor was "now in Italian territory, in the legal care of a couple of Italian nationality and with no prospect of being able to find adequate reception should he return to his homeland" and concluded by observing that "the spouses are not precluded from having the possibility, in the overriding interest of the minor, of adopting the child according to the forms" referred to in Article 44, letter c), Law no. 184/83, provision relating to the non-legitimizing adoption in the event of "ascertained impossibility of pre-adoptive foster care". In short, the judge rejected the application and at the same time suggested filing for

approach, however, is to deny respect for the child's identity while endeavouring to protect the child's rights.

In 2002, the first and most well-known Italian case on the subject came up before Trento's Juvenile Court. It concerned an Italian couple who had been granted the care of a minor by the Moroccan judicial authority under a kafala arrangement. The couple requested adoption of the child, who had also been authorized to reside permanently in Italy by the Commission for Intercountry Adoption. The key point of the reasoning underlying the non-comparability of the institutions rested on the restrictive interpretation of the concept of 'placement for purposes of adoption', qualifying as such "only the provision which in the country in which it is pronounced has the effect of constituting a legal parent-child relationship between the minor and the adopters or at least is open to the establishment of such a relationship in the country of destination. However, this restrictive approach does not consider it necessary for the provision to sever the legal ties with the family of origin". In this specific case for the judge it was "clearly impossible to pronounce the efficacy of a measure that has no correspondent in national law".[337]

In Morocco, natural parents may request and regain custody of the child, which would have harmful consequences for the child. The Court thus deduced that it would be impossible to declare the efficacy of a provision that had no correspondence in national law, as also clarified by the Moroccan Embassy in Italy when consulted by the President-Rapporteur, emphasising that "Moroccan legislation concerning private

---

an adoption under 'special circumstances', insisting on the interest of the minor to remain in Italy and on the circumstance that he had already come to create: a relationship comparable to a parent-child relationship with his foster parents. Cf. G. PIZZOLANTE, *La kafalah islamica e il suo riconoscimento nell'ordinamento italiano*, in *Riv. dir. intern. priv. e proc.*, 2007, p. 947 *et seq*. In these cases, the child does not take on the *status* of legitimate child, does not sever ties with the natural family, whose surname will be kept, though in addition to the adopted parents' surname. Nor does the child lose his/her legal status or citizenship so that if the child moves abroad s/he will still be under the protection of his/her own country. Furthermore, as in the case of kafala, the adoptive parent takes on the duty to raise, educate and support the child and exercises parental authority over the child. The minor does not acquire inheritance rights in the adoptive family. Unlike kafala, the minor under simple adoption acquires inheritance rights and the legal ties that bind him/her to the adoptive parents do not cease with the coming of age.

[337] Cf. Juvenile Court of Trento, Decree of 11th March 2002, cit. In opposition cf. *Court Appel, Paris, 29 avr. 2003*, with comment by F. MBALA, *Adoption internationale: lorsque le pays d'originie prohibe l'adoption*, in *Ree. Dall., Jur.*, 2004, p. 459 *et seq*.

law, which is based in this matter on Muslim law, does not recognize the institution of adoption, but, on the contrary, absolutely prohibits it".

Nevertheless, it is hard not to consider the circumstances of the minor and the fact that the child had already been placed with an Italian couple in Italy, with no prospect of an adequate reception on return to his homeland. The Commission for Intercountry Adoption, specifically called upon to provide clarification, had sent a copy of its own provision showing that the authorization issued to the Moroccan minor upon entering Italy was grounded in the "child's best interests, while also acknowledging the non-comparability of the kafala institution neither to pre-adoptive care nor to adoption. It is clear, as the court pointed out, that "if he were to remain in Italy as a foreign national, in the care of an unrelated family, his psychological situation ... and also his future chances of social inclusion, would be seriously compromised. Indeed, at the age of discernment he would find himself in a distressing situation: a foreigner in Italy and even more so in Morocco".[338]

By rejecting the request for legitimizing adoption, the Court considered the actual situation of the minor – by now permanently resident in Italy – in light of Article 20 of the Convention on the Rights of the Child, deeming that the couple were not precluded from "the possibility of requesting, in the overriding interest of the minor, the adoption of the child according to the forms set out in Articles 44 *et seq*. of Law no. 184 of 1983", thus including the case among the so-called adoptions in 'special circumstances'. It is clear that in the case in question, the Commission for Intercountry Adoption had forced the issue somewhat by authorizing the entry of a minor into Italy pursuant to Article 32, for adoption purposes, well aware of the difficulties of matching kafala to the institutions envisaged in the Italian legal system. The Court thus decided not to make a comparison of the kafala with the public order oriented towards the interest of the minor, but limited its observations on the qualification of the institution.

The use of adoption in 'special circumstances' has the advantage of allowing adoption on the basis of Italian legislation, ensuring full compliance with the national law of the country of origin of the minor, while safeguarding as far as possible the cultural identity of the child, in accordance with the dictates of the 1993 Hague Convention as well as with the general principles of private international law.

---

[338] J. LONG, *Adozione "extraconvenzionale" di minori provenienti da Paesi islamici nota a Trib. min. Trento decreto 5 marzo 2002 e Trib. Min. Trento, decreto 10 settembre 2002*, in *La nuova giurisprudenza civile commentata* ,vol. 2, 2003, p.149 *et seq*.

There is no shortage, however, of doctrinal opinions opposing the use of this method of (non-legitimising) adoption. First of all, though maintaining ties between the minor and the family of origin, adoption in special circumstances pursuant to Article 44 constitutes an 'artificial' parent-child relationship that cannot be recognised by the State of origin of the minor, since the creation of any kind of filial bond other than the biological-natural one is forbidden: "the minor would be the child of the adopters in his/her new country but the child of his/her biological parents in the old".[339] In second place, it could work as a stratagem for all those situations where legitimizing adoption cannot be granted due to lack of minimum requirements, with the twofold risk of unjustifiably broadening the scope of the law itself and of clearing the way for a parallel route to international adoption. Finally, it is not always in the child's best interest to maintain a relationship with the biological family: whether it is actually necessary or appropriate should be assessed case by case.

Article 36 of Law no. 184 lists the existing conditions under which "adoption or foster care for adoption purposes, pronounced in a country not party to the Convention or signatory of bilateral agreements, may be declared effective in Italy". The concept of efficacy could literally be assimilated to an ordinary resolution. Indeed, in the case of adoptions outside the Convention, the Juvenile Court does not limit itself to recognizing the legal effects of a foreign provision, but constitutes the *status familiae*, thus attributing a constitutive nature to the pronouncement of the Italian judge called upon to decide in such a matter. It follows that the foreign provision becomes a mere factual prerequisite for adoption, which must still present all the conditions required by law.

A wider reading of the laws in place might also allow kafala to be transformed into legitimizing adoption. An assessment of the state of abandonment could be inferred from the same provision afforded by kafala in Islamic countries. Secondly, with reference to the actions of the Commission for Intercountry Adoption and authorizing body, simple intervention by these organisations either early on or in the final phase of the adoption could be considered suitable and sufficient. As to compliance with the indications contained in the certificate of suitability and to authorising the child's entry into Italy, pursuant to Article 39. 1. h), no elements emerged from the judgment that could amount to a violation of these conditions, so much so that the couple – who had previously been declared eligible for adoption – had also obtained authorization to enter

[339] J. LONG, *La kafala: una risorsa sociale per i bambini e per le famiglie di religione islamica in Italia*, in *Minorigiustizia*, 2, 2007, p. 177 *et seq*.

the country. Finally, there is one last requirement: that the adoption does not go against the fundamental principles that regulate family and child law in the State, assessed according to the best interests of the minor. The reference here is to international public order and in assessing whether or not the adoption is contrary to it what must be evaluated are the effects of the provision in the legal system, not the act in itself.

The features of adoption in 'special circumstances' (which does seem to be a remnant of the 'ordinary' adoption of old) do show some similarities with the institution of kafala. The adopted child does not take on the status of legitimate child since s/he will not sever the relationship with the family of origin and will keep the surname – to which will be eventually added that of the adoptive parent. The adoptive parent has the duty to raise, educate and support the minor, who does not acquire inheritance rights in the adoptive family. The difference between legitimizing adoption and adoption in 'special circumstances' is the lesser intensity of the resulting effects. However, even this solution is not without criticism since, though it may grant the possibility of maintaining relations with the family of origin, it does create an artificial filial bond that Muslim countries reject and do not recognize. In conclusion, the ruling issued in the Trento decree in itself is "unique and cannot be reproduced as it stands. It should be followed only in the event that equally exceptional circumstances make the pronouncement of adoption appropriate in the specific case".[340]

Case-law has also made a distinction depending on whether the provision for the care of the minor was granted to a foreign *kafil* of Islamic faith or a citizen of a Western country, of a different (or no) religious affiliation. In the event that under kafala the duty of caring for the minor falls to a foreign national, the jurisprudence calmly admitted both the right to recognition of the provision of the foreign judge and the request for family reunification.[341] [342] At first, Italian judges considered that the minor

---

[340] Cf. R. GELLI, *La Kafala di diritto islamico: prospettive di riconoscimento nell'ordinamento italiano*, in *Famiglia e diritto*, no. 1, 2005, p.70 *et seq*.

[341] Pursuant to Article 67, Law no. 218 of 1995.

[342] According to the rules of the Consolidated Immigration Act, Article 29, paragraph 3, Legislative Decree 286/1998. On the relationship of kafala with the law on family reunification, settled case-law considers the Islamic law institution suitable to qualify for reunification by extending Article 29 to kafala. Cf. Court of Biella, 7th March 2000, in *Dir. immigraz. e cittad.*, 2000, 3, p. 121 *et seq*.; Court of Milan, 12th March 2000, *ibidem*, 2, p. 127 *et seq*.; Court of Florence, 9th Nov. 2006, *ivi*; 2007, 1, p. 169 *et seq*.; Court of Turin, 26th June 2009, *ivi*, 2009, 2, p. 216 *et seq*.; Juvenile Court of Reggio Calabria, 10th October 2006, in *Fam.e min*., 2006, 2,

in kafala care could in no circumstances be reunited with foreign nationals residing in Italy, since the law excluded kafala from those institutions equivalent to biological filiation.[343]

A position of closure was thus preferred for fear that the only objective was to circumvent the legislation on adoption, which determines that the recognition of the foreign provision of kafala runs contrary to public order. Adopting the same perspective, but diametrically opposed, however, some trial judges felt that kafala could be a valid condition for reunification on the grounds that the concepts of adoption, foster care and guardianship cannot be measured in terms of legal forms specific to domestic law. They felt that these concepts must be more extensively interpreted so as to ensure that institutions of foreign law producing similar effects (though they may not be *identical*) to those of domestic institutions of child care are taken into consideration.[344]

---

p. 86 *et seq*.; Court of Florence, 9th November 2006, in *Dir. immigraz. e cittad*., 2007, l, p. 169 *et seq*.; Court of Biella, 26th April 2007, in *Dir. fam. e pers*., 2007, p. 1810; Court of Appeal, Turin, 18th July 2007, *ivi*, 2008, p. 143 *et seq*.; Court of Appeal, Turin, 28th June 2007, in *Dir. immigraz. e cittad*, 2008, 3, p. 142 *et seq*.; Court of Appeal, Turin, 30th May 2007, *ibidem*, l, p. 181 *et seq*.; Court of Appeal, Florence, 2nd February 2007, *ivi*, 2007, 4, p. 139 *et seq*.; Court of Brescia, 3rd August 2009, at *www.asgi.it.*

343 Based on an interpretation of Article 29, Consolidated Immigration Act: cf. Court of Reggio Emilia, 9th February 2005, *Dir. imm. e citt*., 2, 2005, p. 183 *et seq*. and in *Quad. dir. e pol. Ecclesiastica*, 2006, p. 906 *et seq*.; subsequently, cf. Government Legal Service, advisory committee opinion, 19th January 2006, no. 7032, in *Rassegna Avvocatura dello Stato*, l, 2006, p.247 *et seq*., which adheres to the interpretation initially practiced by the courts of first instance.

344 Cf. Court of Florence 9th November 2006, in *Quad. dir. e poi. Ecclesiastica*, 2007, p. 846 *et seq*.; Court of Appeal, Turin, 18th July 2007, cit.; Court of Appeal, Turin, 30th May 2007, in *Dir. imm. e citt*., I, 2008, p. 181 *et seq*.; Juvenile Court of Reggio Calabria, 10th October 2006, in *Famiglia e minori*, 2, 2006, p. 86 *et seq*. The possibility that kafala could help to qualify for reunification with foreign kafala parents was also confirmed by the Court of Cassation in 2008, which states that the preferred interpretation is undoubtedly one that achieves a fair balance of the interests at stake: 'the safeguarding of the minor' and 'the democratic protection of state borders', recalling that the Constitutional Court had underlined a 'tendential prevalence' of the principle of protecting the child over and above defending the territory or containing immigration. On the basis of arguments not identical to those already accepted by the trial judges: Court of Cassation 20th March 2008, no. 7472, in *Famiglia e dir*., 2008, p. 675 *et seq*., with note by R. GELLI, *La kafalah tra esigenze di tutela del minore e rischi di aggiramento della disciplina dell'immigrazione*; in *Famiglia, persone e successioni*, 2008, p.891 *et seq*., with note by L. RACHELI, *La kafalah di diritto islamico è un presupposto per*

Part of the doctrine has pointed out that the impossibility of pre-adoptive placement responds to a type of case that is very different from that of a child coming from a legal system that does not provide for adoption, but it is usually cases of repeated pre-adoptive failures, where character issues, physical problems or age factors step in.[345]

Greater consideration of the interest of the minor and appreciation of the Islamic institution was apparent in a provision of the Court of Appeal of Bari relating to the effectiveness of kafala for the purposes of family reunification.[346] The Court had been asked to equate a kafala arrangement issued by the Court of Casablanca in order to allow the minor to be reunited with the Moroccan *kafil* residing in Italy. After qualifying the provision as non-contentious (as such susceptible to automatic recognition pursuant to Article 66 Law no. 218/1995), the Court still declared the application inadmissible because, in the absence of a dispute by the counterparty, it is not necessary to evaluate compliance of the law with public order.

The only apparently viable way for the applicant to obtain an entry visa for the child in her care was to make an application for an entry visa for the purposes of family reunification. For the purposes of the Consolidated Immigration Act, the concepts of adoption, foster care and guardianship must be understood as instruments capable of allowing foreign law institutions, though different from domestic institutions, to be taken into

---

il ricongiungimento familiare. Several subsequent rulings, substantially identical confirm this direction: Court of Cassation 2nd July 2008, no. 18174, in *Giust. civ. Mass*., 7-8, 2008, p. 1083 *et seq*.; Court of Cassation 17th July 2008, no. 19734, in *Foro it*., I, 2009, p. 1179 *et seq*., with note by P. PASSAGLIA. In compliance with the decision of the Court of Cassation 2008 cf. Court of Rovereto 21st May 2009. As regards Court of Cassation see Court of Cassation 28th January 2010, no. 1908, in *Giust. civ. Mass*. 3, 2008, p. 450, rv. 611621, which refers in full to the precedents of 2008; Constitutional Court, 5th July 2003 no. 198, in *Foro it.,* I, 2003, p. 2240 *et seq*., which declared unfounded "in accordance with reasons set out" Article 32. Paragraph 1., Legislative Decree no. 286/98 where it provides that, upon reaching the age of majority, the residence permit may also be issued to foreign minors subject to guardianship.

345 A. GALOPPINI, *L'adozione del piccolo marocchino, ovvero gli scherzi dell'eurocentrismo*, in *Dir. fam. pers*., 2004, p. 140 *et seq*.

346 Court of Appeal, Bari, 16th April 2004, in *Dir. imm. citt*., 2004, no. 2, p. 178 *et seq*. Along the same lines Court of Appeal, Florence, 2nd February 2007, in *Dir. imm. citt*., 2007, p. 139 *et seq*.; Court of Appeal, Turin, 30th May 2007, in *Dir. imm.citt*., 2008, p. 191 *et seq*. With note by J. LONG, *Kafala e ricongiungimento familiare*; and, finally, Court of Appeal, Turin, 28th June 2007, in *Dir. imm. citt*., 2007, p. 142 *et seq*.

account as long as they produce the same effects as domestic measures, especially bearing in mind the child's best interests as regards the family unit.[347] The Court of Appeal of Bari thus opted for a wider reading of the immigration law with regard to the possibility of *makful* - *kafil* family reunification, prioritising the interest of the minor.[348] The purpose of family reunification is clearly the reconstruction of the family, where greater consideration must be afforded to weaker subjects.[349]

It is clear from this ruling – and from others that have followed this interpretative line – that on the one hand kafala does not run against public order and therefore might be considered as effective automatically with the consequent adaptability of the minor. On the other hand, though, a diametrically opposed conclusion may be reached in that according to Italian procedural provisions, *kafils* are not entitled to oppose any decision declaring the state of adoptability because they are not included in the list of the subjects legitimated to do this. The objective of these decisions is obviously to provide an immediate solution to a concrete problem, by justly considering the right of the child as a priority. However, it is up to the jurist and the legislator to arrive at a theoretical evaluation of the

---

[347] Article 29, paragraph 2. of the Consolidated Immigration Act provides that "for the purposes of reunification, children under the age of eighteen are considered minors at the time of filing the request for reunification. Minors adopted, fostered or under guardianship are treated as children". Thus expressed, it seems that the legislator extended reunification not only to those who are joined to the immigrant by a legal relationship of filiation but also by a relationship that, even without relative formal recognition, has substantially a parental content.

[348] Cf. M. ORLANDI, *Adozione 'in casi particolari' di minore straniero presente in Italia per soggiorno temporaneo*, in *Dir. fam. pers.*, 2005, p.654 *et seq*. Cf. in general on the kafala-irnmigration relationship also F. ALICINO, *La legislazione sulla base di intese. I test delle religioni "altre" e degli ateismi*, Bari, Cacucci, 2013, esp. p. 178 *et seq*.; N. ZORZELLA, W. CITTI, L. MIAZZI, *Diritto all'unità familiare e tutela dei minori. Profili sostanziali: la famiglia e i minori*, in *Diritto degli stranieri*, B. NASCINBENE (ed.), Padua, Cedam, 2004, esp. p. 918 *et seq*.

[349] This interpretation was followed also by the Court of Biella, 26th April 2007, in *Dir. fam. pers.*, 2007, p. 1831 *et seq*. with note by J. LONG, *Il ricongiungimento familiare del minore affidato con Kafala* and M. ORLANDI, *La kafalah di diritto islamico e il diritto al ricongiungimento familiare: una interessante pronuncia del Tribunale di Biella.* The Court held that although kafala is not comparable to any specific area of Italian family and child law, it is substantiated in its content and in its purposes, in the power/duty of the kafala parent/guardian to provide the child in need, up to upon reaching the age of majority, guardianship, support and any other precaution and care appropriate to his/her needs, making it abstractly comparable to our own foster care institution (as also stated by the Court of Cassation with decision no. 21395/05).

comparability of legal systems which, though intended to take care of minors, have profound legal differences as regards the resulting effects. Since the production of these effects – limited according to our cultural parameters – is underpinned by the respect of a religious dictate, any normal framework of comparison of the law is extremely reductive as well as misleading. What is needed is a proper reference to a cultural translation.

These observations do not exclude that in any single case it may be considered that kafala goes against public order and is not considered recognizable. Indeed, in 2005 the Court of Reggio Emilia denied recognition by interpreting it in the light of the interest of the minor, as enshrined in Article 23 of EC Regulation 2201/2003. Reasons were based on a consideration of the purpose of the institution which, according to the Court, should be to guarantee the child in a state of neglect or weakness the right to grow and be raised with his/her well-being at heart. In the case in question, it was noted that the biological parents were better placed than the *kafil* to raise and support the child. In this case, then, recognising kafala and thus removing the minor from the natural family environment would have been incompatible with the fundamental right to family unity and the protection of the minor.[350]

4. The Court of Cassation: Family Reunification and Religious Identity

In 2005 and again in 2008, the Court of Cassation stressed that a constitutionally-oriented interpretation of Article 29, Legislative Decree no. 286/98, was required: "where multiple constitutional values of reference are involved (as is the case of family reunification, where, on the one hand, child protection comes into play and, on the other, the safeguarding of state borders), an adequate interpretation of the law should achieve a fair balance of these higher interests, in light also of the values scale provided by the Constituent Assembly".[351] In the specific case, a balance had to be made between the "protection value of the minor, also in relation to a foreign minor, compared to the value of the defence of the territory

[350] Cf. F. MIAZZI, Outline of ruling 9th February 2005, Court of Reggio Emilia, in *Dir. imm. citt.*, 2005, 2, p. 185 *et seq.*

[351] Court of Cassation, 4th November 2005, no. 21395 and three identical decisions of 2008: Court of Cassation, 20th March 2008, no. 7472, Court of Cassation, 2nd July 2008, no.18174 and Court of Cassation, 17th July 2008, no. 19734 at http://www.stranieriinitalia.it/briguglio/immigrazione-e-asilo/2008/aprile/sent-cass-7472-2008.pdf.

and containment of immigration," with the prevalence of the former at the expense of the latter. The case before the Court of Cassation concerned an Italian couple who, through a Rabat lawyer, had managed to locate an abandoned minor and to obtain custody under a kafala arrangement with the Moroccan authorities, after converting to the Islamic religion. Despite the refusal of the Italian Consulate to issue a visa, the couple still brought the minor into Italy. Italian judges then allowed the release of a child's residence permit to subsequently declare the status of adoptability.

In this judgment, the Court of Cassation was called upon for the first time to rule on kafala and excluded the legal representative power of the guardian of the *makful* for the exclusively procedural profile of the (denied) autonomous legitimacy of the *kafil* to oppose the declaration of the child's adoptability status. On a substantial level, however, this decision also recognized that kafala does give guardians indefinite power of custody with the content – in terms of raising the child – of true pre-adoptive foster care.

In the three judgments of 2008, the judges of the Court of Cassation developed this argument, stressing that where the constitutional values of reference are multiple (as mentioned earlier: the protection of minors and the democratic protection of state borders) the only adequate interpretation of this law must be based on striking a fair balance between the interests at stake. In this case the prevalence will tendentially be for the protection of the foreign minor as opposed to the defence of the borders to stem immigration, since this can still be achieved through domestic control of the authorization procedure.

The judgments highlighted the rationale and procedures of kafala, which is generally arranged by judicial procedure, though the degree of detail in which every single Muslim country regulates the discipline may differ. Moreover, kafala was also recognized internationally by the 1989 New York Convention and, in the specific case of Morocco, the institution is provided for by special legislation entitled "*Prise en charge des enfants abandonnés*". It should also be noted that excluding the idea that the institution is exclusively transactional, in the absence of effective controls of the authority, between the Islamic kafala and domestic foster care the areas they have in common should prevail over the differences, since neither of these institutions, unlike adoption, have legitimising effects and do not affect the civil status of the minor.

Kafala might even be said to share greater affinities with adoption, since, while foster care is essentially provisional in nature, kafala tends to last until the child comes of age (even if revocation is admitted). At this point then, the obstacles posed by the Italian consular authorities in

Morocco to the entry of a minor under kafala care into Italy should be definitively overcome, even when the arrangement derives from a notarial deed, albeit approved by the local authority.[352]

It is another question again when it regards the nationality of the subjects entitled to request reunification. If the person requesting reunification with the minor is an Italian national rather than a non-EU citizen, the regulatory point of reference cannot be the same since the Consolidated Immigration Act applies exclusively in the case of a *kafil*/foreign guardian. In this case, the legislative decree of 2007 in the matter of freedom of movement and residence will apply, even though the minor in kafala care cannot be included as a family member, as understood by the Italian legal system.[353]

Clearly there is a risk that kafala might be exploited for the purposes of family reunification, which could occur, for instance, when kafala is

---

[352] So far, Morocco is the only Islamic state to request that a child in kafala care by allowed entry into Italy. Cf. also Court of Cassation, 20th March 2008, cit. For a similar interpretation: Court of Cassation 2nd July 2008, no. 18174, in *Fam. dir.*, 2008, p. 1238 *et seq.*; Court of Cassation 17th July 2008, n. 19734, in *Fam dir.*, 2008, p. 1243 *et seq*. Cf. also J. LONG, *Ancora sul ricongiungimento familiare del minore affidato con kafalah*, in *Dir. imm.citt.*, 2009, p. 112 *et seq.*; E. DE FEIS, *La kafala islamica come strumento di tutela dei minori e presupposti per il riconoscimento in Italia*, in *Fam. Dir.*, 2009, p. 481. The three cases submitted to the Court of Cassation in 2008 all presented a similar description of the facts where the Ministry of Foreign Affairs appealed against the decree authorising a visa for a minor in kafala care with Moroccan guardians who were resident in Italy. The question of law put to the Court was the following: "whether the kafala of Islamic law may be considered relevant for the purposes of reunification pursuant to Article 29, Legislative Decree no. 286 of 1998 despite its exclusively transactional nature and despite the absence of any judicial action aimed at verifying the factual assumptions of the situation of abandonment of the minor or the suitability of the *kafils* (or guardians) themselves". The argument put forward was that the visa for the minor should be refused on the basis of a restrictive interpretation of the provision of Legislative Decree no. 286 of 1998 supporting the exceptional nature of family reunification for which it would be wrong to extend the application of the law envisaged for certain specific relationships to a kafala arrangement: none of these relationships, neither filiation, nor adoption or foster care can be compared, because of its purely transactional nature, to kafala. Cf. also Court of Cassation, 28th January 2010, no. 1908, at legale.savethechildren.it/_DatasImport/pdf/Cassazione_28_1_2010_1908.pdf.

[353] Decree no. 30, 6th February 2007, regarding the implementation of Directive 2004/38/EC on the right of citizens of the Union and their family members to move and reside freely within the territory of the Member States, at www.camera.it/parlam/leggi/deleghe/07030dl.htm.

arranged outside normal institutionalized procedures with an agreement of a purely transactional nature, actually existing in Muslim law. In the usual legislative framework, the state of abandonment of the *makful* and the suitability requirements of the *kafil* are subject to a prior assessment on the basis of which the child's placement will be allowed or not. Otherwise, in kafala by mutual consent, the prerequisites are deemed to speak for themselves in the declaration of the legitimate parent who is transferring parental authority to a third party. In practice, while in the first case control on the legitimacy of the procedure is implemented from the outset, in the second verification is only possible and subsequent to the *kafil* opting to have the agreement approved before the judicial authority.

The Court of Cassation therefore seems to fear that the institution might be exploited in order to circumvent the rules on immigration control, in the event that there is a non-judicial procedure. What is important in this sense is not so much that kafala is adopted in compliance with and on the basis of the efficiency of the controls of the Islamic legal system to which the *kafil* belongs, but that the evidential obligations and procedural filters provided by our own legal system are carried out effectively. It is thus important to underline that, over and above the way kafala is arranged, it will be the task of the Italian administration and of our jurisdiction to verify whether the necessary prerequisites are actually present. The recognition of a legal transaction entered into privately and not examined by the authorities would be contrary to international public order.

Nevertheless, quite clearly the recognition of the social, cultural and legal dignity of kafala should lead us to exclude that it may in itself be contrary to international public order, that is, to a set of fundamental principles which, standing bastion in each national system, must prevent the entry of foreign law if it effectively violates the principles on which the system is based.

This position, however, was completely reversed by the Supreme Court in 2010 where "the admissibility of kafala as a prerequisite for family reunification when the entitled applicant is an Italian national" was denied.[354] In the case in question, an Italian citizen of Moroccan origin

---

[354] Court of Cassation, 1st March 2010, no. 4868, in *Famiglia e dir.*, 2010, p. 780 *et seq.*; in *Riv. dir. intern. prive proc.*, 2010, p. 754 *et seq.*; in *Giur. it.*, 2011, p. 1297 *et seq.*; in *Dir. Famiglia*, 2010, p. 1621 *et seq.*; in *Giust. Civ.*, I, 2011, p. 2180 *et seq.*; in *Nuova giur. civ. Comm.*, 2010, p. *et seq.* 835, with note by J. LONG, *Kafalah: la Cassazione fa il passo del gambero*; in *Minori e giust.*, 2010, p. 325 *et seq.*, with note by ID., *L'ingresso in Italia del minore straniero affidato con kafalah a un cittadino italiano*. Along the same lines cf. also Court of Cassation,

applied for reunification in Italy of a foreign minor residing in Morocco under his legal care through the institution of kafala. The Ministry of Foreign Affairs appealed to the Court of Cassation contesting the decree with which the Court of Appeal had granted the issue of an entry visa (denied by the Italian Consulate in Casablanca) in the interest of the minor seeking family reunification.

The Court reached its conclusion on the basis of a reading of the combined provisions of Legislative Decree 30/2007 and Community Directive 2004/38/CE concerning the right of citizens of the Union and their family members to move and reside freely within the Member States. The judges quashed the contested decree considering the objections posed by the Administration to be founded. Thus, they rejected the entry visa for the Moroccan minor since it was impossible to classify the minor in kafala care as a family member of subjects who were resident in Italy, for the purposes of Legislative Decree no. 286 of 1998 and Legislative Decree no. 30 of 2007.

A careful reading of the same should lead us to believe that there is no room to include minors who are not direct descendants or descendants of the spouse/partner, nor blood relatives, nor dependent or cohabiting in the foreign country. As in the case of Moroccan legislation on kafala, the minor is placed within a family according to a sort of conventional guardianship, to be adapted, aimed at the material and emotional protection of the child, who has no claim to family membership.

Furthermore, nor would a wider interpretation of the Consolidated Immigration Act be possible, since its application is limited to ensuring family unity. Clearly this is not the case here since we are dealing with an Italian citizen, who is unrelated to the child and cannot include him as a child in his family. The only possibility provided for by our system concerns international adoption, according to which Italian nationals are allowed to place an abandoned foreign minor with their family on the basis of Law no. 184 of 1983.

The other argument in support of the Court's decision is to assert the legitimacy of the difference in treatment afforded to the minor placed in kafala care with an Italian citizen compared with the minor placed in kafala care with a foreign national of Islamic faith residing in our country, for whom reunification is currently allowed. As already mentioned,

---

17th December 2010, no. 25661, Mass., 2010, p 1096 *et seq.*; 7th January 2011, n. 20722, (unpublished). Insisting particularly on the need to take into consideration the idea that kafala care may amount to international adoption in disguise also Court of Turin, 14th May 2010, in *Quaderni dir. e politica ecclesiastica*, 2011, p. 803 *et seq.*

reunification cannot be refused *a priori* on the basis of the nationality of the *kafil*, but must be assessed case by case, verifying the existence or not of a substantial relationship between the minor and the guardian, taking into account also the risk of circumventing immigration laws. If the bond between the two is consolidated prior to entry into Italy, the legal procedure of family reunification may be used, applying directly or indirectly the Consolidated Immigration Act since "reunification fulfils the right to unity of two subjects already linked by an existing family bond, while adoption aims to establish a new family bond between two previously unrelated individuals".[355]

The need for a resolution in methodological terms thus led the *Sezioni Unite* of the Court of Cassation to admit a broader interpretation of the notion of "family member" referred to in Legislative Degree 30/2007. They took their starting point from the fundamental legal principle according to which the protection of the child's best interests override any other protected and possibly conflicting legal interests, on the basis of a heuristic criterion and a constitutionally adequate assessment of the regulatory provisions of the legal system. This regulatory interpretation, through the use of the criterion of reasonableness, as developed by the Constitutional Court (which requires that functionally similar circumstances are treated in the same way, by virtue of the "substantial identity of rationale"), should mean, however, that EU and non-EU citizens are treated equally, regardless of their religious faith.

As the most innovative aspect of this jurisprudential intervention has been acutely emphasized, it is the "geographic-symbolic range" of this institution which made it possible not to simply evaluate comparability but to dwell on the real interest of the minor, on the judicial evaluation, allowing the emergence of an "overlap between spatial and semantic translation processes".[356]

In the wake of this ruling, the Court of Appeal of Rome also intervened in 2011.[357] It recognized the exclusive operability of Legislative Decree no. 30/2007 with the consequent impossibility of issuing an entry visa as the child could not be included in the notion of family member – essential

---

[355] R. GELLI, *Questioni relative al ricongiungimento del minore in Kafalah al cittadino italiano. Corte d'appello di Torino, sez. fam. e pers., decr. 19 novembre 2009 e Cassazione civile, 1 marzo 2010 n. 4868*, in *Famiglia e diritto*, 8-9, 2010, p.790 *et seq*.

[356] M. RICCA, *Culture interdette: Modernità, migrazioni, diritto interculturale.* Turin, Bollati Boringhieri, 2013, esp. p. 159.

[357] Court of Appeal, Rome, 31st January 2011, at http://www.marinacastellaneta.it/blog/wp-content/uploads/2013/09/kafala.pdf.

for the reunification between an Italian couple and the Moroccan *makful* in their care. In both rulings reference was made to the most serious consequence of this restrictive interpretation of Legislative Decree 30/2007 – the violation of the main criterion of the child's best interests.

In the same year, the Court of Appeal of Ancona stepped in and completely overturned the position taken by the Court of Cassation the previous year.[358] They provided a constitutionally-oriented reading of the provisions on family reunification contained in the Consolidated Immigration Act, focusing on the primary interest of the minor, given that the child had been placed with a couple not by private agreement but by virtue of the couple's signed undertaking before the local Administration of Social Affairs - Family and Child Directorate representing the country of origin. The Court therefore recognized the *makful's* right of entry into Italy through the instrument of family reunification. On the one hand, it considered that the declaration of kafala made by the State of the minor constitutes a guarantee that the procedures for intercountry adoption will not be violated or circumvented, since kafala is the only remedy that can be implemented according to the law of the minor. On the other, it also based its decision on the recognition of the institution of kafala as practiced by the European legal system.

Again, in the same year, the Appeal Court of Venice granted the issue of an entry visa to two minors in kafala care with their uncle residing in Italy.[359] The request for reunification as well as the entry visa had been denied by the Foreign Affairs office and the Court of Verona itself had rejected the uncle's appeal, arguing that kafala was contrary to public order in that it constitutes an alternative care arrangement – outside the family – has no time limit and does not produce the 'useful' legal effects of adoption. The court of first instance argued that Article 29 of the Consolidated Immigration Act does not allow the reunification of minors in kafala care, as none of the figures within this institution would be attributable to those expressly provided for in the act, in addition to the biological parent-child relationship. The Court of Appeal, however, opted to issue the entry visa.

The decision, however, found itself in contrast with the direction taken by the Court of Cassation of 2010, which stated that kafala may be a suitable condition for family reunification but can only apply to foreign

---

[358] Court of Appeal, Ancona, 16th November 2011, at www.aibi.it/ita/images/Kafala-Sentenza-Corte-Appello-Ancona-11-111.pdf.

[359] Appeal Court of Venice, 9th February 2011, at http://old.asgi.it/public/parser_download/save/corte_appello_venezia_decreto0902 2011.pdf.

nationals pursuant to Article 29 of the Consolidated Immigration Act – not for Italian citizens (in the judgment of the Court of Appeal of Venice it is an Italian citizen).[360] The Venice Court of Appeal, however, argued that the kafala institution, as governed by Moroccan law, which provides for a judicial procedure or a system of legal checks and authorizations, cannot be considered contrary to the principle of public order as it is suitable for ensuring the institutional function of protection of the child, and is also a recognised institution according to the 1989 New York Convention (Article 20). It follows that the institution of kafala, as regulated by Moroccan law, is comparable to that of foster care as provided for by Italian law.

In the legal recognition of kafala, it is also necessary to remember the joint application of the New York Convention and Article 3 e) of the 1996 Hague Convention, which expressly makes reference to the provision of care by kafala or another similar institution. It expressly recognizes kafala measures: Article 23 (2) f) warns that recognition will be refused if Article 33 is not complied with. This establishes that where the foreign provision concerns the placement of the minor in a foster family or institutional care, or the provision of care by kafala or similar institution, then direct consultation between the Central Authorities is necessary, which might also prevent the placement from going through.[361] Italy's ratification of the 1996 Hague Convention, and, importantly, the reference to kafala, should exclude any opposition to public order, without prejudice to the effects and nature of the institution. It is also important to emphasize that Articles 65-67 of Law no. 218/1995 should be suppressed, but obviously this would not entail obligations for non-contracting Islamic States.

In a recent jurisprudential intervention of the *Sezioni Unite* of the Court of Cassation, in 2013, the axis of reasoning once again correctly shifted from the right of the Italian citizen to family reunification to the position of the child.[362] It was emphasised that kafala is first and foremost a protection measure, the only measure of its kind available in Muslim

---

[360] Court of Cassation, 1st March 2010 no. 4868, at http://legale.savethechildren.it/_DatasImport/pdf/Cassazione_1_3_2010_4868.pdf; P. MOROZZO DELLA ROCCA, *Sull'affidamento al cittadino italiano del minore straniero mediante kafalah tornerà a pronunciarsi la Cassazione*, in *Il corriere giuridico*, 6, 2011, p. 848 *et seq*.

[361] At present, Articles 23 f) and 33 are only applicable as far as Morocco is concerned – the only Islamic state to ratify the 1996 Hague Convention.

[362] Published at http://www.meltingpot.org/IMG/pdf/cassazione__sez._unite_civili_sentenza_n.21108-2013.pdf.

countries, and is considered suitable for protecting the best interests of the abandoned child, according to international law.[363] It would therefore be contrary to the best interests of the child not to allow him/her to be reunited with the family with which s/he lived and which guarantees a healthy environment for growth and emotional enrichment.

In addressing the broader issue, the judges recalled what had previously been established by the Court and specifically by the judgments of 2008 and 2010.[364] Adhering to the first of these, the Court ruled that authorisation to enter the country for the purposes of family reunification could not be refused when requested in the interest of a non-EU minor placed in the care of an Italian national residing in Italy with a kafala arrangement pronounced by a foreign judge, in the event that the minor is dependent on or lives in the country of origin with the Italian national or serious health reasons mean that the minor must be personally assisted by them.

In the first place, what is important is the principle that in any circumstances in which the need for protection of the minor emerges, the child's best interests must be assured over and above any other conflicting interests, in compliance with International Treaties. In second place, the *Sezioni Unite* adhered to the constitutionally-oriented interpretation of Article 29 of the Consolidated Immigration Act, confirming the provisions of the 2008 judgment. They felt that interpreting Legislative Decree no. 30/2007, excluding completely its applicability to the Italian citizen seeking reunification with a non-EU minor placed in his/her care under a kafala arrangement would constitute a difference in treatment to the detriment of Italian citizens (so-called reverse disparity) with respect to foreign nationals for whom reunification with a minor placed with them under a similar arrangement would be allowed. On the basis of these observations, judges came to define the issue without recognizing any impediment to the extensive interpretation "especially when it is the only

---

[363] Court of Cassation, *Sezioni Unite*, 16th September 2013, no. 2118, in *Fam. Min.*, 2014, p. 127 *et seq.*, with comment by R. GELLI, *Il ricongiungimento del minore in kafalah al cittadino italiano: la svolta delle Sezioni Unite* and at www.personaedanno.it/attachments/article/43614/Cassazione_-_sez._unite_civili,_sentenza_n.21108-2013.pdf.

[364] Court of Cassation no. 7472/2008 and no. 4868/2010, cit. The first affirmed the possibility of granting an entry visa to Italy for the reunification between Moroccan citizens residing in Italy and Moroccan minors placed in their care under a kafala arrangement, on the basis of the constitutionally-oriented interpretation of Article 29, Legislative Decree no. 286/98. The second ruling opted for a diametrically opposed outcome based on the application of Legislative Decree no. 30/2007.

constitutionally-oriented interpretation and is in accordance with the principles stated in supranational laws, pacts or EU sources".

But this breadth in meaning is also required by the principle of the child's best interests prevailing over other interests. The argument is supported and further specified also by a statement to Parliament which declared that "fostered children and foster parents with temporary custody may enjoy the rights conferred by the directive on the basis of the solidity of the bond established in the particular case".[365] Therefore, a formal comparison between legal institutions is not required, but it is intended to emphasize the substantial aspect of the relationship by virtue of the combined provisions of the principle of the child's best interests and non-discrimination. In essence, what forges the meaning of comprehensive family member of the child in kafala care is not the abstract legal area of this legal institution, but the substantial relationship between child and guardian. For the Court of Cassation, this does not mean recognizing the same effects as adoption for a kafala measure in our legal system (which may only be resolved at a regulatory level), but instead means acknowledging the relationship generated by it, in which the rights of the child are fulfilled.

Similarities with our foster care and adoption institutions, the principle of non-discrimination also in terms of religious faith and the protection of the child's best interests justify the inclusion of kafala in the concept of family reunification, though limited to nationals from Islamic states. The situation is different for Italian nationals, albeit converted to Islam, who have sought intercountry adoption but in an Islamic state and thus not in possession of a provision that can be translated into adoption. In these cases, the jurisprudence has applied Legislative Decree no. 30/2007, which does not count the minor - *makful* as a family member. It might, however, concern Italian nationals who have converted to Islam and must respect the rules of the Quran.

With reference to the legal effectiveness of kafala granted to a 'western' citizen, the issue essentially turns on the compatibility of this protection measure with intercountry adoption law. In such cases,

---

[365] Statement from the Commission to the Parliament and Government of 2009 concerning guidelines to difficult aspects of transposition and application of Directive 2004/38/EC. Cf. also Legislative Decree of 2017, concerning urgent provisions for the acceleration of international protection proceedings, as well as the fight against illegal immigration and, the same year, March 29 2017, amendments to the Consolidated Immigration Act pursuant to Legislative Decree 25 July 1998, no. 286, and other provisions concerning protection measures for unaccompanied foreign minors.

however, the principle of the child's best interests appears to be decisive in a consolidated jurisprudential orientation that tends towards the strongest protection of these interests. Theoretically, the legislative framework of Article 41, Law no. 218 of 1995 could also be used. According to this, a foreign provision may be recognized in Italy if it does not fall within the scope of application of the laws on adoption in special circumstances.[366] However, the possible operability of the limitation to public order should be established, stressing that the reform law of private international law only required an assessment with reference to the effects of the application of the foreign law (and not of the foreign law itself).[367] Moreover, in view of the sensitive nature of this kind of protection, great care would be needed in using this limitation in the international system of child protection.[368]

Another decision by the Court of Cassation in 2015, again centred on the need for enhanced protection of the child's interest, also recognized a conventional-transactional kafala arrangement as a valid condition for

---

[366] Specifically, the case occurred with regard to action pursuant to Articles 66 and 67 of Law no. 218/95 concerning a couple with whom a *makful* had been placed by order of the Moroccan judge. In support of their application, the couple claimed that it was in the best interests of the minor – suffering from a serious illness – to access the medical care guaranteed by the Italian National Health Service. The application had been accepted by the Court of Appeal on the grounds that kafala was comparable to foster care as envisaged by domestic law and in the absence, according to the characteristic features of the institution, of any element that might run contrary to public order or mandatory regulations of national law that could prevent the recognition of the effectiveness of the measure in Italy. The Court of Cassation reversed the decision of the trial judge establishing that the request for resolution could not be proposed pursuant to Article 67, paragraph 2, Law no. 218/95, but should have been proposed pursuant to Law no. n. 183/8446. Cf. also Court of Cassation, 23rd September 2011, no. 19450, *Corr. Giur.*, 2012, p.197 *et seq.*, with comments by P. MAROZZO DELLA ROCCA.

[367] See Court of Verona 12th July 2010, in *Quaderni dir. e politica ecclesiastica*, 2011, p. 811 *et seq.*

[368] Cf. R. CLERICI, *La compatibilità del diritto di famiglia mussulmano con l'ordine pubblico internazionale*, in *Famiglia e diritto*, 2009, p. 197 *et seq.*, according to whom "the current or future validity of these two international acts [International Convention on the Rights of the Child and the 1996 Hague Convention] thus imposes on the Italian State the obligation to recognize the effectiveness of this institution and to exclude, at the same time, its opposition to public order". The Court of Appeal of Turin, 18th July 2007, excluded any opposition to public order by reason of kafala being specifically mentioned in the 1989 New York Convention, in *Dir. fam. Pers.*, 2008, p. 143 *et seq.*

family reunification.[369] The Court observed, *inter alia*, that it would be discriminatory if a citizen of an Islamic country who moves to a 'western' state and acquires citizenship, was obliged to cease identifying with the culture of his homeland when kafala is neither criminally relevant nor contrary to the fundamental principles of public order in the new country. In general, it is also worth noting that intrafamily guardianship, which is typical with kafala by mutual consent, is not entirely unknown to the family culture of western countries nor can it be said to deny the right to family life or to live in the family of origin. Rather, it represents a form of expansion of the family protection network, aimed at helping the child enjoy better opportunities for growth and better living conditions, safeguarding the relationship with the parents and family of origin. Among other things, it is also important to note that intrafamily guardianship allows the child to live not only within the extended family environment, but within an environment that shares the values and identities of origin.

Recently, the Regional Administrative Court of Piedmont (2016) accepted the appeal of a 17-year-old Egyptian girl who arrived in Italy after she had been placed in the care of an uncle residing in Italy through the institution of kafala.[370] Faced with the refusal of a residence permit for work purposes, she filed an appeal for the incorrect configuration of her circumstances as 'unaccompanied minor'. It should be noted that when a legal form of guardianship entailing effective custody by an adult comes into play, as in the case of a kafala arrangement, this phrase should cease to exist. For reasons outside her control or the uncle's failure to apply for formal recognition of the arrangement on time, a formal provision of placement in kafala care had not been granted in in Italy as well, nor had the opinion of the General Directorate of Immigration of the Ministry of Labour and Social Policies come to light.

Again, recalling the decision of the *Sezioni Unite* of 2013 on a similar issue, the Juvenile Court of Salerno (2017), transformed kafala into

---

[369] Court of Cassation, 2nd February 2015, no. 1843, in *Nuova Giurisprudenza civile commentata*, 2015 p. 707 *et seq*. with a comment by M. DI MASI, *La Cassazione apre alla kafalah negoziale per garantire in concreto il best interest of the child*. The ruling underlines that "holding that the rules on adoption and specifically those on international adoption may apply to this institution, means negatively prejudging the meaning and relevance of the institution of kafala in the legal systems that provide for it".

[370] Regional Administrative Court of Piedmont, Judgment no. 281 of 3rd March 2006 at
http://www.osservatoriofamiglia.it/moduli/17506191_tarpiemonte281%20MINORE%20KAFALA%20PERMESS0%20SOGGIORNO.pdf.

adoption pursuant to Article 44, with the child getting a new surname in addition to the old one and a visa to remain in Italy.[371]

Finally, a Tutelary Judge of the Court of Mantua, 10/05/2018, recognised in full a foreign provision ordering the placement of a foreign minor with an Italian national under a kafala arrangement. At the basis of the ruling in question was the measure issued by the Court of Khenchela (Algeria), which ordered an Algerian minor to be placed in kafala care with an Italian woman. She subsequently returned to Italy, taking the child with her, who, from that moment on, lived with the *kafil* and her husband. The social services reported to the local Tutelary Judge the presence of an unaccompanied foreign minor and requested foster care, in particular the appointment of the woman as her guardian. Noting that the measure issued by the Algerian Court had full and direct effect in the Italian legal system pursuant to Articles 65 and 66, Law no. 218/1995, Article 20 of the New York Convention on the Rights of the Child and Articles 3, e) and 33 of the Hague Convention of 19 October 1996 on jurisdiction, the judge held that there was no need to proceed with the request to appoint the woman guardian of the minor, since the protection and legal representation of the child had already been attributed to her by the foreign provision that ordered kafala. The Court, in essence, conformed to the consolidated orientation of the case-law of the Court of Cassation, which equates the institution of kafala under Islamic law with the Italian institution of foster care.

5. Ratification of the Hague Convention in Italy Excluding Kafala

With its law of 2015, Italy finally ratified the 1996 Hague Convention[372] applicable to questions relating to the attribution, exercise and total or partial revocation of parental responsibility, custody rights, the protection of the child as well as care, upbringing and other similar systems, to the administration, conservation or disposition of the child's assets, the placement of the child in a foster family or in alternative care facilities or to child support. Ascertaining filiation, maintenance obligations, adoption

---

[371] Juvenile Court of Salerno, no.7, 26th January 2017.

[372] *Ratifica ed esecuzione della Convenzione sulla competenza, la legge applicabile, il riconoscimento, l'esecuzione e la cooperazione in materia di responsabilità genitoriale e di misure di protezione dei minori, fatta all'Aja il 19 ottobre 1996, published in Gazzetta Uff.* n. 157, 9th July 2015 and at http://www.aiafavvocati.it/files/2015/07/RESPONSABILITA_GENITORIALE.pdf.

and the matter of asylum or immigration remain outside the Convention. In force internationally since 2002, the Convention has been ratified by 41 states (only Italy was missing among the EU countries). Law no. 101 identified the Presidency of the Council of Ministers as "Central Authority". As clarified in the explanatory report, Italy felt that it should "set down specific rules for the adaptation of domestic legislation both with reference to the recognition of certain protection measures, and for the need to modify Law no. 218, 31st May 1995, concerning the reform of the Italian system of private international law".

The difficulties that emerged in the course of the parliamentary ratification process highlight the problems that Italian legislation has had to face in family matters, which the law should only 'touch upon' lightly when it comes to legal institutions of other systems.[373] This with a view to supporting the gradual process of integration of foreign minors into the new host country, without severing the sense of identity with the homeland, directed towards a democratic pluralism.

Ever since the Hague Convention came into being, the complexity of the issues to be addressed has been apparent. It also made a cultural and legal transition, favouring habitual residence over citizenship in attributing jurisdiction to Member States.[374]

Italy last intervened with Bill no. 1589 presented by the government in 2013, proposing the frameworks of previous legislatures, in which it had initially decided not to proceed with the simple ratification of the Convention, and proposing a text that intervened in a partially autonomous manner. It aimed to introduce new and independent systems – international foster care, for instance – and assimilate *kafala* and adoption in terms of procedure and requirements, though its effects remained unclear. This legislative proposal envisaged two distinct possibilities as regards Articles 4 and 5 but presented an inconsistency in the process of recognition in Italy regarding the "legal assistance" of an abandoned child, clearly evident in the *kafala* system. It was based on the distinction between the protection by *kafala* of a child not in a state of abandonment, Article 4, and that of the abandoned child, Article 5, both designed to arrange placement in Italy though failing to take into account the need for harmonization with its legislative system. In addition, further problems arose with the neglected child who, while providing for by a series of

[373] For centuries the family has been an island that the sea of law should only touch upon lightly, according to A.C. JEMOLO, *La famiglia e il diritto*, in *Ann. Sen. Giur. Università di Catania*, 1948, III, p. 3.

[374] The Council of the European Union adopted the 2008/431 / CE regulation with the aim of authorizing member states to join or ratify the Convention.

guarantees similar to those used for intercountry adoption, was not placed in a position of equality with other children.

The only possible outcome was thus foster care, since the parents were appointed only as guardians and protectors, without considering that this was a child in a state of neglect. Thus, legal measures such as temporary foster care would be put in place, which obviously did not count in the case of abandonment. In particular, the child would find him/herself with a residence permit to be renewed every two years. On reaching adulthood s/he would not be guaranteed Italian citizenship, nor take the surname of the foster parent, establish any legal relationship, or have any inheritance rights. In essence, the child's legal status would be comparable to that of an unaccompanied foreign minor.

It would have been more appropriate to equate the Islamic *kafala* with legitimizing adoption or adoption in special circumstances pursuant to Article 44, Law 184/1983, especially in consideration of the rationale behind the law, whose primary objective is the protection of the child and must therefore aim at a stable family status within a real family unit, in which the child is integrated both socially and legally. Here, again, it would have been advisable to entrust this task to the Commission for Intercountry Adoption rather than the Juvenile Justice Department, as envisaged in this draft bill, both because of its affinity and its greater expertise and capacity in terms of vigilance in the field. It should be made clear that reference is made to the juridical institution of *kafala* rather than similar systems not clearly defined, systems which could lead to the introduction of other forms of international family childcare into our system which may not be easily identified or identifiable.

Also for the child who has not been abandoned, Article 4 did not seem to bear any reference to Italian legislation on temporary foster care. From the tone of the law it appeared that children within Italy's borders benefitting from the protection provided by Law 184/1983 were discriminated against. A reading of the bill points to a difference between legal assistance and custody that derive from the legal systems of the countries of origin: in the first case the reference is to the *kafala* system, in the second it is not clear to which system reference is made. Determining abandonment cannot be left to arbitrary assessment by the Juvenile Court, but should result from certain criteria of the foreign provision: the parents being temporarily prevented from taking care of the child; absence of measures curtailing parental authority; permanence of family cohabitation.

Furthermore, no assessment of the suitability of the applicants prior to the start of the procedure, as would normally be expected, was called for by the Juvenile Court, whose task was simply to ratify the work carried out by the central Authorities and authorized organisations. Clearly, the risk was that national and international legislation regarding adoption might be circumvented.

The regulatory provision also referred to "spouses residing in Italy", with no mention made of mixed couples. It was established that it was the duty of the Tutelary Judge to confer the functions of guardian/protector on the couple: this provision was useless, automatic attribution by law would have been preferable. Another point that was not clear was the reference to Article 37, which seemed to introduce an attempt to circumvent the Hague Convention, which explicitly excludes the ascertainment and contestation of filiation, the decision on adoption, etc. from its scope of application. Again, the juridical configuration of potentially permanent legal assistance was not made clear, appearing, as it did, to fall in line with the premises and procedures of intercountry adoption, to which it should be fully equated to avoid dangerous forms of discrimination. It must also be remembered that, pursuant to new regulation on registration, "the effects of the family registry are understood to mean a group of people bound by marriage, kinship, affinity, adoption, protection or by emotional ties, cohabiting and dwelling in the same Municipality" and which also appears to include children placed within the family unit through *kafala.*[375] This draft law was not fully incorporated into the 2015 law, which opted for a more meagre text and to remove the section relating to *kafala*, to be approved at a later date with more legislation.

Another regulatory solution could be envisaged, more in keeping with the rationale of the system and more respectful of the legal and cultural context, using the recognition pursuant to Articles 65 and 66 of Law no. 218/1995, thus as a foreign provision of non-contentious jurisdiction. This idea, however, would still leave numerous issues unresolved both in terms of the stability of the system and the powers of representation of the *kafil*. It is also important to reiterate that our Court of Cassation's body of case-law has demonstrated a growing interest in the legal importance of *kafala,* independent of adoption.

Automatic recognition is difficult to accept in that *kafala* and adoption do not merely represent similar or comparable legal systems and automatic acceptance. Nor would it allow the cultural differences of the legal frameworks in which these systems lie, and which are an integral part of the identity of the child, to be taken into due consideration. What is vital is that in the name of an excessive respect for the child's cultural traditions,

[375] Cf. Article 4, Presidential Decree, 30th May 1989.

s/he does not end up in a legal context that is worse than any other subjects protected under law.

The solution might be to opt for a special mode of access to citizenship, consciously chosen by the child after a period of stay in Italy. From this perspective, access to *status civitatis* could lead to a redefinition of the *status filiationis*, if the interested parties agree.[376]

An examination of the rationale behind Italy's legislation and jurisprudential provisions seems to suggest full recognition of the *kafala* as a tool for the reception of the child with full parental responsibility, with reference to care, moral and material support, emotional bonds, maintenance, education and upbringing, but without representation of the child, which still remains in the hands of the foreign authority.

Another viable solution in the interests of the child could be to pursue fostering for non-abandoned children and intercountry adoption for the others, with a clear attribution of responsibility, rights and duties for to the parents/guardians, also considering the *kafala* system in the countries of origin. Indeed, particular attention must be paid to the concept of abandonment in the state of origin. Experience shows that this declaration is made by one of the parents who forgoes care of the child for different reasons, *inter alia*, related to economic difficulties. In Islamic countries the parent signs this declaration with *kafala* in mind – thus this sort of foster care – up to the age of eighteen, keeping ties with the biological family.

What must be avoided is the risk of a dual misunderstanding that also affects the fostering family. In this sense agreements with the *kafala* child's homeland would be appropriate, which may also possibly provide for ways of relating with the natural family, preparing the families and, if necessary, the possibility to transform *kafala* into adoption when the child comes of age.

It should also be noted that the text of the bill referred to "legal assistance" which, although used in Article 3, sub-paragraph e) of the Italian version of the Hague Convention, in our system usually indicates the technical defence in proceedings through the mediation of a jurist qualified as a lawyer. Parental support, instead, does not need to be granted to qualified subjects and includes a wider power of moral and material care of the child, analogous to parental responsibility/guardianship, with the

---

376 Cf. in a broad sense N. YASSARI, *Adding by Choice: Adoption and Functional Equivalents in Islamic and Middle Easter Law*, in *American Journal of Comparative Law*, 2015, 63, 4, pp. 927-962 in which, by comparing certain national legal systems of Islamic countries with the category of "functional equivalents", it defines forms of protection for children outside the family, while respecting the Quran's prohibition of adoption.

exclusion of legal representation. It would be better to refer to "juridical assistance", making it clear that it involves the rights and duties of parental responsibility. In the French text of the Hague Convention the term is *recueil légal*, more correctly translatable as reception rather than legal assistance. As to protection measures, the English text provides for family custody, placement of the child in a foster family, and placement under the *kafala* system, provision of care by *kafala* or similar institution.

In addition, the bill did not clearly outline the procedures necessary to provide legal assistance or to obtain the consent of the parents/guardians of the country of origin; nor did it indicate the channels through which Italian parents should proceed with foster care or what shape the relationship between the two families should take. Finally, the possibility of acquiring citizenship at the age of majority was not clearly stated.

Article 5 seemed to superimpose various types of assistance, confusing systems that do not create a parent-child relationship with legitimizing national or international adoption. It should be noted, indeed, that to provide this form of assistance an Italian couple must possess the requisites required for adoption pursuant to Article 6 Law no. 184/1983 and contact an authorized body. Islamic legal systems of child protection are not easily comparable to 'western' systems. Furthermore, it must be considered that by not mentioning the kafala system, the 1983 Hague Convention does not consider itself applicable to *kafala,* also because it does not create a relationship of filiation – not even partial.

Italian case law, especially in the past, converted *kafala* measures first into pre-adoptive fostering and then into actual adoption, especially when the former Law no. 184 was in force.[377] The current regulation in Article 35 requires that the validity of adoptions made in member countries of the 1993 Hague Convention be recognized, using the term "adoptions" or provisions issued in foreign states intended to allow adoption in the country of arrival. For non-signatory countries of the Hague Convention, the terms of adoption or pre-adoptive fostering are used instead.[378] The use of different terminology has the precise purpose of making sure that any

---

[377] In articles 31 and 32 it provided for the jurisdiction of the Juvenile Court to declare "the effectiveness in the State of the adoption or pre-adoption custody of the child issued by a foreign authority regarding Italian citizens residing in Italy or in the foreign state, or other provision in terms of protection and other child protection systems". Given the generic nature of the reference to child protection systems, this could be used for the *kafala* system.

[378] Article 36. It should also be noted that in paragraph 4 it uses only the term adoptions for the recognition of adoptions established in the countries where the adoptive parents have resided for at least two years.

adoption provision pronounced in Italy does not distort the meaning of the original provision. Article 37a of Law no. 184, which provides that "the Italian adoption law applies to the foreign minor who is in a state of neglect", should be applied.

The 1996 Hague Convention is set to replace that of 1961 and also requires a reform to be made of Article 42 of Law no. 218/1995. This determines a reformulation of the conceptual categories in terms of protection of minors which can easily be brought back to the notion of parental responsibility. Using this as the only category could lead to a uniformity of international private law, characterized by greater certainty about the qualification of the specific case. Consequently, the only distinction useful for the purpose of identifying the source of a regulation derives from the location of the child's residence in a Member State of the European Union or in a third State.

Clearly there is an urgent need for a commitment to use every means possible to find a solution from a multicultural perspective, respecting the cultural and juridical traditions of our country and of the countries of Islamic religion, but above all aimed at satisfying the interest of the child and his/her psychological and physical development in respect of the child's rights. To this end, it might be worth reconsidering among a range of alternative solutions the *kafala* system as well.

6. Legal Instruments Related to a Religious Command and Principle of Secularism. Issues and Perspectives

It is well known that in France the Mission de l'adoption internationale (MAI), an institution similar to our own Intercountry Adoption Commission (IAC), does not authorize the entry of minors whose national law prohibits adoption, and kafala is understood as a Muslim institution that "*ne peut en aucune façon être comparée à une adoption, simple ou plénière, laquelle emporte création d'un lien de filiation, ce qui est totalement proscrit par la Charia et par la législation familiale en vigueur notamment au Maroc et en Algérie. Dans ces conditions, le droit international privé français, respectueux des législations étrangères et soucieux d'éviter le prononcé en France de décisions conférant à des étrangers un statut non susceptible d'être reconnu dans leur pays d'origine, s'oppose à l'adoption en France d'enfants dont la loi nationale interdit l'adoption*".[379]

---

379 Note on "La Kafala de droit musulman", website of the Ministry of Foreign and European Affairs:

This approach was legally consecrated with the enactment of Law no. 2001-111 (relating to international adoption), which introduced provisions into the Civil Code preventing legitimising/full adoption of foreign minors whose national law prohibits such an institution.[380] The only exception allowed, pursuant to Article 370-3, 2 paragraph of the Civil Code, regards minors who were born or habitually reside in France. Prior to the introduction of this law, France used a single criterion for the distributive application of the personal laws of the parties involved: the adopter's law was applied with reference to the conditions and effects of adoption, while the adoptee's *lex fori* determined the conditions and modalities of the valid provision of consent or representation.

The problematic nature of this lay in the fact that, in practice, the French court, revealing a certain legal nationalism, used its own *forma mentis* to assess the content and validity of that consent. With the Fanthou case in 1995, the French Court of Cassation stated that two spouses could adopt a child whose national law does not recognise adoption or prohibits it if, regardless of the provisions of that law, the child's legal representative has given his/her consent in full knowledge of the effects, which, according to French law, derive from full adoption, i.e. the complete severance of all legal ties between the adopted child and his/her natural family.[381]

In Switzerland, a 2002 law established the need for certain additional requirements for the adoption of a child, if prohibited by national law. This consisted of documentary evidence of parental consent to the adoption of the child or a declaration of the country of origin indicating the reasons for which consent cannot be given and certifying the placement of the child with the future adoptive parents.

Belgium intervened with a law in 2005.[382] The only preconditions required are that the child be an orphan who has lost both parents, the

---

http://www.diplomatie.gouv.fr/fr/adopter-a-1-etranger/comment-adopter-a-1-etranger/leglossaire-de-1-adoption/tous-les-termes-de-1-adoption/article/kafala-de-droit-musulman. Besides the law of 2001, the legislative reference is to the Circular of 22nd October 2014 relative to the legal effects of *recueil légal* in France, at http://www.textes.justice.gouv.fr/art_pix/JUSC1416688C.pdf.

380 Law no. 2001-111, 6th February 2001, on international adoption. For comments cf. P. L AGARDE, *La loi du 6 février 2001 relative à l'adoption internationale: une opportune clarification*, in *Rev. crit. drot internal. privé*, 2001, p.275 *et seq*.

381 Court of Cassation, *I chambre civile*, 10th May 1995, at https:/www.legifrance.gouv.fr/affichJuriJudi.do?idTexte=JURITEXT000007033183.

382 In its Civil Code Belgium recognized adoption of minors from countries where national law does not provide for adoption or pre-adoptive custody (Article 361-5). In this way, couples who intend to adopt a minor from a country that does not

recipient of an abandonment order and subject to the protection of the public authorities. The relevant organisation of the child's country of origin should provide a form of protection for the child in addition to authorizing his/her transfer in order to guarantee the child a permanent stay abroad. Both authorities concerned must provide written approval of the decision to place the child with a guardian. In 2008, the Brussels Court of Appeal ruled that "*l'adoption plénière d'un enfant n'est pas fondée sur de justes motifs et n'a pas lieu dans son intérêt supérieur ni dans le respect des droits fondamentaux qui lui sont reconnus en droit international, lorsque l'adoptant est le père biologique de l'adopté et que le lien de filiation peut être établi. La filiation adoptive ne sera envisagée que s'il n'est pas - ou plus - possible d'établir la filiation biologique*".[383] This highlights the desire to contrast intrafamily adoption, which is common in kafala arrangements.

In 2007, a Spanish law also intervened in the matter.[384] Where the adoption of a minor is requested by Spanish nationals, a sort of 'pre-nationality' status is afforded to the child, applying the domestic law

---

recognise adoption can apply to the Belgian Central Authority for placement. The authorities of the child's country of origin authorize the expatriation of the minor and the consulate issues a temporary visa for entry into Belgium for pre-adoption purposes. Once the child has arrived in Belgium, the couple can register him/her in their municipality of residence and, where it concerns orphans of both parents, ask the court to declare the adoption. The reform corresponds to the coming into force, on 1st September. 2005 of *loi du 24 avr. 2003 réformant l'adoption, de la loi du 13 mars 2003 modifiant le Code judiciaire et du décret du 31 mars 2004 relatif à l'adoption, cui si somma la loi du 6 déc. 2005*. Cf. S. SAROLEA, *L'adoption internationale en droit belge à l'aune de la jurisprudence de la cour européenne des droits de l'homme*, in *Rev. trim. dr. Fam.*, 2009, l, p.11 *et seq.*

383 *Cour d'appel de la jeunesse de Bruxelles*, 7th May 2008, *Rev. trim. dr. Fam.*, 2009, 3, p. 737 *et seq.*

384 *Real Decreto 240/2007, de 16 feb. sobre entrada, libre circulación y residencia en España de ciudadanos de los Estados miembros de la Unión Europea y de otros Estados parte en el Acuerdo sobre el Espacio Económico Europeo*, in *BOE* no. 51, 28th February 2007. Cf. A.L. CALVO CARAVACA, J. CARRASCOSA GONZÁLEZ, *La ley 54/2007 de 28 de diciembre 2007 sobre adopción internacional (reflexiones y comentarios)*, Granada, Comares, 2008 who note, among other things that "*l'adopción se concibe como una institución de protección del menor y de integración de éste en una familia*" (p.8); M. DIAGO, *La kafala islamica en España*, in *Cuadernos de Der. Transnacional*, 2, 2010, pp. 140-164 and at http://www.millenniumdipr.com/archivos/1350316352.pdf; N. MARCHAL ESCALONA, *La kafala marroquí: problemas de ayer, hoy y mañana*, in *Rev. Int. doctr. y jusispr.*, and at
http://www.fundacionadopcionvivirenfamilia.org/fotosbd/25092013190243413l.pdf.

aimed at ensuring child protection measures are in place. An identical legal framework has been adopted in Luxembourg.[385] In Germany, on the other hand, in the event of a couple seeking to take care of an abandoned child under a kafala arrangement, it is sufficient that the applicants are of German nationality or at least spouses whose marriage has been regulated by German law. This system allows the German law to apply rather than that of the nationality of the minor when this corresponds to the child's best interests. In the United Kingdom, the kafala measure was in some cases qualified as an act of child protection and the consent of the guardians was deemed valid for adoption purposes.[386]

This rapid excursus must be viewed in relation to the basic consideration that western European secular law has for some time been based on the principle of non-identification with a religious system. Respect for this principle is effectively guaranteed by the more or less perfect feasibility of any ethical action, at least at a theoretical level. As can also be seen from a legal comparison with the institution of kafala, complex changes to the classical model of the modern state require the search for a more adequate balance, but especially for fresh new rules of legal expression in the complex sector of human rights and religious freedom in particular.

These rules should be sought not as some sort of regulatory utopia with the inclusion of as many values as possible, but in an attempt to avoid a radicalization of the parameters to be included. It has been emphasised that "*l'égalité de droits est incompatible avec la valorisation privilégiées d'une croyance*".[387] Through its neutrality – *neuter* = neither one nor the other, the state – *res publica* in the full sense of the term – guarantees its impartiality, so that each individual, regardless of his or her private religious feeling, can identify him/herself with the common context of society and state. This should not simply be a negative concept – the doctrine has long since settled on positions that deny the manifestation of religious freedom simply on the basis of the state's absence in the matter. What it should be is an approach to the law with a clear and identifiable

---

[385] *Loi du 16 juin 2010 portant approbation de la Convention de La Haye*, 19th October 1996, at http://legilux.public.lu/eli/etat/leg/trep/2010/07/15/nl/jo.

[386] The Adoption and Children Act of 2002 introduced the institution of 'special guardianship': cf. A. McFarlane, M. Reardon, *Child care and adoption law*, Bristol, Jordan Publishing, 2006, no. 5, noting that "it is intended to combine the advantages of a continued legal relationship with the birth family with the security of a long-term placement." (p.138); K. O'Donovan, *L'adoption dans le droit du Royaume-Uni*, in *L'adoption internationale en droit comparé*, Paris, Les Petites affiches, p. 149 *et seq*.

[387] H. Pena Riuz, *Qu'est-ce que la laïcité?* Paris, Gallimard, p. 10.

positive meaning, which manifests itself in the duty on the political authority to guarantee its full and effective deployment. It is about this approach and the correct identification of this positive action that the main issues arise, issues that still need to be discussed. Respect for mutual values is what must be pursued. In this way, the old conceptions, typical of the western world, of state neutrality and religious freedom, could still play an important and positive part.

The religious factor is crucial in the process of transformation of legal systems and allows us to reshape the issue of *identity*, which represents the cultural basis of subsequent political integration. It has been emphasized that respect for identity is susceptible to two different readings. In the first place, it may be understood as respect for the origins of the child, hence the emphasis on nationality to ensure the stability of the child's position in the move from one country to another. But it might also be taken to mean respect for the cultural and emotional environment of the child, hence the emphasis on integration in the environment that is geographically and culturally closer to the child.[388] The 1993 Hague Convention gives priority to the first consideration. Thus, maintaining the principle of subsidiarity in international adoption, it tends to preferentially grant the maintenance of the child in his/her native environment. The desire to maintain strong ties with the homeland would in this sense prevail over other interests of the child, such as being adopted by culturally distant foreign naturals. It is important, however, to stress that the phenomenon of hetero-integration is closely connected to the change of state sovereignty and requires a more broadminded, open view on the part of the legal system, which is destined to increase over time due to the process of global interdependence and related forms of international coordination.[389]

The narrow-minded, closed view of the law towards the legitimacy of the kafala would seem to be based essentially on the protection of the child's best interests in an anti-avoidance perspective of the legislation on international adoption or family reunification. According to this view, the entry of a foreign child into a 'western' context must necessarily be implemented through domestic regulation, which represents the only reasonable balance between the need to protect the abandoned foreign child and requests to place a child within a family.

---

388 P. HAMMJE, *L'intérêt de l'enfant face aux sources internationales du droit international privé*, in *Le droit international privé: esprit et méthodes. Mélang es en l'honneur de Paul Lagarde*, Paris, Dalloz, 2005, p. 365 *et seq.*

389 Cf. M. RICCA, *Metamorfosi della sovranità e ordinamenti confessionali. Profili teorici dell'integrazione tra ordinamenti nel diritto ecclesiastico italiano*, Turin, Giappichelli, 1999.

The issue, however, as amply demonstrated, is much more complex because it is linked to a legal construct of religious origin with important repercussions both on the legal status of the minor and on his/her fundamental rights. It is also part of the non-recognition of religiously-oriented legal constructs in the secular public space. Again, in the name of the child's best interests, the need to apply the regulatory structure most favourable to the child should be emphasized, which, in the specific area of parenting, involves the acquisition of the name and patrimony of the adopters and a status that is equal to that of any legitimate or adopted children in the family unit. Finally, the right to recognise and protect the religious freedom of the child cannot be subject to a law based solely on the country of origin (in which the child does not live and where s/he might have lived for just a few months) and a supposed membership of the *Umma*/community of believers.

The secularism at the basis of our democratic structure cannot allow such passive inclusion in a 'group', since it is a simple ideal but should be more properly configured as a method, a tool, an axiological paradigm of a modern, democratic and pluralist state. It is also true, though, that a defence of legal instruments with a religious connotation and which demand public recognition, cannot constitute a threat *tout court* or an involution of the secular ideal. The challenge of a modern, democratic and pluralist community, in the name of a broader idea of tolerance, is the capacity to accept different identities, to manage the inevitable conflicts that arise within the system harmoniously, to encourage the search for a delicate balance between freedom and equality. This guarantee should include the foundations of the structuring of a country but also its evolutionary dynamics, though they may be destabilizing, strengthening a real *identity policy* with respect for *diversity*.

The problem is then that of a redefinition of a public space that is totally and truly common to all. The preservation/protection of the bonds of social cohesion and the fight against discrimination should be the watchword for this constructive phase of open, globalized, multicultural societies, which cannot and must not allow religion to penetrate the *res publica*. Nor should it leave room for any form or process of political particularism, but allow each and every one free religious expression, provided that it does not spill over into the common sphere to undermine the democratic process, as understood in modern cultures, and the ideals at its core.

The future evolution of human rights, even within 'western' dynamics, will necessarily develop in the relationship between our culture, which is basically secularized/neutral and the Islamic world. The phenomenon of migration means that such religious rather than political communities are becoming increasingly present, each claiming independent space to exercise their rights. The problem of protecting cultural diversity is the possibility, granted to groups that may be homogeneous within themselves but in contrast to the majority of the population, to develop and use their spaces of freedom independently. This requires that the political powers allow their use in full. Naturally, within the limits in which constitutionally significant cases or, as in the case of the kafala, absolute universal rights such as the protection of the minor are not affected, it is necessary to guarantee the recognition of the child's status within the new family unit and the protection of his/her freedom of conscience and religion (naturally besides that of his/her parents).

These demands for visibility in the *res publica* not only concern the sphere of religious freedom, but the problem of religion as culture, of a religious vision within the public, common space. In *fluid* societies, freedom of religion is configured as cultural freedom and from being part of first-generation civil law is transformed into expanding law, taking a new evolutionary direction but also representing a parameter upon which the level of stability of the democratic nature of an open legal system may be evaluated. A new secularism must therefore be based on a legal valorization of the differences, abandoning the principle of neutrality to incorporate pluralism, not as an uncritical reception of the different demands for recognition but based on cultural openness towards dialogue.

An anthropological rather than juridical-formal basis might suggest that kafala could be recognized as a *cultural* model of adoption. The ratification of the 1996 Hague Convention requires a legal solution to be found alongside the rules to identify a possible alternative capable of removing this very delicate matter from the arbitrariness of jurisprudential decisions entrusted to the diverse sensitivity of the judging bodies and valid 'case by case'.

Religious motivation should not be used as a tool for choosing a different regulatory regime that may create unequal treatment. The use of religion and any conditioning dependant on the cultural belonging of an individual should be excluded at all costs from a democratic legal system so as not to create its own *ad personam* regulatory system. In the legal translation of different cultural systems, a secularised perspective that characterizes democratic social structures must always be used. If the kafala is linked to certain religious parameters, it may have relevance domestically but cannot lay claim to a public space in multicultural and pluralist systems. The consideration of the law of origin of the child, though it may protect domestic jurisdiction, leads to discrimination on a religious basis, which is absolutely unacceptable.

In Italy, if the focus, as we correctly believe, is to be centred on the child's best interests, what is needed is a clear and valid *erga omnes* regulatory intervention that does not create second class or even invisible citizens, as is still happening in France following the adoption of the 2001 law. The legal status of the child, especially if the child is very young, cannot be conditioned by the religious choices of the country of origin or the child's natural parents. Within the context of the western world, the child should be able to take advantage of the same rights and guarantees that our countries grant all adoptive and natural children.

A clear regulatory position would make it clear for the country of origin that a kafala arrangement will automatically be transformed into a real, legitimising adoption when the child leaves the homeland to enter that of his/her new parents and in which s/he will acquire citizenship, which will be retroactive from the moment in which the child is taken into care/adoption. This would also make sure that any legal disparities with legitimate or adopted children present in the family are avoided. A sort of 'pre-nationality' status could be used, or it might simply be the case of providing for further requirements, as practised by Swiss and Belgian legislation.

Social and juridical progress and the transformation of the family and the figure of the child within it, holding full rights, recognition of natural filiation, and equal status to the adopted child are irrepressible rights within a democratic legal system. Naturally, this approach can be easily reserved for minors who have lost both their parents and are thus subject to public protection. When faced with a kafala arrangement by common consent the situation is different and more complex. This will normally be of an intrafamily nature and should be assessed case by case, taking into account also the child's age and the possibility that s/he may be heard or may express his/her consent.

Any willingness to preserve the faith may be attributed to the minor, but only after reaching the age of majority. On coming of age, the child may choose, if in possession of dual citizenship, the legislation to adhere to and possibly re-transform the provision of adoption into kafala with all its legal consequences and with full awareness of this decision. No choice should be left to the adoptive parents who, though Muslims residing in a western country, will have to adapt to national legislation.

It should be emphasized, therefore, that in such a complex issue, the construction of a regulatory solution must take into account first and foremost the child's best interests, not only of an emotional nature but also at a social and economic level. Nor should it flounder with respect to its founding secular values and religious freedom. Any other needs, such as those related to avoiding new adoptive or semi-adoptive practices or limiting the entry of non-EU citizens into Europe, should seek other legislative solutions. If the democratic model, as developed and structured in western Europe, can be considered a universally shared form, its efficiency is always going to be conditioned culturally speaking by the evolution of socio-juridical models and will need constantly evolving forms of shared ethics. The idea of secularism must therefore be aimed at creating a space truly open to all "to exercise the rights of moral freedom (of conscience, of thought, religion and worship, etc.) in conditions of freedom and equality, and to build their existence from these: a space desired by men and women, independently of God."[390]

[390] G. ZAGREBLESKY, *Scambiarsi la veste. Stato e Chiesa al governo dell'uomo*, Roma-Bari, Laterza, 2010, p. 9. Cf. also S. FERRARI, *Libertà religiosa e sicurezza nazionale in Europa dopo l'11 settembre*, in *Quaderni di diritto e politica ecclesiastica*, 2005, pp. 161-184.

BIBLIOGRAPHY

A. Adinolfi, *Il diritto alla vita familiare nella giurisprudenza della Corte di giustizia dell'Unione europea*, in *Rivista di diritto internazionale*, n. 1, 2011.

P. Alston, B. Gilmour-Wish, *The best interest of the Child, Towards a sinthesis of Children's Rights and cultural values*, Unicef, 1996.

F. Astiggiano & M. Dogliotti, *Il procedimento di adottabilità*, in *Famiglia e diritto*, fasc.3, 2014.

T. Ballarino, E. Ballarino, and I. Petrelli, *Diritto Internazionale Privato Italiano*, Padova, Cedam, 2016.

B. Barel & S. Armellini, *Manuale breve di diritto internazionale privato*, Milano, Giuffrè, 2016.

J. Bargach, *Adoption and Wardship (Kafala) in Morocco*, 18 Recht van de Islam 77, 91, 2001.

J. Bargach, *Orphans of Islam. Family, abandonment, and secret adoption in Morocco*, New York, Rowman & Littlefield Publishers, 2002.

E. Bartholet, *International Adoption: a Way Forward*, in *New York Law School Rev.*, 2010-2011.

M.C. Baruffi, *La cittadinanza dell'Unione e i diritti dei minori nello spazio giudiziario europeo*, in *Cittadinanza e diversità culturale nello spazio giuridico europeo*, ID. (ed.), Milano, Giuffrè, 2010.

A. Beghè Loreti, *La legislazione dell'adozione dei minori nei Paesi dell'America Latina*, Milano, Giuffrè, 1984.

A. Beghè Loreti, *La tutela internazionale dei diritti del fanciullo*, Padova, Cedam, 1995.

H.J. Berman, *Law and Revolution: The Formation of the Western Legal Tradition*, Harvard University Press, 1983.

A. Bisio, I. Roagna, *L'adozione internazionale dei minori. Normativa interna e giurisprudenza*, Milano. Giuffrè, 2009.

C. Breen, *The standard of the best interest of the child*, The Hague-London-New York, 2002.

C. Breen, *The Standard of the Best Interests of the Child: A Western Tradition in International and Comparative Law*, The Hague, Kluwer Law International, 2002.

A. Büchler, *Islamic family law in Europe? From dichotomies to discourse – or: beyond cultural and religious identity in family law, International Journal of Law in Context*, 2012.

G. Campanato, V. Rossi, S. Rossi, *La tutela giuridica del minore*, Padova, Cedam, 2005.

C. Campiglio, *Il diritto di famiglia islamico nella prassi italiana*, *Rivista di diritto internazionale privato e processuale,* 1, 2008.

C. Campiglio, *La famiglia "islamica" in Italia*, in A. G. Danovi and S. Bariatti (eds), *La famiglia senza frontiere, Atti del convegno tenuto presso la Facoltà di Giurisprudenza dell'Università degli Studi di Milano il 25 maggio 2007,* Padova, Cedam, 2008.

A. Canac, *Reflexions sur l'inexistence de l'adoption en droit musulman*, 75 *Revue algerienne, tunisienne et marocaine de legislation et de jurisprudence 27*, 1959.

N. Cantwell, *Monitoring the Convention through the idea of the "3P"*, in *Politics of Childhood and Children at Risk: Provision, Protection, Participation*, P.L. Heilö, E. Lauronen, M. Bardy (eds.), Vienna, European Centre, 1993.

L. Carroll, *Orphaned grandchildren in Islamic law of succession. Reform and Islamization in Pakistan*, *Islamic Law and Society*, 5,3, 1998.

S.M. Carbone, C. Tuo, *Gli strumenti di diritto dell'Unione Europea in materia di famiglia e il Trattato di Lisbona*, in *Studi sull'integrazione europea,* n. 2, 2010.

G. Carobene, *Sulla protezione internazionale della libertà religiosa*, in *Il Diritto Ecclesiastico*, 1998, 2.

G. Casaburi, *Dai diversi modelli di adozione di minore nella giurisprudenza della Cassazione alla novellazione legislativa della nozione di stato di abbandono*, in *Foro. it*., I, c. 60, 2014.

F. Castro, *Il modello islamico*, edited by G. M. Piccinelli, Torino, Giappichelli, 2007.

E. Chaumont, "Yatīm", *Encyclopaedia of Islam, Second Edition*, Vol. XI, 2002.

J. Chelhod, «Rada'», *Encyclopaedia of Islam, Second Edition*, Vol. VIII.

A. Cilardo, *Il minore nel diritto islamico. Il nuovo istituto della kafala,* in A. Cilardo (ed), *La tutela dei minori di cultura islamica nell'area mediterranea. Aspetti sociali, giuridici e medici,* Napoli, ESI, 2011.

R. Clerici, *La cittadinanza nell'ordinamento giuridico italiano*, Padova, Cedam, 1993.

N. Colaianni, *Eguaglianza e diversità culturali e religiose. Un percorso costituzionale*, Bologna, Il Mulino, 2006.

M. Corsaro, *L'affidamento preadottivo nelle procedure per l'adozione internazionale*, in *Fam. dir.*, 2002.

M. Cossutta, *Dai diritti dell'uomo ai diritti del fanciullo*, in *La protezione internazionale dei diritti del fanciullo*, Trieste, Proxima Scientific press, 1993.

N.J. Coulson, *A History of Islamic Law*, 9, Edinburgh, 1964.

J. de Coninck, T*he Functional Method of Comparative Law: Quo Vadis?*, 74 Rabel J. Comp. & Int'l Private L. 318, 2010.

A.O. Cozzi, *Parità fra I coniugi*, in *Commentario breve alla Convenzione Europea dei Diritti dell'Uomo*, S. Bartole, P. De Sena, V. Zagrebelsky (a cura di), Padova, Cedam, 2012.

L.M. Craciunean, *The European Court of Human Rights Approach to Cultural Rights and Cultural Diversity*, in *Rom. J. Comp. L.*, 2, 2013.

E. De La Rosa, *Cultural diversity, European public policy exception and family law of Muslim Countries*, *Beijing Law Review*, 6, 2015.

J. De Verda & R. Beamonte, *La kafala ni es adopción, ni puede llegar a serlo, Actualidad Jurídica Iberoamericana*, 4, 2016.

F. Di Pietro, *La kafalah islamica e le sue applicazioni alla luce della giurisprudenza della Corte europea dei diritti dell'uomo, Ordine internazionale e diritti umani*, 2016.

M. Di Masi, *La Cassazione apre alla kafalah negoziale per garantire in concreto il best interest of the child*, *La nuova giurisprudenza civile commentata*, 2015.

M. Dien & Y. Izzi, "Wilāya", *Encyclopaedia of Islam, Second Edition*, vol. 11, 2002.

M. Distefano, *Interesse superiore del minore e sottrazione internazionale di minori: in margine al caso Neulinger*, in *Studi in onore di Claudio Zanghì*, edited by L. Panella and E. Spatafora, Torino, Giappichelli, 2011.

M. Dogliotti, *Adozione di maggiorenni e minori,* in *Codice civile*, Commentario, fondato da P. Schlesinger, diretto da F. D. Busnelli, Milano 2002.

M. Dogliotti, *L'adozione dei minori*, in *Trattato Bessone*, Diritto di famiglia, edited by Auletta, IV, Torino, 2011.

Y. Donders, *Human Rights: Eye for Cultural Diversity*, Inaugural Lecture delivered upon appointment to the chair of Professor of International Human Rights and Cultural Diversity at the University of Amsterdam on 29 june 2012, Amsterdam, University of Amsterdam, 2012.

R. Duca, *Family reunification: the case of the Muslim migrant children in Europe, Athens Journal of Social Sciences*, 2014.

H.G. Ebert, *The Problem of Adoption Under Modern Islamic Legislation in the Arab States*, in *Proceedings of the Arabic and Islamic Sections of the 35th International Congress of Asian and North African Studies*, Budapest, 1999.

A.A. Ehrenzweig, *Conflict of Laws*, St. Paul, West Publishing Co., pt. 1, 1959.

L. Fadiga, *L'adozione legittimante*, in *Trattato di diritto di famiglia*, diretto da P. Zatti, II, Filiazione edited by G. Collura, L. Lenti, M. Mantovani, 2° ed., Milano, 2012.

M. Farina, *In senso favorevole all'adozione*, v. Cass., 22 giugno 2016, n. 12962, in *Nuova giurisprudenza civile commentata*, 2016.

A. Fekry Ibrahim, *The Best Interests of the Child in Pre-modern Islamic Juristic Discourse and Practice*, 63 Am. J. Comp. L. 859, 2015.

L. Ferrari Bravo, M. Di Majo, A. Rizzo, *Carta dei diritti fondamentali dell'Unione Europea*, Milano, Giuffrè, 2001.

A.M. Finocchiaro, *Adozione e affidamento dei minori*, Milano, 2001.

A.M. Finocchiaro, *Responsabilità genitoriale; dal 1 Marzo 2005 va in soffitta l'istituto della patria potestà*, in *Guida al Diritto (Diritto Comunitario e Internazionale)*, n. 1, 2005.

C. Fioravanti, *i diritti del bambino tra protezione garanzie: l'entrata in vigore, per la Repubblica Italiana, della Convenzione di Strasburgo*, in *Le nuove leggi civili commentate*, n. 3, 2003.

C. Focarelli, *La convenzione di New York sui diritti del fanciullo e il concetto di «best interest of the child»*, in *Rivista di diritto internazionale*, n. 4, 2010.

M. Franchi, *Protezione dei minori e diritto internazionale privato*, Milano, Giuffrè, 1997.

M. Freeman, *Article 3. The best interests of the child, in A commentary on the United Nations Convention on the rights of the child*, A. Alen, J. Vande Lanotte, E. Verhellen, F. Ang, E. Berghmans, M. Verheyde (ed.), Leiden-Boston, Matinius Nijhoff, 2007.

A. Fuccillo, *La tutela dei minori e l'identità religiosa*, in *Giustizia e religione*, edited by A. Fuccillo, Torino, Giappichelli, 2011.

A. Furia, *L'Unione europea*, in *Promozione, protezione ed attuazione dei diritti dei minori*, C. Carletti (ed.), Torino, Giappichelli, 2009.

A. Gambaro, P.G. Monateri and R. Sacco, *voce Comparazione giuridica*, in Digesto IV, Disc. priv., sez. civ., Torino, 1995.

R. Gelli, *La Kafala tra esigenze di tutela del minore e rischi di aggiramento della disciplina dell'immigrazione*, in Fam. e diritto, 2008.

C. Ghionni, *Adozione internazionale e diritto alla famiglia*, Napoli, ESI, 2016.

A. Giladi, *Children of Islam. Concepts of childhood in medieval Muslim society,* London 1992.

A. Giladi, *Infants, parents and wet nurses. Medieval Islamic views on breastfeeding and their social implications*, Leiden, Brill, 1999.

S. Gilmore, *The limits of Parental Responsability*, in *Responsible Parents and Parental Responsibility*, R. Probert, S. Gilmore, J. Herring (eds.), Oxford, Hart Publishing, 2009.

J. Gordley, *The Functional Method*, in Methods of Comparative Law 107, Pier Giuseppe Monateri ed., 2012.

A. Glander, *The Oriental child not born in wedlock. A study of the anthropological parameters, religious motivations and sociological phenomena of child care in Islam and Judaism*, Frankfurt am Main, Peter Lang Publishing, 2001.

JR. A. Glenn Mower, *The Convention on the rights of the child*, London, Greenwod Publishing Group, 1997.

S. Grataloup, *L'enfant et sa famille dans les normes europennes*, Paris, LGDJ, 1998.

C. Honorati, *Verso una competenza della Comunità Europea in materia di diritto di famiglia?* in *La famiglia nel diritto internazionale privato e comunitario*, S. Boriatti (ed.), Milano, Giuffrè, 2007.

S. Ishaque, *Islamic Principles on Adoption: Examining the Impact of Illegitimacy and Inheritance Related Concerns in Context of a Child's Right to an Identity*, 22 Int'l J.L. Pol'y & Fam. 393, 2008.

C. Kalfat, *Les aspirations conflictuelles du droit de l'adoption*, 1 Revue algerienne des sciences juridiques, economiques et politiques 7, 1994.

J.M. Kelly, *A Short History of Western Legal Theory*, Oxford, 1992.

F. Kutty, *Islamic "Adoptions": Kafalah, Raadah, Istilhaq and the Best Interests of the Child*, in *The Intercountry Adoption Debate* 526, 539, Robert L. Ballard et al. eds., 2015.

T. Krüger, *The family: a state of the art.* Religare – Working Paper, 2, 2010.

F. Kutty, *Islamic 'adoptions': kafalah, raadah, istilhaq and the best interest of the child*, in *The Intercountry Adoption Debate: Dialogues Across Disciplines*, edited by Robert L. Ballard, Naomi H. Goodno, Robert F. Cochran, Newcastle upon Tyne, Cambridge Scholars Publishing, 2015.

E. Landau-Tasseron, *Adoption, Acknowledgement of Paternity and False Genealogical Claims in Arabian and Islamic Societies*, *Bulletin of the School of Oriental and African Studies*, 66, 2003.

D. Latifi, *Adoption and the Muslim law, Journal of the Indian Law Institute*, 1974.

M.C. Le Boursicot, *La kafala ou recueil lègal des mineurs en droit musulman: une adoption sans filiation*, in *Droit et Culture*, n. 59, 2010.

L. Lenti, *Introduzione. Vicende storiche e modelli di legislazione in materia adottiva*, in *Trattato di diritto di famiglia* diretto da P. Zatti, III, edited by G. Collura, L. Lenti, M. Mantovani, Milano, 2002.

Y. Linant de Bellefonds, *Traité de droit musulman comparé, Tome IIIeme, Filiation, Incapacités, Libéralités entre vifs*, Parigi-L'Aia, Mouton & Co, 1965.

J. Long, *Adozione e Islam. Gli ordinamenti giuridici occidentali e il divieto islamico di adozione, Studi urbinati di Scienze giuridiche, politiche, economiche,* 55, 2004.

J. Long, *Il ricongiungimento familiare del minore affidato con Kafala*, in *Dir. famiglia*, 2007.

J. Long, *Ordinamenti giuridici occidentali, kafala e divieto di adozione: un'occasione per riflettere sull'adozione legittimante*, in *La nuova giurisprudenza civile commentata,* Volume 2, 2003.

J. Long, *Si al ricongiungimento familiare del minore affidato con Kafalah*, in *Nuova giur. Civ. comm*, 2008.

E.G. Lorenzen, *Qualification, classification, or characterization problem in the conflict of laws*, *Yale Law Journal*, 50, 1941.

G. Magno, *Il minore come soggetto processuale. Commento alla Convenzione Europea sull'esercizio dei diritti dei fanciulli*, Milano, Giuffrè, 2001.

J. Malingreau, *International kafala: a right for the child to enter and stay in the EU Member States?, European Journal of Law Reform*, 16, 2014.

C. Mallat, *Introduction to Middle Eastern Law*, Oxford, 2007.

M. Marchegiani, *Diritti dei minori*, in *Codice della Famiglia*, edited by Sesta M., vol. II, Milano, Giuffrè, 2007.

M. Martinelli, *I rapporti di filiazione nell'ambito della famiglia islamica e in quella occidentale*, in C. Cardia and G. Dalla Torre (eds), *Comunità islamiche in Italia: Identità e forme giuridiche*, Torino, Giappichelli, 2015.

P. Martinelli, F. Mazza Galanti, *Diritto del bambino, in la Carta dei diritti dell'Unione Europea. Casi e materiali*, G. Bisogni, G. Bronzini, V. Piccone (eds), Taranto, Chimienti Editore, 2009.

N. Mathieu, *Séparation des parents et garde d'enfant – Le point e vue sur la jurisprudence de la Cour Européenne des droits de l'homme*, in *Rev. Trim. dr. Homme*, 93, 2013.

Y.M. Mattar, *Trafficking in Persons, Especially Women and Children, in Countries of the Middle East: the Scope of the Problem and the Appropriate Legislative Responses*, in *Fordham Int. Law Journal*, 721, 2003.

N. Meyer-Fabre, *La Convention de La Haye du 29 mai 1993 sur la protection des enfants et la coopération en matière d'adoption internationale*, in *Rev. crit. dr. privé*, 1994.

R. Michaels, *The Functional Methods of Comparative Law*, in *Oxford Handbook of Comparative Law,* 339, Mathias Reiman & Reinhard Zimmermann eds., 2006.

F. Milanese, *Il Garante per l'infanzia nella promozione di una cultura dei diritti dei bambini*, in *Il garante dell'infanzia e dell'adolescenza, un sistema di garanzia nazionale nella prospettiva europea*, L. Strumendo (ed.), Milano, Guerini, 2007.

M. Moinuddin Khan, *Encyclopaedia of Islamic Law and Jurisprudence: Islamic Law and Family*, 2010.

L. Mollica, *Osservazioni a Cass. 23 luglio 1997, n. 6899*, in *Dir. fam. pers.*, 1998.

A.C. Moro, *Manuale di diritto minorile*, Bologna, Zanichelli, 2008.

P. Morozzo della Rocca, *Adozione "plena, minus plena e tutela delle radici del minore"*, in *Rivista di diritto privato*, 1996.

P. Morozzo della Rocca, *Il nuovo status di figlio e le adozioni in casi particolari*, in *Famiglia e diritto*, 2013.

P. Morozzo della Rocca, *La condizione giuridica del minore straniero*, in *Minorigiustizia*, 2002.

P. Morozzo della Rocca, *Sull'affidamento al cittadino italiano del minore straniero mediante kafala tornerà a pronunciarsi la Cassazione*, in *Il corriere giuridico*, 6, 2011.

E. Moscati, *Il minore nel diritto privato, da soggetto da proteggere a persona da valorizzare* (contributo allo studio dell'interesse del minore"), in *Dir. fam. pers.*, 2014.

F. Mosconi, *La protezione dei minori*, in *Convenzioni internazionali e legge di riforma del diritto internazionale privato*, F. Salerno (ed.), Padova, Cedam, 1997.

F. Mosconi & C. Campiglio, *Diritto internazionale privato e processuale. Volume I. Parte generale e obbligazioni*, Torino, Utet, 2015.

S. Muckel, *Islam in Germany*, in R. Potz, and W. Wieshaider (eds), *Islam and the European Union*, Leuven, Peeters, 2004.

K. Murphy, *The traditional view of public policy and ordre public in private international law, Georgia Journal of International and Comparative Law*, 11, 1981.

J.L. Murray, *The Influence of the European Convention of Fundamental Rights on Community Law*, in *Fordham International Law Journal*, 33, n. 5, 2011.

J.J. Nasir, *The Islamic Law of Personal Status*, Graham & Trotman, London, 1990.

M. Nisticò, *Kafala islamica e condizione del figlio minore. La rilevanza della kafala nell'ordinamento italiano*, available at: https://www.gruppodipisa.it/, 2013.

C. Novi, *La tutela dei diritti dei minori nell'ordinamento comunitario*, in *Diritto pubblico comparato ed europeo*, n. 1, 2007.

Th.J. O'Shaughnessy, "The qurʾānic view of youth and old age", *Zeitschrift der Deutschen Morgenländischen Gesellschaft*, 141, 1991.

M. Orlandi, *La kafala islamica e la sua riconoscibilità quale adozione,* in *Diritto e Famiglia*, 2005.

T. Oubrou, "La kafala et la sharia", *Droit de la famille – Revue mensuelle lexisnexis juris classeur*, 2009.

S. Parker, *The best interests of the child – Principles and problems*, in *The best interests of the child. Reconciling culture and Human Rights*, P. Alston (eds.), Oxford, Clarendon Press, 1994.

C. Peraro, *Il riconoscimento degli effetti della kafala: una questione non ancora risolta,* in *Rivista di diritto internazionale privato e processuale*, 2015.

O. Pesle, *L'adoption en droit musulman*, 16, Alger, 1919.

R. Peters, "Guarantee", in: *Encyclopaedia of Islam*, Third Edition, edited by: Kate Fleet, Gudrun Krämer, Denis Matringe, John Nawas, Everett Rowson

B. Poletti Di Teodoro, *La Convenzione intramericana di La Paz del 24 maggio 1984 sui conflitti di legge in materia di adozione dei minori, in Riv. dir. civ.*, 1984.

D. Pollack, Bleich M., Reid C. Jr., Fadel M.H., "*Classical religious perspectives of adoption law*", *Notre Dame law review*, 79, 2, 2004.

D. Powers, *The Abolition of Adoption in Islam, Reconsidered*, in *Droit et Religions*, 2010.

D.S. Powers, *Muḥammad is not the father of any of your men*, University of Pennsylvania Press, Philadelphia, 2011.

I. Queirolo, *La disciplina della responsabilità genitoriale: il Regolamento CE 2201/2003*, in *Lezioni di diritto dell'Unione Europea e relazioni familiari*, I. Queirolo, L. Schiano Di Pepe (eds.), Torino, Giappichelli, 2014.

C. Ravera, *Art. 5, Uguaglianza degli sposi, in La Convenzione Europea dei Diritti dell'uomo e delle libertà fondamentali commentata ed annotata*, C. Defilippi, D. Bosi, R. Harvey (eds.), Napoli, ESI, 2006.

A. Raza Naqvi, *Adoption in Muslim Law*, 19 Islamic Stud. 283, 1980.

J. Rehman, *Religion, Human Rights Law and the Rights of the Child: Complexities in Applying the Sharia in Modern State Practices*, 62 N. Ir. Legal Q. 153, 2011.

F. Rigaux, *La Convenzione delle Nazioni Unite sui diritti dell'Infanzia*, in *Violazioni dei diritti dei bambini – un metodo di approccio*, Roma, Abele, 1995.

J. Ringelheim, *Diversité culturelle et droits de l'homme – L'émergence de la problématique des minorités dans le droit de la Convention Européenne des droits de l'homme*, Bruxelles, Bruylant, 2006.

R. Rivello, *L'interesse del minore fra diritto internazionale e multiculturalità*, in *Minorigiustizia*, n. 3, 2011.

S.A.H. Rizvi *et alii*, "*The concept of adoption. Islamic socio-legal view point*", *Islamic and Comparative Law Quarterly*, 2, 1982.

M. Rohe, *Islamic Law in Past and Present*, Leiden-Boston, Brill, 2015.

L. Sacchetti, *Il nuovo istituto dell'adozione internazionale*, Rimini, Maggioli ed., 2000.

L. Sandrini, *Protezione dei minori (dir. int. priv.), Matrimonio, (dir. int. priv.)*, in *Dizionario giuridico* diretto da N. Irti, Milano, Giuffrè, 2010.

D. Santillana, *Istituzioni di diritto musulmano malichita con riguardo anche al sistema sciafiita*, Vol. I, Roma, ARE, 1926.

C.L. Santili, *Sussidiarietà e residualità nell'adozione internazionale*, in *Le nuove regole delle adozioni*, P. Morozzo Della Rocca, (ed.), Napoli, ESI, 2002.

S. Sardar Ali, *A Comparative Perspective of the Convention on the Rights of the Child and the Principles of Islamic Law*, in *Protecting the World's Children* 142, UNICEF ed., 2008.

M. Sayed, *The kafala of Islamic law: how to approach it in the West*. In P. Lindskoug, U. Maunsbach and G. Millkvist (eds), *Essays in honor of Michael Bodgan*, Lund, Juristforlaget, 2013.

G. Sciancalepore, P. Stanzione, *Minori e diritti fondamentali*, Milano, Giuffrè, 2006.

G. Sergio, *La Convenzion Europea sull'esercizio dei diritti dei fanciulli: una tappa decisiva verso il riconoscimento della soggettività dei minori*, in *Cittadini in crescita*, 1, 2003.

W.R. Smith, *Kinship & Marriage in Early Arabia*, 52, BiblioLife 2009, 1903.

A.E. Sonbol, "*Adoption in Islamic society. A historical survey*", in E. W. Fernea (ed.), *Children in the Muslim Middle East*, Austin, University of Texas Press, 1995, 45–67.

P. Stanzione, *Garanti per l'infanzia e interesse del minore*, Salerno, Università degli Studi di Salerno, 2000.

L. Strumendo, P. De Stefani, *Il Garante dell'infanzia e dell'adolescenza*, in *Tutela civile del minore e diritto sociale della famiglia*, L. Lenti (ed.), vol. VI (II ed.), Trattato di diritto di famiglia, diretto da P. Zatti, Milano, Giuffrè, 2012.

L.E. Teitz, *Children crossing borders: internationalizing the restatement of the conflict of laws, Duke Journal of Comparative and International Law*, 27, 2017.

T. Tomeo, *La kafala, Comparazione e diritto civile*, available at: http://www.comparazionedirittocivile.it, 2013.

F. Tommaseo, *Il processo civile familiare e minorile italiano nel contesto dei principi europei*, in *Dir. fam. pers.*, 3, 2012.

G. Turri, *I grandi principi europei di tutela dei minori*, in *Minorigiustizia*, n. 2, 2008.

A. Vaccaro, *L'adozione internazionale e la Convenzione dell'Aja*, in *Dir. fam. e pers.*, 1996.

G. Van Bueren, *The international Law on the Rights of the Child*, The Hague-Boston-London, Martinus Nijhoff Publishers, 1998.

H. Van Loon, *The accomodation of religious laws in crossborder situations: the contribution of the Hague Conference on private international law, Cuadernos de Derecho Transnacional*, 2, 2010.

N. Yassari, *Adding by Choice: Adoption and Functional Equivalents* in *Islamic and Middle Eastern Law*, 63 Am. J. Comp. L. 92, 2015.

N. Yassari, *Intestate Succession in Islamic Countries*, in *Comparative Succession Law: Intestate Succession* 421, Kenneth G.C. Reid et al. eds., 2015.

K. Zweigert & H. Kotz, *An Introduction to Comparative Law*, Oxford, 1998.